A More Perfect Union:

Vermont Becomes a State, 1777-1816

Michael Sherman, Editor

Vermont Historical Society
Montpelier, Vermont
and
Vermont Statehood Bicentennial Commission

Library of Congress Cataloging-in-Publication Data

A More perfect union : Vermont becomes a state, 1777-1816 /
    Michael Sherman, editor.
        p. cm.
    Includes bibliographical references.
    ISBN 0-934720-33-9
        1. Vermont—Politics and government—1775-1865. 2. Statehood
(American politics) I. Sherman, Michael, 1944-   .
F52.M67   1991   90-20967
974.3'03—dc20   CIP

A joint publication of the Vermont Statehood Bicentennial
Commission and the Vermont Historical Society
Managing editor: Susan Bartlett Weber
Designed by The Laughing Bear Associates
Printed by Northlight Studio Press

A More Perfect Union:

Vermont Becomes a State, 1777-1816

Michael Sherman, Editor

Contents

Preface

This book is the product of many hands and minds. It began as a collection of facsimile documents from the middle and late eighteenth century with commentaries by historian Marilyn Blackwell, expanded into a series of short books on topics related to statehood, then "sugared off," to use a well-worn but appropriate Vermont phrase, to this compact volume of essays and documents. My thanks to State Archivist D. Gregory Sanford and *Vermont Life* editor Tom Slayton — both members of the Vermont Statehood Bicentennial Commission's Publications Committee — for their help in shaping and guiding to completion the final product.

With a workable plan in mind we turned next to finding or encouraging the scholarship that would meet our needs. Marilyn Blackwell gave us permission to adapt her work to our new needs; Gary Aichele and Peter Onuf allowed us to reprint their essays, previously published in *Vermont History* and *Lake Champlain: Reflections on Our Past*, and I revised my article from a talk prepared for induction into the Phi Alpha Theta history honor society. Our thanks to the Vermont Historical Society, publishers of *Vermont History*, the Center for Research on Vermont, publishers of *Lake Champlain: Reflections on Our Past*, and Professor Albert Andrea, head of the Alpha Alpha Psi chapter, Vermont, of Phi Alpha Theta.

We next turned to the more challenging task of commissioning new scholarship and writing for our book. Paul Gillies volunteered to write on the legal and constitutional aspects of adjustment to statehood. Michael Bellesiles, already engrossed in reading Levi Allen's diaries, which had recently become available as the result of a project to conserve and microfilm documents in the Henry Stevens Papers, offered to write an article based on this rediscovered source. Samuel B. Hand and P. Jeffrey Potash, who had made a joint presentation on Nathaniel Chipman for a meeting of the Chittenden County Historical Society, graciously agreed to transform an informal talk on research in progress into a finished work of scholarship.

Editing these essays has been a challenging but immensely rewarding task. My thanks to D. Gregory Sanford for carefully reading each; offering his knowledge, comments, and suggestions to supplement my own; and for his own contribution of the introduction to the January 1791 debate between Nathaniel Chipman and Daniel Buck on ratification of the U.S. Constitution.

Special thanks to Susan Bartlett Weber for her excellent work copyediting the manuscripts and for managing this Hydra of a publication project. Her high standards, helpful recommendations, and experience working with authors, editors, designers, and printers have kept this publication on track and on time.

Thanks to Colleen Pixley and Kathy White, both on the staff of the State Archives, for transcribing and typing the documents included in this book.

Finally, thanks to the Vermont Statehood Bicentennial Commission for its support and encouragement. Early in its life the commission was determined that the celebration of Vermont's two hundredth anniversary of statehood would include lasting contributions to scholarship. The commission's two chairmen, William Schubart and William Gray, and Executive Director Carolyn Crowley stuck to that goal and the commission has backed it with generous financial support.

The Vermont Historical Society, through a special publication fund, is pleased to be a partner with the bicentennial commission in presenting this book to the public. We hope that our joint effort will add to an understanding of the events and ideas that led to and were consequent to Vermont becoming one of the United States of America in 1791. We hope, too, that this publication will stimulate thought about the implications of those events two hundred years ago and by doing so will serve some of the needs of contemporary readers and future generations of Vermonters and American citizens.

MICHAEL SHERMAN,
Editor

Introduction

The constitution that was proposed to the original thirteen states of the United States on September 28, 1787, and ratified by the required two-thirds of them by the end of July 1788, went into effect on March 4, 1789. Exactly two years later, on March 4, 1791, Vermont became the fourteenth state, the first to enter the union under the new Constitution.

Since 1777 the people who called themselves Vermonters had enjoyed *de facto* if not *de jure* independence. They had declared themselves free of the jurisdiction of Great Britain, New Hampshire, and New York; created an independent state; adopted a constitution; elected their own governors and representatives; written their own laws; minted their own coins; even naturalized foreigners as citizens of the state. But for fourteen years Vermont had failed to win acknowledgement of its independence by the Continental Congress, failed in its persistent efforts to join the new nation or obtain a voice in Congress.

For Vermont, therefore, becoming one of the United States had many meanings, consequences, and implications. It meant surrendering a measure of sovereignty for as yet uncertain and — among some Vermonters — disputable advantages, redefining allegiances and identities, tieing fortunes and futures to the emerging nation, and turning away once and for all from both continued existence as an independent state and the potential advantages of political and economic union with the government of Canada. These choices had been weighed against the promises and expectations of life under the Constitution, succinctly expressed in its preamble:

"We the People of the United States, in Order to form a more perfect Union, establish Justice, insure domestic Tranquility, provide for the common defence, promote the general Welfare, and secure the Blessings of Liberty to ourselves and our Posterity, do ordain and establish this Constitution for the United States of America."

The bond that the framers had anticipated in 1787 and that many but certainly not all Vermonters anticipated in 1791 was not made merely at the stroke of a pen. It would take another twenty-five years to sort out the implications and adjust to the realities of what Vermonters committed themselves to and what the nation as a whole sought to accomplish in that episode of forming a more perfect union.

This book explores some of the issues that troubled the minds and disturbed the political, economic, and social lives of Vermonters from 1791 to 1816 as they and their fellow citizens of the United States adjusted to union with each other. The authors use the perspectives of constitutional, legal, social, economic, and cultural history, and biography to examine documents, institutions, ideologies, careers, and motives in the early statehood period. They ask how late eighteenth-century Vermonters saw themselves, how their contemporaries saw them both inside Vermont and from elsewhere within the new nation, and how successive generations of historians have seen them over the distance of time and through the changing lenses of historical interpretation.

The essays in this book do not tell the story of Vermont's statehood. They tell many stories about how Vermont became a state. They offer, moreover, several perspectives on the meanings and implications of statehood in the late eighteenth century and in our own day.

Part one of the book provides a constitutional prologue, exploring both the rationale behind Vermont's constitution-making of 1777 and the 1791 debate over ratification of the U.S. Constitution. Underlying these events is not only the theme of constitutional government in eighteenth-century America, but also the timeless debate over how to keep government responsive to the people it represents.

Part two expands on this debate by reminding us that while a clear and vocal majority favored union in 1791, that sentiment was by no means unanimous. To some Vermonters possibilities for a more perfect union were to be found in Canada, not the United States, while others felt that an independent Vermont already constituted perfection.

Vermont's quest for political recognition and acceptance lasted fourteen years. But once the goal was attained and the celebrations of March 1791 quieted down, Vermont and the United States had to confront the realities of statemaking and living under the same Constitution. The third section examines how the nation and the state adjusted to these realities.

The final essay looks at the interplay of myth, commemoration, and history. Celebrations such as those occasioned by the bicentennial of Vermont statehood provide opportunities for confirming popular self-perceptions through interpretation of the past. Understanding how we celebrate is often as important as understanding what we celebrate.

Indeed, the process of historical interpretation is a theme of this book. Because the starting point for new interpretation is the historical record, we include as our final section a selection of source documents relating to Vermont's 1777 constitution (Thomas Young), the struggles of Vermont for recognition (Ira Allen), the concern about Vermont's potential for disturbing national tranquillity and security on the eve of statehood (George Washington), the Acts and Resolutions of the Convention in Bennington in 1791 that ratified the U.S. Constitution and cleared the last hurdle to statehood, and the actual celebration of statehood (*Vermont Gazette*).

Vermonters and historians of Vermont have not in the past devoted a great deal of attention to describing or analyzing how Vermont became a state in 1791. Perhaps it is because the story contains too many ambiguities of motive; because it is too complex to be narrated easily and smoothly; because it is riddled with party politics, factional fighting, and divisiveness — all alien to the general tendency in an earlier era of American scholarship toward creating a unified and unifying history — or perhaps because statehood was the anticlimax to what have been the consistently more attractive stories of settlement on the New Hampshire Grants, the struggle against New York by the Green Mountain Boys, the declaration of an independent state of Vermont, and the participation of the new state in the American Revolution.

Until recently, our national historiography has focused on the creation of a national identity, where regional differences, economic barriers, social distinctions, and diverse political goals have ultimately found resolution through time and by means of institutions. This synthetic goal, which has driven our historical writing from the early nineteenth century into the most recent quarter-century, has self-consciously obliterated from the record and from popular historical consciousness deep and enduring divisions over ideology and goals at all levels of American society: community, state, region, and nation.

The results of a century and a half of consensus historiography have been to de-emphasize controversies such as those that surrounded Vermont's transition from an independent state to one of the United States of America. Our historical writers have assumed that statehood was the inevitable outcome of American independence from Great Britain and the first episode in physical, political, and economic growth of the American republic. "Manifest Destiny" — a doctrine of mid-nineteenth century politics — supplemented later in that century by the popularization of Darwin's biological model of growth and change and its application to social and political change, formed the elements of a historiography that obscured details of choice, controversy, and internal divisions. Operating on our history like a template, this nationalist historiography cut away as irrelevant the thoughts and actions of men, women, social and economic groups and subcultures that fell outside the grand pattern of our national history. Thus, we know less about how we became the fourteenth state in the new nation than how we separated ourselves fourteen years earlier from New York or New Hampshire. We have accepted almost without concern a gap in our historical consciousness between the Battle of Bennington in 1777 and the Battle of Plattsburgh in 1814 — neither of which was fought on Vermont soil and both of which demonstrated our commitment to a larger national goal.

When Vermonters have turned their attention to the period of becoming a state, it has been as an act of self-denial. Vermont, in such an interpretation, chose to surrender its status as an independent republic to join the union. Just what was involved in that decision, how it came to be made, how the already existing states of the union and the federal government responded to this act of political suicide and resurrection have received scant attention.

Chance has been an ally of intention in diverting popular and scholarly attention from the period 1783 to 1816. Much of the documentation that could have supported close analysis of the post-Revolutionary period was either never created or has disappeared. Vermont had no equivalent to James Madison, whose notes at the Constitutional Convention of 1787 give us a detailed account of debates, issues, solutions proposed, abandoned, or adopted. Thus we have little first-hand information concerning the drafting of Vermont's constitution in 1777 or the debates fourteen years later over ratification of the U.S. Constitution and the decision to join the nation. We have few biographical studies of the founders or key figures in the early years—Thomas Chittenden, Nathaniel Chipman, Ira Allen, Moses Robinson, Isaac Tichenor—although some of that work is now in progress and some appears in this book. Some material has recently re-emerged, such as the diary of Levi Allen quoted extensively by Michael Bellesiles in his contribution to this volume, and some well-known sources are being re-examined, such as the biographical information on Nathaniel Chipman and his own published writing discussed here by Samuel Hand and Jeffrey Potash. But much of what we know about the period still comes from mid-nineteenth century transcriptions and editions of official documents and the close scrutiny of a few primary sources—such as Gary Aichele's examination of the Vermont and Pennsylvania constitutions, the summary of speeches on January 10, 1791, by Nathaniel Chipman and Daniel Buck as reported in the Newspaper, *Vermont Gazette*, or Paul Gillies's study of laws and official correspondence for the period 1791-1816.

These studies of readily available, long-known, and, in some ways, formulaic sources give us new insights into the period, however, because historians since the 1960s have broken away from the profession's attachment to consensus history. Responding to the cultural and intellectual impact of the politics of dissent in the 1960s and 70s, historians have begun to study the ideological, social, and economic rifts in late eighteenth-century society and assess the impact of those divisions on politics and culture. Confronted with the history of genocide, racial warfare, and repression in the twentieth century, scholars now ask how identifiable racial and economic groups fared within late eighteenth-century society. Historians sensitized to the history and struggles of minority groups in contemporary America now examine how the emerging majority in the early years of the nation dominated, ignored, repressed, or occasionally took into account the minority in the new democratic society.

In addition, as Peter Onuf's essay demonstrates, contemporary historiography is beginning to take into account the interaction between regional and national politics. The story of how Vermont became a state can no longer be told effectively or usefully without understanding the context of national politics as the United States Constitution was being drafted. The off-stage thunder of Vermont's agitation for statehood, its ongoing struggle with New York, its attempts to incorporate the border towns of New York and New Hampshire, and its negotiations with British government officials in Canada raised important questions about the meaning of statehood and governance. The other background noise of sectional politics—long since identified as an important issue in debates over the Constitution—likewise had an echo in Vermont's bid for statehood and the response of the original thirteen states.

Finally, as contemporary historiography retreats from the scientific pretenses of the nineteenth century and even from some of the statistically based social science methods of more recent decades, we are beginning to ask new questions about the relationships between what we know and how we tell what we know. Thus, my contribution to this book acknowledges that although we may have imperfect knowledge of the past we can and do use historical narratives, myths, and civic celebrations to perform important cultural and political tasks.

Our picture of how Vermont became a state, why Vermonters chose that option, why some opposed it, and what were the consequences of those choices for Vermont and its neighbors has thus become broader and deeper as we have begun to ask new questions. It has not become an easier story to tell, however. More knowledge has not always produced clarity and simplicity or eliminated controversy. On the contrary, as the essays on Nathaniel Chipman and Levi Allen demonstrate, a historiography that focuses attention on factions and diversity presents new opportunities for arguments about motives and consequences.

Nor are these merely academic questions. Dissent and doubt in the eighteenth century have echoes in our own day. The debates two hundred years ago between champions of a national politics and culture and those who endeavored to protect local institutions and regional cultural patterns are heard today in Congress, our statehouses, and town meetings. For we, like our eighteenth-century predecessors, continue to examine the roles of the states in a large national government. We ponder the role of constitutions in setting political, moral, social, and economic agendas. We look for international or even global solutions to problems that have local consequences, such as environmental protection, energy policy, industrial and agricultural productivity, and hunger. And we struggle with the most durable problem of democratic society: hearing the voice of dissent, acknowledging the rights of the minority, and extending the benefits of good governance to all those who live among us.

MICHAEL SHERMAN

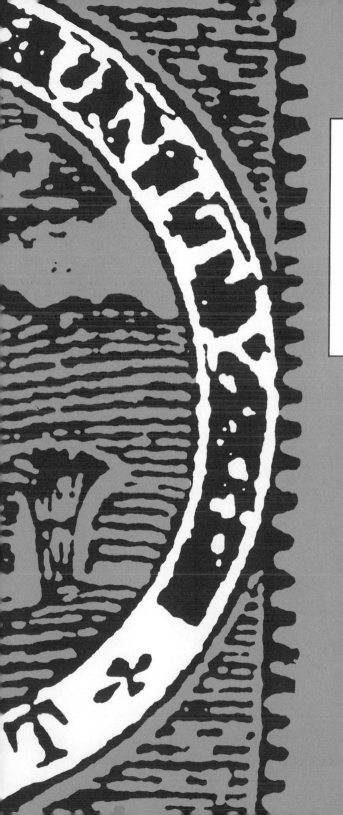

PART I

Constitutional Beginnings

Making the Vermont Constitution: 1777-1824

by Gary J. Aichele

 As a result of renewed interest in constitutional origins stimulated by the national constitutional bicentennial, scholars have begun to take a closer look at the constitutional "foundings" of the individual states. Regrettably, primary sources concerning the framing and ratification of the Vermont constitution are sparse, which may account for the relative paucity of secondary commentary concerning this important period in Vermont's political history. Nevertheless, from the materials that are available, it is possible to develop a view of the creation of the Vermont republic that distinguishes it rather significantly from the original thirteen states in the federal union and provides an important perspective on the meaning and consequences of constitutionalism in America during the waning years of the eighteenth century. Specifically, this essay will investigate three aspects of the Vermont constitution of 1777 — its historical context, its constitutional content, and its political consequences.

HISTORICAL CONTEXT

The political community known today as "Vermont" had no historical existence prior to the creation of the Vermont Republic in 1777. Long known as the New Hampshire Grants, the territory and inhabitants of the region existed in a state of political limbo brought about by the ambiguous territorial claim decision of the British Privy Council in 1764. Intended to resolve permanently the disputed claims of the rival colonies of New York and New Hampshire, the order declared the western bank of the Connecticut River "to be" the boundary between the royal colonies of New York and New Hampshire. The decision left unclear what the legal boundary between the two colonies "had been." This complicated further the legal status of titles west of the Connecticut River originating in New Hampshire patents. [1] New Hampshire governor Benning Wentworth had precipitated the struggle for control of the territory when he granted a charter to the town of "Bennington" in 1749. Located at the westernmost periphery of the land Wentworth claimed under New Hampshire's royal charter, Bennington lay within the territory claimed by the colonial governor of New York under New York's charter. Thus, from the beginning, the land that would become Vermont was the subject of a legal dispute, the outcome of which would be determined by fundamentally political forces. [2]

Demographically, people had moved into the Grants from more densely populated neighboring colonies; town names and the records of early settlements suggest that a majority of new settlers were from Connecticut. Together with other "Yankees" from New Hampshire and Massachusetts, they cut the first roads and cleared the first farms. But especially after 1764, they were followed by other settlers, newcomers who were less committed to the New England town-meeting tradition, and more willing to adapt to any form of civil authority that could protect their property and maintain the peace of the community. These settlers, soon to be called "Yorkers" as a result of their willingness to recognize the provincial authority of New York over the Grants, often found themselves at odds with their Yankee neighbors. Perhaps the most important factor affecting settlement in the Grants, however, was the rough competition that developed between Yankee and Yorker land speculators, the most

3

significant including the Allens and their supporters on the one side, and James Duane, John Tabor Kempe, and William Smith on the other. Each side actively promoted settlement throughout the Grants as a means of solidifying its claims and increasing its profits. Thus, differences in political traditions, social sympathy, and financial self-interest all played a role in fanning the flames of controversy ignited by the Privy Council order of 1764. [3]

By the spring of 1770 the issue of political sovereignty over the Grants had come to a head in two separate parts of the Grants over two separate issues. In April 1768 New York had created Cumberland County, a new jurisdiction responsible for the governance of towns situated in the southeastern region of the Grants. Largely through the efforts of Thomas Chandler, Chester was selected as the first county seat, where the first county court was held in 1769. This exercise of authority by New York, and specifically the imposition of a county court system over a region that historically had known only local town courts, was met with considerable opposition. The problem was made worse by the fact that inhabitants of the new county were unrepresented in the New York provincial assembly. In May 1770 Cumberland Sheriff Daniel Whipple was seized while trying to execute an arrest warrant for Nathan and Simon Stone and Joseph and Benjamin Waite, all prominent men of the town of Windsor. A month later, an angry mob led by Nathan Stone kept the county court from sitting in Chester, principally by seizing and holding John Grout, a Yorker lawyer who had brought an earlier suit against Stone. Though the actions of the men of Cumberland County in the spring and summer of 1770 clearly evidenced dissatisfaction with the county court system, the riots had nothing to do with land titles. Most of the settlers in the Connecticut River valley had petitioned New York for confirmatory titles; for a fee New York executed new titles confirming the rights of holders under their original Wentworth grants. [4]

The situation west of the mountains was, however, quite different. If the provincial government of New York headed by Governor William Tryon was prepared to confirm Eastern titles for a fee, it was not able to use the same device to quiet contested grants west of the mountains; Wentworth patents frequently conflicted with grants for the same land made by the governor of New York. In 1770 holders of Wentworth titles lying west of the Green Mountains appointed Ethan Allen to present their case before the New York courts. Allen was personally faced with a difficult problem. While many of the owners he represented actually hoped that New York would confirm their Wentworth titles, Allen and other large land speculators claiming to own thousands of acres could not have raised the capital required to pay the legal fees involved. Moreover, in seeking confirmatory titles from New York, the owners were at least implicitly acknowledging the authority of New York over the Grants and their obligation to begin paying taxes known as "quitrents." If small farmers and townspeople were prepared to accept this burden to secure quiet title to their property, the Allens were not. Winning the lawsuits heard in Albany early in 1770 might have brought peace to the Grants, but such a victory would clearly have bankrupted the Allens and other large Yankee land speculators. [5]

Such was not the case, however. The New York court, presided over by Chief Justice Robert Livingston, who himself was heavily involved in land speculation in the Grants, refused to admit evidence presented by Allen proving the existence of Wentworth patents; a verdict was directed in favor of Major John Small, a New York speculator, against Isaiah Carpenter, a Bennington farmer. It is also important to note that James Duane and Attorney General John Tabor Kempe were also large investors in land speculations involving the Grants. Through the court's decision in the Albany ejectment suits brought in 1770, the leading political figures of provincial New York made it clear that they intended to profit personally by throwing Grant inhabitants off their farms and out of their homes. [6]

Not surprisingly, trouble developed the following year when the victors in these lawsuits attempted to consolidate their gains. In a series of skirmishes along the old border, inhabitants of the Grants dealt roughly with New York surveyors and other officials of Albany County who attempted to dispossess them of their land. The dispute was especially keen along the Walloomsac River and in the Manchester-Arlington area, land lying in the large New York patents known as the "Walloomsac Patent" and "Princetown." Having unsuccessfully attempted to evict Isaiah Carpenter of Shaftsbury and Samuel Rose of Manchester, Henry Ten Eyck and Abraham Cuyler, the sheriff and mayor of Albany, assembled a posse of some two hundred men and crossed the Walloomsac near the farm of James Breakenridge, west of Bennington. There on July 19, 1771, the Yorkers were confronted by an armed force of more than one hundred "Green Mountain Boys" from the surrounding area. When the sheriff tried to execute his eviction notice, it became clear that Breakenridge and his friends had no intention of giving up the farm; it also became clear that Ten Eyck's posse had no stomach for a real fight over the place. As the Yorker officials withdrew, aware perhaps for the first time that many Albany County farmers on the New York side of the Walloomsac were sympathetic to the claims of their neighbors in the Grants, military companies began to organize in the Grants under the captaincies of men like Seth Warner, Remember Baker, and Robert Cochran. Over them Ethan Allen exercised general authority either by election or tacit acquiescence. [7]

The rout of Sheriff Ten Eyck's force exerted a powerful influence over the subsequent affairs of the Grants. From that time, New York's capacity to enforce its claim to sovereignty over the Grants existed in theory only. Emboldened by their vic-

6

tory, and perhaps recalling New York's ineffectual efforts to enforce its authority during its "Anti-Rent Wars" with residents of western Massachusetts in 1755 and 1766, Ethan Allen and his supporters became increasingly bold in their opposition to New York officials and Yorker sympathizers. From 1771 to 1775, the Green Mountain Boys burned out Yorker settlers, harassed and banished Yorker sympathizers, and whipped with the "beech seal" New York officials and surveyors. During this same period, the Allens and several close associates had consolidated their land holdings in the Champlain and Winooski river valleys, culminating in the creation of the Onion River Land Company in January 1773. Perhaps as a consequence, their anti-Yorker actions escalated during the summer of 1773 when they "reclaimed" Allen's property at Otter Creek by burning out Col. John Reid's Scottish tenants, bringing to an abrupt end a temporary truce between the New York authorities and the inhabitants of the Grants agreed to at a meeting in Bennington in July. The first formal meeting of the leaders of the opposition was held at Eliakim Weller's tavern in Manchester in early 1774 to consider an appropriate response to Governor Tryon's proclamation offering rewards for the arrest of the leaders of the Green Mountain Boys. At this and a subsequent meeting held at Capt. Jehiel Hawley's home in Arlington in April 1774, the leadership of what was quickly becoming an organized rebellion openly challenged the continued authority of New York over the Grants and, at least indirectly, the authority of the king. Not long after, Dr. Samuel Adams, a prominent Arlington leader and Yorker supporter, was seized and taken to Stephen Fay's tavern in Bennington, where he was bound to an armchair and ceremoniously hoisted to the top of the signpole. He hung for hours just below the old stuffed "catamount" at the top of the staff, as Green Mountain Boys drank to his health. Intended as an obvious warning, their message was clear. Those who openly sided with New York would do so at their own risk. In January

1775, the Green Mountain Boys took considerably stronger action against the Rev. Benjamin Hough of Socialborough, who had continued to serve as a justice of the peace under New York authority despite repeated warnings to resign the position. Tried by the leaders of the Green Mountain Boys, Hough was severely whipped and escorted out of the Grants under armed guard. [8]

On the eastern side of the mountains, events transpired that would provide the Green Mountain Boys with an important opportunity to broaden their campaign against New York. Trouble with the Cumberland County court had continued; in January 1772 an angry mob had openly defied an order of the court by "liberating" property seized by the sheriff from Leonard Spaulding of Putney in payment of a debt owed Jonas Moore. The matter was subsequently resolved when the rioters agreed to pay the forty pounds Spaulding owed Moore. [9] During the summer of 1774, Spaulding was again at the center of an anti-court mob, but this time for a different reason. Arrested for speaking out disparagingly against the king in connection with the passage of the Quebec Act, Spaulding had been forcibly released from jail by an angry group of his friends. [10] Not surprisingly, Issac Low, chairman of the New York Committee of Correspondence, wrote the supervisors of Cumberland County inquiring into the revolutionary sentiment among its inhabitants. Though the supervisors attempted to suppress the inquiry, Dr. Reuben Jones of Rockingham and Capt. Azariah Wright of Westminster forced the calling of a convention on the issue, which was held at Westminster in October 1774. At this and two subsequent conventions held at Westminster in November 1774 and February 1775, the people of Cumberland County defended their rights as British subjects against the unjust acts of Parliament, appointed a large standing Committee of Correspondence, and took preliminary measures to organize a provisional county government. [11]

The regular sitting of the Cumberland Court of Common

Pleas was scheduled to be held in Westminster on March 14, 1775. In light of the actions taken at the recent convention, Judge Chandler was urged to postpone the session, which he initially agreed to do. Unfortunately, Judge Noah Sabin let it be known that he intended to hold court as usual, and a group of towns-people opposing him determined to take possession of the courthouse. On March 12 Sheriff William Patterson of Hinsdale (Vernon) raised an armed force in Brattleboro and other Yorker towns and marched to Westminster. After refreshing themselves at John Norton's tavern, the group attacked the courthouse late in the evening. After several attempts to storm the door and dislodge the defenders failed, the sheriff ordered his men to open fire; ten men inside the courthouse were seriously wounded, and two — William French and Daniel Houghton — died of their wounds. Word soon spread of what was called the "Westminster Massacre," and by noon of the fourteenth over four hundred men had assembled in front of the courthouse, prepared to support the rioters against the sheriff and judges. Several hundred additional men, including Robert Cochran at the head of a company of Green Mountain Boys, arrived the following day. By a vote of those assembled, the officers of the court were taken under a guard of twenty-five Green Mountain Boys commanded by Cochran, and twenty-five New Hampshire militia commanded by a Captain Butterfield, to Northampton, Massachusetts, where they remained in jail until released to New York under a writ of *habeas corpus*.[12]

Though the inhabitants of the Grants had not been immune to the spirit of revolt against royal authority sweeping the American colonies, the claim that young William French was a martyr to the cause of independence is difficult to support. The clash at Westminster was only indirectly related to the growing independence movement in Cumberland County, while popular dissatisfaction with the conduct of local judges and lawyers was the immediate provocation. Though totally unrelated

9

to the situation west of the mountains, the problems resulting from their armed resistance to New York authority led the inhabitants of Cumberland County in a convention called at Westminster a month later to "renounce and resist the administration of the government of New York till such time as they can have opportunity to lay their grievances before his most gracious Majesty in Council." Significantly, the resolution included the first public sentiment that the Grants should be removed from "so oppressive a jurisdiction" as New York, and "either annexed to some other government or erected and incorporated into a new one."[13]

Thus, when Ethan Allen and the Green Mountain Boys captured Fort Ticonderoga on May 10, 1775, liberating its cannon and stores for the Revolution, it was as much a revolution against the tyranny of the colonial government of New York as it was against the British Crown. This "revolt within a revolt" provided the perfect opportunity for Ethan Allen and his cronies to reverse serious erosion in support for their cause west of the mountains and to extend their influence east of the mountains. Anxious to protect his reckless investments in the Onion River Land Company, and convinced of the strategic and commercial importance of the Richelieu-Champlain valley corridor to Montreal and Quebec, Allen had joined Col. Philip Skene's efforts to secure a royal charter for a new and independent colony in the Champlain region. Skene had gone to London to seek such a charter in 1774. When the rising tide of the American Revolution caused Allen to abandon his hopes for such a royal colony, he quickly joined the patriot cause as the only acceptable alternative. The battles of Lexington and Concord in mid-April 1775 had signaled a critical change in American-British relations, and when the Massachusetts Committee of Safety authorized Capt. Benedict Arnold to raise a company of militia in western Massachusetts to capture Fort Ticonderoga, Allen seized the moment. Capturing the dilapidated and poorly defended garrison at Ticonderoga not only gained the Green Mountain Boys badly needed recognition among respected patriot leaders, but also advanced Allen's larger motive—opening the way for an American assault on British Canada. Allen considered the success of such an adventure likely and was anxious to secure American domination of commerce and trade in the region. [14]

Following the lead of the other colonies, eastsiders declared their support for the American Revolution in a convention at Westminster in early June 1775. A month later, westside leaders met at Cephas Kent's tavern in Dorset to elect officers to command the Green Mountain Rangers, a new battalion of Gen. Philip Schuyler's New York regiment raised to defend New York against the threatened invasion of Sir Guy Carleton, the British commander in Canada. Schuyler was undoubtedly relieved that Seth Warner was elected to command the battalion with the rank of lieutenant colonel rather than Ethan Allen. Whether as a result of his disappointment at not being chosen to lead or his reluctance to wait until the regiment was ready to move north against Canada, Allen headed north almost immediately and was captured in an ill-conceived assault near Montreal in September 1775. Under the command of Brig. Gen. Richard Montgomery, the regiment succeeded in capturing St. Johns and Montreal during the fall of 1775; on December 31, however, Montgomery was killed in an assault launched against the Citadel in Quebec, which ended in disaster for the Americans. [15]

In January 1776 eighteen westside towns sent representatives to Kent's Tavern in Dorset to reconsider the status of the Green Mountain Rangers; a committee was appointed to draft a "Remonstrance and Petition" to the Continental Congress requesting permission for the unit to serve as a part of the Continental forces rather than as a New York battalion. The petition also sought recognition for the Grants as a "separate district" from New York. [16] The petition was presented to the Continental Congress in Philadelphia in May, but was withdrawn in June

11

when it became clear that the Congress was unprepared to support independence for the Grants. In early July, Congress did vote to raise a new regiment of the Continental Army. Despite objections from the New York delegation, Seth Warner received a commission as colonel, and the roster of officers included many of the old leaders of the Green Mountain Boys. [17] A second convention was held in Dorset on July 24, 1776, at which representatives from thirty-one westside towns and one eastside town — Townsend — resolved to form "a separate district." Known as the "Dorset Resolution," the statement was promptly circulated throughout the Grants, together with the call for another convention to be held in Dorset in late September. On the twenty-fifth, representatives of twenty-five westside and seventeen eastside towns voted unanimously to endorse the "Dorset Resolution" and to form a separate district.

During this phase of the campaign for independence, the leadership of Thomas Chittenden of Williston and Dr. Reuben Jones of Rockingham became increasingly significant in broadening support for the movement throughout the Grants. If initially Capt. Heman Allen and Dr. Jonas Fay of Bennington, together with Col. William Marsh of Manchester, had been the primary political proponents of independence, it was Chittenden and Jones who encouraged eastsiders to endorse the "Dorset Resolution"; while Joseph Bowker of Rutland was routinely elected to preside over this series of carefully orchestrated conventions, it was Chittenden and Jones who were principally responsible for securing participants. [18]

On October 30, 1776, yet another convention convened at Westminster, but attendance was seriously reduced by the threat of an invasion following Arnold's defeat off Valcour Island, and the meeting was adjourned until the following January. At the reconvened meeting, twenty-four delegates representing seven westside and ten eastside towns unanimously declared the Grants to be a separate and independent state named "New Connecticut." Neither Fay nor Marsh attended, and Nathan Clark of Bennington and Thomas Chittenden were entrusted with the task of drafting an appropriate declaration. Though actual representation at the convention was relatively sparse, there is evidence that the action of those present was widely supported throughout the Grants. [19]

In early April 1777, several events occurred that would have a critical impact on the future of the new "state." Early in the month, a petition was presented to the Continental Congress in Philadelphia seeking recognition and the right to send delegates. About the same time, a new state constitution was ratified in New York. Characterized by a strong governor and appointed judges who served for life, the constitution was far too "aristocratic" for the tastes of most inhabitants of the Grants. More important, it provided that the Grants would be entitled to elect only nine of the seventy members of the new state assembly and three of twenty-four members of the state senate. Such an arrangement reflected the serious tensions that existed between the coastal and back-country regions of the country. In February 1777, Col. Jacob Bayley of Newbury and Dr. Eleazer Wheelock of Hanover, president of Dartmouth College and leader of the so-called "College Party," a group of prominent upper Connecticut River Valley inhabitants who supported a plan for both sides of the river community to remain united regardless of larger jurisdictional issues, had met in Lebanon, New Hampshire, with representatives of the "Exeter Party," the political faction in control of the New Hampshire state government in Portsmouth. Reflecting the underlying discontent of the back-country with the New Hampshire constitution of 1775, which perpetuated coastal domination of the state, an accommodation was agreed to which would have revived New Hampshire's claim to towns along the western bank of the Connecticut River and significantly increased the political influence of the region. By early April, however, it was clear that arrangements had fallen

13

through, and no union of the river towns under New Hampshire authority would be agreed to by the Exeter Party. [20]

The combined failures of the New Hampshire negotiations and the unacceptable New York constitution of 1777 finally convinced reluctant eastside leaders like Jacob Bayley, who had been elected to represent Gloucester County in the New York assembly, and Charles Phelps of Marlboro, an important leader who had preferred union with Massachusetts, to support the formation of the new state of "New Connecticut." Consequently, attempts made by the old Cumberland Committee of Safety in June 1777 to elect officers under the recently ratified New York constitution met with marked failure; in a series of conventions convened in Westminster and Brattleboro only a handful of towns were represented. Though many staunch eastside Congregationalists agreed with Jacob Bayley that Bennington radicals like the Allens were "friends of Hell," they were now prepared to make a pact with the devil himself to preserve the independence of the Grants. [21]

On June 4, 1777, seventy-two delegates representing twenty-two westside towns and twenty-six eastside towns gathered in Windsor. In addition to proposing a "Declaration of Rights" and "Frame of Government" the convention adopted "Vermont" as the name of the new state, aware that a group of Connecticut inhabitants of the Wyoming Valley in northeastern Pennsylvania had already established themselves as "New Connecticut." A month later, on July 2, 1777, the convention reconvened in Windsor, with fifty delegates representing some thirty-one towns about evenly divided east and west. Confronted with the possibility of imminent invasion from General Burgoyne's army, the delegates unanimously endorsed the proposed constitution. Following the unsuccessful engagement at Hubbardton on the seventh, a Vermont Council of Safety was appointed, with Thomas Chittenden elected its first president. [22]

From this summary of the history of the Grants between

1764 and 1777, several important points should be established concerning the significance of the historical context of the Vermont constitution of 1777. First, the inhabitants of the New Hampshire Grants had lived in a virtual "state of nature" after 1764; law and order were both in short supply with the safety of one's person and property more dependent upon his standing in the community than on the protection of any provincial government or royal officials. Second, the political unrest caused by New York's feeble attempts to assert its physical control over the Grants broke into open and armed resistance at approximately the same time that relations between the Crown and its colonies were becoming seriously strained. As a result, Governor Tryon could not depend on units of the regular British army that might otherwise have been available to establish effective colonial control over the Grants. Finally, rejecting New York's claims of sovereignty, the inhabitants of the Grants, relying increasingly upon community consensus to determine the legitimacy of state action, declared their independence from both the State of New York and the British Empire. Reflecting a political tradition that included both the Mayflower Compact and the Fundamental Orders, a rugged and self-reliant people used town meetings to address essentially local matters and repeatedly sent representatives to conventions called to resolve issues concerning the larger polity. In practice, if not in theory, Vermont was the product of Hobbesian and Lockean philosophy experienced firsthand.

CONSTITUTIONAL CONTENT

For many years, the conventional wisdom was that the constitution proposed by the Windsor convention of June 1777, and subsequently adopted by the Windsor convention of July 1777, was essentially a copy of the Pennsylvania constitution of 1776. [23] Early commentators claimed that with the exception of some ten minor alterations, the Vermont constitution duplicated

15

the major provisions of the Pennsylvania model. Both constitutions created a unicameral legislative assembly with powers reflecting the radical republican philosophy of the times. Both created a "Council of Censors," which would ensure that the people's command as expressed in the constitution would not be altered or abridged by their elected representatives or officials. Both created executive officers who would serve for relatively brief terms and who would in theory exercise limited authority and whose discretion would be strictly limited. [24]

More recent scholarship, however, has suggested that despite the striking similarities between the two documents, the framers of the Vermont constitution actually made some twenty-seven changes from the Pennsylvania original. Though several of these changes altered the text of the instrument only slightly, their political effect was substantial. Under the Pennsylvania constitution of 1776, the government of Pennsylvania grew increasingly unstable until the constitution was significantly amended. In contrast, Vermont established a "closed regime," which was initially quite stable and essentially governed the state without interruption until its political support eroded during the first decade of the nineteenth century as a result of popular opposition to the Embargo Acts of 1807-8 and partisan controversy concerning the War of 1812. [25]

The most significant differences between the two texts concerned the way in which state executive officers and censors were to be elected and the nature and authority of the judiciary. Although the Pennsylvania constitution provided for no statewide elective offices, the framers of the Vermont constitution provided for twenty-eight—the governor, lieutenant governor, treasurer, twelve members of the Governor's Council, and thirteen members of the Council of Censors. In sharp contrast to their alleged model, the Vermont framers also eliminated the Pennsylvania prohibition on reelection, as well as the prohibition of holding multiple offices under the constitution at the same

16

time. Most strikingly, the Vermont constitution omitted entirely the section of the Pennsylvania constitution concerning the organization of the judiciary. While the Vermont instrument mentioned a "supreme court" and provided that "courts of justice be established in every county" of the state, it was completely silent concerning the important issues of judicial qualifications, method of selection, composition, jurisdiction, tenure, and compensation. Unfortunately, no record of the Vermont framers' deliberations or debates survives. It might have helped to explain why they followed the Pennsylvania constitution so closely in some areas and deviated from it so dramatically in others; what little evidence there is suggests that Thomas Chittenden may have played a critical role in transforming the Pennsylvania model into the fundamental law of Vermont. [26]

POLITICAL CONSEQUENCES

The basic challenge precipitating Vermont's constituent act was to create a new political commonwealth where no true political community had previously existed. In this sense, the founding of the state of Vermont represented quite a different experience from that of the other American states. In contrast to the popular enthusiasm that met the declaration throughout the colonies, political leaders in the New Hampshire Grants had difficulty convincing their people that they had the right to self-government. [27] Specifically, the new government faced the immediate challenge of demonstrating that it could exercise sovereign authority by protecting the lives and property rights of those living within its jurisdiction. Only over the course of time did the citizens of the new state of Vermont come to accept the legal status and authority of their self-proclaimed "constitution." [28]

This challenge was compounded by the presence of factional rivalry, regional jealousy, and the misapprehension of a generation of settlers who had experienced only limited political stability. In particular, the evolution of the Bennington faction into a cohesive political alliance known as the "Arlington Junto" did little to assuage the fears of men like Jacob Bayley and Charles Phelps that decisions of state were being made by Thomas Chittenden and Ira Allen — principals of the Onion River Land Company — to advance their own private financial interests. There were also the old Yorkers like Judge Samuel Wells of Brattleboro and Judge Thomas Chandler of Chester, who continued to resist the formation of an independent Vermont. Finally, the decision of the new state government to fund the war effort through the confiscation and sale of property of "Loyalists" rather than through new taxes provided a direct means of rewarding supporters of independence at the expense of less enthusiastic citizens.

Unlike the American colonies, leaders in the Grants could not simply adopt a revised or amended colonial charter as the new revolutionary state constitution. Thus, the nature of Vermont's "statehood" was considerably more ambiguous from the outset. Vermont had joined the American revolution against British colonial tyranny at least partly as a result of what the people considered the "illegal measures" and "oppressive acts" of the colonial government of New York. In their "Declaration of Independence" of January 15, 1777, representatives of the people of the Grants had explicitly declared their independence from "the arbitrary acts of the crown," including "the jurisdiction by said crown granted to New York government over the people of the New Hampshire Grants."[29] Ironically, it was precisely for this reason that the new commonwealth's claim to statehood was not embraced or recognized by the other states. Vermonters had been instrumental in capturing Fort Ticonderoga in 1775 and thwarting Burgoyne's invasion of New England in 1777; not surprisingly, they expected to be welcomed into the new nation as a fully equal partner. Instead, the Continental Congress refused to act favorably upon Vermont's petition to join the union of new American states. Although partly due to New York's adamant insistence that the Grants remain a part of New York, the debates in Congress during the summer of 1777, and later, suggested more far-reaching questions raised by the "Vermont Problem." The issue provoked potent antagonisms of ancient origin between New York and New England and heightened existing tensions between coastal and backcountry delegates. More important, it undermined the tenuous and limited alliance between the new states to such an extent that discussion of the Articles of Confederation was delayed. Seriously threatening the cooperation necessary to pursue the war successfully, further debate over the "Vermont Question" was postponed until a future date. [30]

Vermont's assertion of its right to independence fundamentally challenged the authority of the status of Congress as successor to the Crown. The new state claimed the same right to independence and self-government that the colonies had relied upon in asserting their independence from Great Britain. Recognition of an independent state of Vermont would also have invited further "dissolution" and "disunion" among the original thirteen states. Pennsylvania's jurisdiction over the Wyoming Valley was already being challenged, and Virginia in particular was confronted with the political aspirations of frontier communities in Kentucky and Tennessee. Despite these circumstances, inhabitants of Vermont fully expected Congressional recognition, and the failure of Congress to seat delegates from Vermont in 1777 resulted in a politically precarious existence for the new commonwealth. No longer part of the British Empire and not yet a part of the American union of states, Vermont found itself in the unanticipated circumstance of proclaiming itself to be an independent — if isolated and vulnerable — republic. [31]

Though an independent royal colony may have been considered desirable by Ethan Allen in 1774, by 1778 the American Revolution had rendered such a plan impossible; moreover, the creation of a "Vermont" regiment in the Continental Army had suggested a more favorable reaction by Congress to Vermont statehood. Relying on the political advice of Dr. Thomas Young, an old friend of the Allens who became the chief supporter of Vermont's independence movement in Philadelphia, Congressional recognition was virtually guaranteed. A radical democrat steeped in the traditions of English republicanism, Dr. Young wrote an open letter to his friends in the Grants in April, 1777:

> You have nothing to do but send attested copies of the recommendation to take up government to every township in your district and invite all your freeholders and inhabitants to meet in their respective townships and choose members for a general convention to meet at an early date to choose delegates to the general congress, a committee of safety and to form a constitution for your state.[32]

Realizing that the Grants had no colonial identity or charter upon which to rely, Dr. Young sent along a copy of the Pennsylvania constitution of 1776, which had been modeled on William Penn's famous colonial charter of 1681 and framed and ratified within weeks of the signing of the Declaration of Independence. It was also Dr. Young who had suggested in his letter that the new commonwealth might better be named "Vermont" than "New Connecticut." Having provided both a model frame of government and a new name for state, Young encouraged his friends to "organize fairly and make the experiment." To those who were concerned that Congress might not endorse statehood, he wrote:

> I have taken the mind of several leading Members in the Honorable Continental Congress . . . I ensure your success at the risk of my reputation as a man of honor or common sense. Indeed, they can by no means refuse you! You have as good a right to choose how you will be governed, and by whom, as they had.[33]

Following Dr. Young's advice, seventy-two delegates assembled in Windsor on June 4, 1777. The largest gathering

20

of representatives of towns in the Grants to that time, the delegates elected a committee of safety and appointed a committee to draft a proposed constitution. Joseph Bowker, the president of the first Windsor convention, sent a letter to all the towns of the Grants, informing them of the convention's work, and recommending that they elect delegates "to meet the grand convention at Windsor . . . to form a constitution for the state of Vermont."[34] On July 2, 1777, the first constitution for the State of Vermont was adopted by the Windsor convention.[35]

Although it was believed for some time that as a result of difficulties associated with the war the constitution of 1777 was never ratified by the people of Vermont, more recent scholarship suggests otherwise.[36] Though there has been little detailed historical work done in Vermont's early constitutional period, contemporary scholarship challenges the traditional assumption that the work of the Windsor convention was never submitted directly to the people. Available evidence calls into considerable question Ira Allen's assertion that the constitution was not submitted to the people of Vermont for ratification, ostensibly as a result of difficulties encountered in having the constitution published, but in fact because of fear that the people might have rejected it. In February 1778, Thomas Chittenden, president of the Council of Safety, sent a letter to the inhabitants of "the state of Vermont" encouraging them to "adopt" the new constitution and choose delegates to the first General Assembly.[37] Interestingly, records indicate that several towns, notably Brattleboro and Guilford, either initially abstained or voted against the constitution.[38] By March 12, 1778, however, a sufficient number of towns had ratified the document and elected representatives at town meeting to enable the first legislative General Assembly to convene at Windsor. It elected Thomas Chittenden the state's first governor as well as the twelve men who formed the first executive council.[39] Though the Windsor convention had been called principally for the purpose of drafting a constitution, the method by which Vermont's constitution was implemented at least presaged the formal practice of submitting constitutions to the people for popular ratification.

Thomas Chittenden. Engraving. Vermont Historical Society

Chittenden's election was significant. A seasoned political leader with prior experience in the Connecticut assembly, he had been instrumental in securing east-west cooperation, assuring the ultimate success of the independence movement. Moreover, his election as the president of the Council of Safety and membership on the committee responsible for drafting the constitution distinguished him from other likely contenders. Had Ethan Allen been released by the British through a prisoner exchange a month earlier or Col. Seth Warner been interested in the position, the situation might have been different. Despite Chittenden's close ties to the Allens and membership in the "Arlington Junto," he was nevertheless the man most qualified for the position. The clear "consensus" candidate, his election demonstrated that the people of Vermont had successfully met the first challenge of statehood — finding a way to integrate the east-west political schism of the state's political factions.

Throughout the early constitutional period, Ethan and Ira Allen and their Bennington friends had dominated the politics of the Champlain Valley, as Col. Jacob Bayley and Dr. Eleazar Wheelock and their various allies had the politics of the Connecticut River Valley. These two rival forces, together with lingering Yorker sentiment in Brattleboro, Guilford, and Putney, threatened to destroy the fragile foundations upon which the new state was to be built. Although Chittenden was closely associated with the political forces west of the mountains, his election revealed a willingness on the part of the easterners to compromise. Motivated in large measure by the unpopular state constitutions adopted in New Hampshire and New York, which seemed to ignore the interests of both these areas, and the complete inability of either New Hampshire or New York to govern effectively at the fringes of their territories, the Allen and Bayley factions accepted internal compromise as the only acceptable alternative available. [40]

Despite the appearance of unanimity, however, the scope of the compromise between these two groups was relatively limited; they continued to compete rather ruthlessly within the new polity for political control of the new government as well as for control of Vermont's economic future. Despite their continuing dispute over whether the region's economic growth and prosperity lay to the north via the Richelieu-Champlain Valley corridor or to the south via the Hudson and Connecticut River valleys, the mutual accommodation of these two powerful factions did reflect a common commitment to independence for the Grants.

Vermont's tentative statehood created serious problems within both the territorial limits claimed by the new state and the larger political entity increasingly referred to as the United States of America. On June 25, 1777, Roger Sherman introduced a motion at the Continental Congress requesting official recognition of the new state of Vermont and granting permission for the state to send delegates to Congress. Led by James Duane and other members of the New York delegation who were adamantly opposed to this explicit dismemberment of an existing state, the Congress voted down Sherman's motion. [41] In time, at the insistence of Gov. George Clinton and other powerful voices in the new union, the Congress would adopt in June 1779 a resolution preserving the rights of the original states — no new state was to be formed out of an existing state without the consent of both Congress and the legislature of the existing state. [42] Proposed and accepted in order to keep Vermont out of the union, this resolution would be preserved intact as part of Article IV, Section 3 of the federal constitution of 1787.

Unwilling to rejoin the state of New York, and unable to join the new nation as an independent state, Vermont was forced to prove in fact what until 1777 had existed only in theory — the right of a free and sovereign people to form themselves into an independent body politic through their voluntary consent. Lying at the heart of what became known as "the Vermont Doctrine," this assertion both affirmed and challenged the republican principles of the American Revolution and the ensuing union under the Articles of Confederation. The inhabitants of the Grants had found themselves, as they had proclaimed in their "Declaration of Independence," without the benefit of "law or government"; returned to "a state of nature," they enjoyed the inherent natural right to form a government "best suited to secure their property, well being and happiness." [43] In his famous "Vindication of the Opposition of the Inhabitants of Vermont to the Government of New York," Ethan Allen wrote in 1779 that "the inhabitants of these contested lands governed themselves, and managed their internal police under the direction of committees and conventions" in a manner entirely similar to that of the several states following the Declaration of Independence. The thrust of Allen's argument was quite plain — Vermont's claim to the right of self-government was precisely the same right claimed by the colonies in their declaration against Great Britain. [44]

Dr. Young had believed as much when he wrote in 1777 that "such bodies of men as looked upon themselves [as] returned to a state of nature" needed only to take the initiative

24

to draft and adopt a plan of government and thus "become a body politic," as had the original thirteen states. [45] It was in this spirit that Governor Chittenden wrote to Congress in 1782:

> How inconsistent then, is it in Congress, to assume the same arbitrary stretch of prerogative over Vermont, for which they waged war against Great Britain? Is the liberty and natural rights of mankind a mere bubble, and the sport of state politicians? [46]

But Dr. Young's brand of republicanism was not shared by everyone. If it was the unusually stringent requirements of consensus under the Articles of Confederation that had initially kept Vermont out of the union, it was the growing fear of anarchy among Federalist leaders that would continue to frustrate admission. Sounding more like the British of 1776 than American patriots, leading men began to argue that the people of Vermont had never been returned to a state of nature, nor had they ever really existed as a separate and distinct body politic. Rather than fellow patriots fighting for the Republic, these lawless frontiersmen were outlaws and bandits who had refused to recognize the legitimate authority of the laws of New York. Such men were little interested in the claim that immediately prior to the Revolution the British Crown had established an independent colony and had granted a new charter to Philip Skene, its royal governor. The effort invested by the government of Vermont to prove the existence of such a charter suggests the important if not critical role colonial charters played in defining rights and establishing legitimacy during the early constitutional period in America. Vermont's claim to equal status was initially based more on its asserted claim of independent colonial existence than upon the right of its people to form their own government. [47]

Vermont's hesitancy to base its claim of statehood on the will of its own citizens is significant. Contemporary Americans consider it an article of faith that self-determination exercised through representative forms of government and republican government are synonomous expressions of the same ideal. In fact, Vermont's founding and its relations with the American states seriously call into question whether America's founding generation really shared this view. While the continental union confirmed the legitimacy, autonomy, and territorial integrity of the original thirteen colonies, the implicit assumption of the Articles of Confederation was that the source of the sovereignty of the several states could be traced to the original sovereignty of the British Crown. The critical link in this evolution was, of course, the colonial charter. Absent such a charter, the necessary source of sovereignty simply did not exist. As one commentator wrote, "Many gentlemen . . . are fully of the opinion that Congress has no authority to admit those people [of Vermont] into the federal union as a separate state on the present principles."[48] Others shared this sentiment: "If every district so disposed may for themselves determine that they are not within the claim of the thirteen states . . . we may have ten hundred states, all free and independent."[49] Not surprisingly, the terrible consequences of such a prospect caused one writer to instruct James Madison to "fix the boundaries" and "let the people . . . know that they are citizens and must submit to their government."[50]

Despite the fact that Vermont could prove no legitimate past and could derive none of the benefits of Congressional recognition, it clung to its assertion of the right of its citizens to determine for themselves how they would be governed. As one newspaper argued:

> When it is for the interest and happiness of the people, for which all governments are, or ought to be formed or constituted, no good reason can be assigned why new states and empires should not arise and branch out from old ones."[51]

If in June 1779 it had been the opinion of Governor Chittenden that "a public acknowledgement of the powers of the earth" was essential to the continued existence of the state of Vermont, by the following summer his view and that of many other Vermonters had become more positive. Increasingly, the argument of Vermonters was that their right to independence depended less upon the existence of a colonial charter or the recognition of the federal Congress than it did upon the simple fact that they would only consent to be governed as Vermonters. Forced to "go it alone," Governor Chittenden entered into a series of secret negotiations with Gen. Frederick Haldimand, British Commander-General of Canada. Though considerable scholarly debate exists over Chittenden's motivation for attempting to negotiate Vermont's reentry into the British Empire as a separate colony, Chittenden's questionable diplomatic overture had the effect of protecting Vermont's neutrality when it became clear that Vermont could not expect protection from the Continental Congress. [52]

The new government also moved to shore up the people's confidence in its ability to guarantee land titles and protect life and limb within its jurisdiction. After a tenuous and troubled start, it was soon established that the new government was in fact taking hold and providing the first reliable authority the people of the Grants had experienced. In the final analysis, Vermonters began to realize that as only the government of Vermont had demonstrated the capacity and will to govern the territory of Vermont effectively, no other justification was necessary to support its legitimacy. As Peter Onuf concluded:

> Only in Vermont was the concept of a state as a self-constituted political community fully and radically tested . . . In this sense, Vermont was the only true American republic, for it alone had truly created itself. [53]

By 1780, the success of Vermont's "experiment" and the unpalatable New York and New Hampshire constitutions of 1779 had encouraged some thirty-five New Hampshire towns along the Connecticut River and twelve New York towns along the western shores of Lake Champlain to seek admission into the Vermont republic. In the republic's only military campaign, Vermont militia had convincingly routed the forces of New York in the abortive "Border War" of December 1781.[54] Vermont's aggressive territorial expansion dramatically demonstrated the costs of Congress's policy of non-recognition; if the states were unwilling to accept Vermont's sovereignty, Vermonters saw no reason to respect the sovereignty of their neighboring states. The fact that the Allen faction had been politically outmaneuvered by the first Eastern Union of sixteen New Hampshire towns in June 1778, which had the effect of shifting control in the legislature to the Bayley faction, explains why the "Arlington Junto" utilized Congressional outrage and threats from New Hampshire governor Meseach Weare and Gen. John Stark of the Continental Army's northern command to have the Union dissolved in February 1780. By the spring of 1781, however, circumstances had changed significantly with both the Allen and Bayley factions supporting the creation of a "Greater Vermont" through the territorial expansion that accompanied the second Eastern Union with New Hampshire towns and the first Western Union with twelve New York towns. Exposed to the risks of the independent status that non-recognition created, Vermont needed to expand its territory significantly. Lying between British Canada to the north and the United States to the south, the independent republic of Vermont could scarcely expect to survive without expansion. The only other alternative was recognition and incorporation into one adjoining empire or the other.[55]

The Haldimand Negotiations of 1781 made this situation explicit. While most Vermonters would never have tolerated a reunion of Vermont and the British Empire, which explains the serious scandal that developed when the existence of these secret diplomatic negotiations became known, the fact that such an eventuality was even considered by Vermont's leading political figures reveals the fragile nature of the Vermont republic during those early years. Whether undertaken to secure Vermont's neutrality during the war or to protect the personal financial investments of the principals in the Onion River Land Trust by securing access to the strategic Richelieu-Champlain Valley corridor, the plan lost support following Cornwallis's defeat at the Battle of Yorktown in October 1781.[56] While the British recognized the sovereignty of the thirteen original states through the Treaty of Paris signed in September 1783, and implicitly recognized American claims to what had been the New Hampshire Grants by agreeing to a Canadian boundary that lay north of the Grants, Vermont's status remained unsettled. At the insistence of George Washington, Vermont had abandoned its eastern and western unions in February 1782; the question of the admission into the American union of states, however, remained unsettled. Thus, from 1783 until 1791, when Vermont was finally offered admission to the United States, it remained necessary for the government of the Republic of Vermont to prove itself to the citizens of the United States of America as well as to its own citizens.

Though little has been written on the subject, existing historical research suggests that Vermont developed a system of government in substance, if not in form, remarkably similiar to party or parliamentary government.[57] As mentioned, the text of the Vermont constitution of 1777 resembled the Pennsylvania constitution of 1776 in many ways, but the differences between the two permitted a concentration of power in executive officers elected on a statewide basis in Vermont. Consequently, a single party or faction within the state was able to control executive decisions and thus dominate politics for the first decade of its existence.[58] Prior to a constitutional revision in 1786, which provided that the three branches of government "shall be separate and distinct so that neither shall exercise the powers properly belonging to the others," the concept of separation of powers did not operate in Vermont.[59] The unicameral legislature and

29

Governor's Council created in 1777 continued as essential elements of Vermont's government until the creation of the Vermont state senate and the abolition of the Governor's Council in 1836.[60] The provision of the constitution of 1777 creating the Council of Censors, which was abolished as unworkable in Pennsylvania in 1790, was retained in Vermont until 1870. Unlike Pennsylvania's council, which was comprised of two censors elected from each county, Vermont's constitution provided for thirteen censors to be elected statewide.[61] As mentioned above, the governor, lieutenant governor, and the twelve additional members of the Governor's Council were also to be elected statewide under the Vermont constitution. Only the members of the state's unicameral General Assembly were to be elected by the people of each town at town meeting, initially two from the larger towns and one each from the smaller towns. The absence of any prohibition against multiple office-holding in the Vermont constitution of 1777 also contributed significantly to the concentration of political power in Vermont and the evolution of a unique style of party government.[62]

Consistent with the tentative nature of Vermonters' acceptance of the theoretical underpinnings of their independence, few citizens of the new republic believed the constitution of 1777 to be anything other than a legislative act of a statewide convention. The constitution was not formally declared to be "the supreme law of the land" until 1796 and was ceremoniously reenacted by succeeding General Assemblies as a gesture of allegiance and reaffirmation.[63] This "habit" of reconstituting the republic calls into question what has become a rather traditional acceptance of the differentiated roles played by constitutional conventions and General Assemblies in the founding period. The practice in Vermont suggests that at a minimum the significance of such a formal difference had not yet been accepted by the citizens of the state of Vermont.

This practice also suggests the extent to which the first

citizens of Vermont viewed their constitution instrumentally. As the preamble stated, the constitution was instituted "for the security and protection of the community as such," "to enable the individuals who compose it to enjoy their natural rights," and "to take such measures as may to them appear necessary to promote their safety and happiness."[64] The experience of the early years of the Vermont republic confirms that the citizens of the state were far more concerned that the broad ends of the new government be achieved than they were with the specific means employed.

Perhaps as a result of the unsettled conditions confronting them, the citizens of Vermont accepted the leadership of what can only be described as the oligarchy of a small but powerful group of men who dominated Vermont politics for over two decades.[65] From the outset, members of the Governor's Council participated in and dominated the legislative process. Members of the council drafted legislation and reported bills to the assembly. Members of the council also participated more directly in the work of the assembly, serving as members of legislative committees until 1791.[66] Thomas Chittenden, the first governor, held that office for all but one year (1789-90) prior to his death in 1797; during the same period of time barely more than twenty men sat in the Governor's Council.[67] It is also significant that until 1786, judges of the state's supreme court were almost always either members of the council or members of the General Assembly; from 1777 until 1779 they were elected annually by joint ballot of the governor, council, and assembly, after which time they were elected by the legislature.[68] Between 1779 and 1786, members of the Governor's Council held all but one of the five seats on the supreme court, and for five of these years all five of the justices were also members of the council.[69] Nor was such multiple office-holding limited to the high court. From 1777 to 1824, twenty-one of the twenty-three members of the Chittenden County court had served in either the General Assembly or the Governor's Council, either before or during their tenure on the court. In Windsor County, the figure was twenty-six of twenty-eight, suggesting that such a pattern was probably typical throughout the state.[70] In the absence of a constitutional article providing for the organization of the state's judiciary, the General Assembly in 1782 established a court system modeled after the Massachusetts Courts of General Session. In such a system, there was no distinction made between trial and appellate courts; moreover, county courts possessed broad supervisory powers over town government and over local economies. Together with local town officials, the courts served in effect as the county governments. Thus, the overlapping personnel on the Governor's Council, General Assembly, and county courts operated to ensure party control of government at all levels of state government.[71]

As might be expected under such a system, the General Assembly concurred with every recommendation of the Governor's Council from 1777 through 1781. In that year and the one following, the assembly required an accounting from the state treasurer and passed a tax measure and two private bills over the objection of the council. While the assembly remained generally content to follow the executive's lead, it increasingly asserted its independence.[72] In particular, the legislature reserved jurisdiction over certain types of disputes, including those over land titles, and asserted the right to amend through private bills decisions of the courts that it deemed unwise. This practice challenged directly the judiciary's authority to interpret and apply the law of the land as well as the Council of Censors' role in reviewing the constitutionality of all governmental acts.

It is a particularly fascinating aspect of Vermont's early constitutional period that an important alliance developed between the Council of Censors and an increasingly professional judiciary. Originally staffed by lay judges, Vermont's judiciary became predominantly the domain of professional lawyers after 1789;

lawyers also began to assume a leadership role among the Council of Censors.[73] Between 1800 and 1814, the Council of Censors and the courts began to attack actions of the legislature as contrary to the constitution—the fundamental law of the land. Though initially unsuccessful in persuading the people of Vermont that there was anything wrong with the legislature interpreting and informally amending the constitution through ordinary legislation, the arguments of the censors and the courts ultimately prevailed. Undoubtedly, the organization and growth of the Federalist Party under the able leadership of such men as Nathaniel Chipman, Isaac Tichenor, and Moses Robinson and the strong public opposition to the Embargo of 1807-8 and ensuing War of 1812 helped to weaken the hold of the incumbent government. The Governor's Council elected in 1808, for example, was the first council on which incumbents did not constitute a majority. Competition between the Federalists and the Jeffersonian successors to the old Allen-Chittenden "Junto"— like former Green Mountain Boy Matthew Lyon, the successful and popular political leader who founded the town of Fair Haven—had become increasingly fierce during the late 1790s. Reflecting fundamental philosophical differences as well as the emergence of nascent national political parties, this political rivalry had important consequences for constitutional developments in Vermont.[74]

In one especially important case, *Bates v. Kimball*, 2 D. Chipman 77 (1824), Justice Asa Aikens ruled an act of the legislature unconstitutional—the first time a Vermont court had explicitly invoked the power of judicial review. Asserting that it was the duty of the judicial branch to "declare the law," Aikens held that "interpretation of the laws is the proper and peculiar province of the courts." In language that could only have been taken from Marshall's famous decision in *Marbury v. Madison*, Aiken relied on the republican principle that the constitution was the embodiment of the will of the sovereign people of Ver-

33

mont, which only they could amend or alter through the specific means set forth in the constitution.[75] The victory of Aikens' view of the constitution was confirmed the following year when the General Assembly passed a bill reorganizing the state's judicial system, creating a politically independent state supreme court, and accepting at least implicitly the court's authority concerning judicial review.[76]

Thus, by 1824 Vermont's constitutional "founding" had been completed. The Vermont constitution of 1777 served the state well during a particularly trying period in its history. The only source of political identity for the new commonwealth, the constitution held the state of Vermont together both legally and socially during its fourteen-year struggle as an independent nation-state. During the time that elapsed from 1777 to 1824, the people of Vermont had come to view their constitution rather differently than they had originally. When the future of their political community had been uncertain at best, they were prepared to consider the constitution as little more than the provisional guidelines of the polity, a declaration of the rights and liberties of free men, and a frame of government that each annual legislature was free to revise, subject only to occasional review by the Council of Censors. But as greater stability and prosperity developed — perhaps as a result of the success of their constitution — Vermonters began to treat the constitution as something more than a mere legislative act. In time, the constitution became the "fundamental law" as well as the organic founding act of their polity.

NOTES

[1] William Slade (ed.), *Vermont State Papers* (Middlebury, Vt.: J. W. Copeland, 1823), 19-20. See also Chilton Williamson, *Vermont in Quandary, 1763-1825* (Montpelier, Vt.: Vermont Historical Society, 1949), 10-11.

[2] Allan R. Raymond, "Benning Wentworth's Claims in the New Hampshire-New York Border Controversy," *Vermont History* 43 (January 1975): 20.

[3] David M. Ludlum, *Social Ferment in Vermont, 1791-1850* (New York: Columbia University Press, 1939), 16. See also Donald A. Smith, *Legacy of Dissent: Religion and Politics in Revolutionary Vermont, 1749-1784* (Ph.D. diss., Clark University, 1980), Vermont Historical Society, manuscript collection, 152; and Winn L. Taplin, Jr., *The Vermont Problem in the Continental Congress and in Interstate Relations, 1776-1787* (Ph.D. diss., University of Michigan, 1956), Vermont Historical Society, manuscript collection, 1-2.

[4] Matt Bushnell Jones, *Vermont in the Making, 1750-1777* (? Archon Books, 1968), 257-263; Charles Miner Thompson, *Independent Vermont* (Boston: Houghton Mifflin Co., 1942), 87-91.

[5] Frederic F. Van DeWater, *The Reluctant Republic: Vermont, 1724-1791* (New York: John Day Company, 1941), 81-83; Williamson, 18.

[6] Van DeWater, 82.

[7] Jones, 284-5.

[8] Ibid., 280-1, 321-3, 331-2, 334-5.

[9] Ibid., 264-5.

[10] Ibid., 267.

[11] Ibid.

[12] Ibid., 268-73; See also H. Nicholas Muller, III, "Myth and Reality: The Politics of Independence in Vermont, 1776-1777," in *Perspectives '76* (Hanover, N.H.: Regional Center for Educational Training, 1976), 63-4; and Thompson, 163.

[13] Jones, 275; Taplin, 22. See also William Doyle, *The Vermont Political Tradition* (Barre, Vt.: Northlight Studio Press, 1984), 15-21.

[14] Taplin, 2, 16-19; Charles Jellison, *Ethan Allen: Frontier Rebel* (New York: Syracuse University Press, 1969), 84.

[15] Jones, 355-6; Williamson, 52-4.

[16] Jones, 358-9; Williamson, 55-6.

[17] Jones, 351, n. 14; Taplin, 67.

[18] Jones, 358-74; Williamson, 58-60.

[19] Jones, 375-6.

[20] Williamson, 79-81.

[21] Taplin, 28-30; Jones, 351-2.

[22] Jones, 383-6; Williamson, 63-6.

[23] John N. Shaeffer, "A Comparison of the First Constitutions of Vermont and Pennsylvania," *Vermont History* 34 (January 1966): 34-5.

[24] E. P. Walton (ed.), *Records of the Governor and Council of the State of Vermont*, (Montpelier, Vt.: J. M. Poland, 1873), I, 83-103.

[25] Shaeffer, 33; Doyle, 26-29.

[26] Jones, 389-93; Marshall True, "Why Are There No Biographies of Thomas Chittenden?" in *Lake Champlain: Reflections on Our Past*, Jennie G. Versteeg, ed., (Burlington, Vt.: Center for Research on Vermont, University of Vermont, 1987), 213.

[27] Peter S. Onuf, "State-Making in Revolutionary America: Independent Vermont as a Case Study," *Journal of American History* 67 (March 1981): 799.

[28] Onuf, 803.

[29] Vermont "Declaration of Independence," *Vermont and the New Nation: Selected documents illustrating Vermont's founding period and the national context of issues*

affecting Vermont, Marshall True and William Doyle, eds. (Hyde Park, Vt.: Vermont Council on the Humanities and Public Issues, 1987), 34.

[30] Taplin, 44-9; Peter S. Onuf, "Vermont and the Union" in *Lake Champlain*, 189-92; also reprinted in this volume, pp. 150–169.

[31] Shaeffer, 797-9.

[32] *Vermont and the New Nation*, 35. See also Nathaniel Hendricks, "The Experiment in Vermont Constitutional Government," *Vermont History* 34 (January 1966): 63.

[33] *Vermont and the New Nation*, 35.

[34] Hendricks, 64-5.

[35] Ibid.

[36] Nathaniel Hendricks, "A New Look at the Ratification of the Vermont Constitution of 1777," *Vermont History* 34 (April 1966): 136-7.

[37] Ibid., 137.

[38] Ibid., 138-9. See also Ira Allen, *History of the State of Vermont, 1798* (Rutland, Vt.: Charles Tuttle, 1969), 72.

[39] Hendricks, "A New Look at Ratification," 139.

[40] Doyle, 33-42. See also True, "Why Are There No Biographies of Thomas Chittenden?" 210-12.

[41] Taplin, 57-59. See also Larry R. Gerlach, "Connecticut, the Continental Congress, and the Independence of Vermont," *Vermont History* 34 (July 1966): 190.

[42] Gerlach, 190.

[43] *Vermont and the New Nation*, 34.

[44] Ethan Allen, "A Vindication of the Opposition of the Inhabitants of Vermont to the Government of New York," (Dresden/Hanover, N.H.: 1779), quoted in Onuf, "State-Making in Revolutionary America," 803.

[45] *Vermont and the New Nation*, 35; Onuf, "State-Making in Revolutionary America," 806; Hendricks, "The Experiment," 72.

[46] Thomas Chittenden to the President of the Congress, *Collections of the Vermont Historical Society* (Montpelier, Vt.: Vermont Historical Society, 1871), vol. 2, 319.

[47] Onuf, "State-Making in Revolutionary America," 805; Doyle, 47-50.

[48] Ezra L'Hommedieu to George Clinton (8 September 1781), quoted in Onuf, "State-Making in Revolutionary America," 800, n. 12.

[49] "Report of the Committee," *Conventions of Towns in Cheshire County, New Hampshire* (Cheshire County, N.H.: 1780), quoted in Onuf, "State-Making in Revolutionary America," 801.

[50] Joseph Jones to James Madison (2 October 1780), quoted in Onuf, "State-Making in Revolutionary America," 801.

[51] *The Pennsylvania Herald* (11 June 1785), quoted in Onuf, "State-Making in Revolutionary America," 801.

[52] Onuf, "Vermont and the Union," 194-5.

[53] Onuf, "State-Making in Revolutionary America," 815.

[54] Earle Newton, *The Vermont Story: A History of the People of the Green Mountain State, 1749-1849* (Montpelier, Vt.: Vermont Historical Society, 1949), 87-8.

[55] Doyle, 33-45.

[56] Ibid., 42-5.

[57] See H. Nicholas Muller, III, "Early Vermont State Government: Oligarchy or Democracy? 1778-1815," in *In A State of Nature: Readings in Vermont History*, H. Nicholas Muller, III, and Samuel B. Hand, eds. (Montpelier, Vt.: Vermont Historical Society, 1982), 80-1.

[58] Onuf, "State-Making in Revolutionary America," 798-9, 808-9.

[59] Muller, "Early Vermont State Government," 80.

[60] Newton, 77.

[61] Shaeffer, 38.

[62] Ibid., 36.

[63] Newton, 77. See also Gordon Wood, *The Creation of the American Republic, 1777-1787* (Chapel Hill, N.C.: University of North Carolina Press, 1969), 306-8.

[64] *Vermont and the Nation*, 36.

[65] Shaeffer, 36.

[66] Ibid., 38-9.

[67] Ibid., 36.

[68] Ibid., 39-40.

[69] Muller, "Early Vermont Government," 82-3.

[70] Samuel B. Hand and P. Jeffrey Potash, "Litigious Vermonters: Court Records to 1825," *Occasional Paper #2* (Burlington, Vt.: Center for Research on Vermont / University of Vermont, 1979), 11.

[71] Ibid., 4. See also Samuel B. Hand, "Lay Judges and the Vermont Judiciary to 1825," in *A State of Nature*, 94-104, at 99.

[72] Shaeffer, 42-3.

[73] Hand, "Litigious Vermonters," 13; Hand, "Lay Judges," 101.

[74] Aleine Austin, "Vermont Politics in the 1790's: The Emergence of Rival Leadership," *Vermont History* 42 (Spring 1974): 140; see also Edward Brynn, "Patterns of Dissent: Vermont's Opposition to the War of 1812," *Vermont History* 40 (1972): 10.

[75] James L. Bickford, "The Council of Censors and its Role in the Development of Judicial Review in Early Vermont, 1783-1824" (Master's thesis, Vermont Law School, 1978), 17-26. See also Lewis Meader, "The Council of Censors in Vermont," *Vermont Historical Society Proceedings (1898)*, (Montpelier, Vt.: Vermont Historical Society, 1899), 105.

[76] Bickford, 27-8.

Joining the United States: Ratification of the U.S. Constitution

by D. Gregory Sanford

 Though most Vermonters anticipated union with the United States soon after passage of Vermont's 1777 constitution, fourteen years elapsed before statehood was achieved. Crucial to statehood was settlement in October 1790 of New York's claims to Vermont. On October 27 Vermont's General Assembly called for an election, on the first Tuesday of December, of delegates to a convention to be convened in Bennington on January 6, 1791.

The act calling for the election declared that "[i]n the opinion of this legislature the future interest and welfare of this State render it necessary that the constitution of the United States . . . should be laid before the people of this State for their approbation." Such approbation, by delegates elected by the people, was essential to Vermont's admission to the union.

The delegates met from January 6 to 10. While the vast majority of delegates supported ratification, Daniel Buck of Norwich, Benjamin Emmons of Woodstock, and Beriah Loomis of Thetford voiced reservations. As Emmons argued, the convention's action "may not perhaps be unaptly applied to the act of Adam in eating the forbidden fruit. . . . We are now acting for future generations, and the determination of this body will most probably affect posterity even to the end of time."

The key points of debate were raised by Nathaniel Chipman who favored ratification and Daniel Buck who argued for continued independence. On January 10, 1791, the delegates voted 105 to 4 in favor of ratification. In the end, only Daniel Heald of Chester, Moses Warner of Andover, Benjamin Perkins of Bridgewater, and Enoch Emerson of Rochester dissented.

No records were kept of the convention and the only documentation that survives is the report on the convention proceedings that appeared in the *Vermont Gazette*, January 10 to February 14, 1791. The following excerpts from the *Gazette* feature the main arguments of Nathaniel Chipman and Daniel Buck.

Proceedings and Debates of the Convention for Adopting the Constitution of the United States.

BENNINGTON, *January 10, 1791*

A list of members of the convention, for adopting the constitution of the united states.

THOMAS CHITTENDEN, *president.*
MOSES ROBINSON, *vice president.*
ROSWELL HOPKINS, *secretary.*

Bennington County.

Bennington, Moses Robinson. Sunderland, Tim Brownson. Shaftsbury, Gideon Olin. Pownal, Thomas Jewett. Stamford, Andrew Selden. Arlington, Timothy Todd. Manchester, Martin Powell. Rupert, Israel Smith. Dorset, John Shumway. Sandgate, Reuben Thomas.

Windham County.
Hinsdill, [Vernon] *Jonathan Hunt. Westminster,
Stephen R. Bradley. Athens, James Shafter.
Londonderry, Edward Aiken. Townsend, Joshua
Wood. Guilford, Peter Briggs. Brattleborough,
Gardiner Chandler. Newfane, Calvin Knoulton.
Whitingham, Isaac Lyman. Putney, Daniel Jewet.
Rockingham, Elijah Lovewell. Halifax, Benjamin
Henry. Dummerston, Jason Duncan. Wilmington,
Timothy Castle. Thomlinson,* [Grafton] *David Palmer.
Marlborough, Jonas Whitney.*

Rutland County.
*Rutland, Nathaniel Chipman. Hubbardston, James
Churchill. Orwell, Ebenezer Wilson. Danby, Daniel
Sherman. Pittsford, Thomas Hammond. Pawlet,
Lemuel Chipman. Castleton, Noah Lee. Middletown,
Jonathan Brewster. Wells, Samuel Lathrop. Brandon,
Nathan Daniels. Sudbury, Joseph Warner. Benson,
Asahel Smith. Fairhaven, Simeon Smith. Poultney,
William Ward. Shrewsbury, Emmanuel Case.
Tinmouth, John Spafford. Wallingford, Asahel
Jackson. Chittenden, Samuel Harrison.*

Windsor County.
*Springfield, Simon Stevens. Chester, Daniel Heald.
Hartland, Oliver Gallup. Windsor, Benjamin Greene.
Hartford, John Marsh. Cavendish, Asaph Fletcher.
Bethel, Michael Flynn. Andover, Moses Warner.
Weathersfield, Nathaniel Stoughton. Woodstock,
Benjamin Emmons. Sharon, Daniel Gilbert. Bernard*
[Barnard], *Silas Tupper. Bridgewater, Benjamin
Perkins. Pomfret, William Perry. Royalton, Heman
Durkee. Norwich, Daniel Buck. Rochester, Enoch
Emmerson.*

40

Addison County.

Addison, John Strong. Ferrisburgh, Abel Thompson. Panton, Benjamin Holcomb. Middlebury, Samuel Miller. Monkton, John Ferguson. Bridport, John N. Bennet. Newhaven, Oliver Pier. Vergennes, Alexander Brush. Salisbury, Eleazer Claghorn. Leicester, John Smith. Shoreham, Josiah Pond. Cornwall, William Slade. Whiting, Samuel Beach.

Orange County.

Fairlee, Nathaniel Niles. St. Johnsbury, Jonathan Arnold. Randolph, Josiah Edson. Maidstone, John Rich. Guildhall, David Hopkinson. Brookfield, Daniel Kingsbury. Williamstown, Cornelius Lynde. Tunbridge, Elias Curtiss. Vershire, Thomas Porter. Strafford, Peter Pennock. Bradford, John Barron. Corinth, Peter Sleeman. Barnet, Alexander Harvey. Peacham, William Chamberlain. Danville, Abraham Morrill. Newbury, Daniel Farrand. Thetford, Beriah Loomis. Lunenburgh, Samuel Gates.

Chittenden County.

Williston, Thomas Chittenden. Cambridge, John Fassett. Colchester, Ira Allen. Georgia, John White. Milton, Abel Waters. Charlotte, John M'Neil. Essex, Timothy Bliss. Shelburne, William C. Harrington. Newhuntington, Amos Brownson. Johnson, Jonathan M'Connel. St. Albans, Silas Hathaway. Hinesburgh, Elisha Barber. Fairfax, Joseph Beeman. Jericho, Martin Chittenden. Southhero, Ebenezer Allen. Northhero, Enos Wood. Burlington, Samuel. Hitchcock.

ROSWELL HOPKINS, *secretary.*

41

IN CONVENTION,

Friday morning. [Jan. 7.] Mr. N. Chipman then rose, and addressed the house, as follows;

MR. PRESIDENT,

The subject, on which we are now called to deliberate, is a subject of great importance, and involves in it many and mighty consequences. I shall wave at present any consideration of the particular circumstance in which we may be supposed to stand with the united states, on account of the former claim of Newyork, and the late compromise between Vermont and that state — and shall first make a few observations on our local and relative situation as a state and the consequences that will attend the event, either of our continuing independent, or of our accession to the union. I will then briefly observe on the principles and tendency of the federal constitution.

In viewing our situation, the first thing that strikes the mind, is the narrow limits of our territory: wholly inadequate to support the dignity, or to defend the rights of sovereignty — not can we but reflect on the fortune that usually pursues such limited independencies.

The division of an extensive territory into small independent sovereignties greatly retards civil improvements — this was formerly the case in Europe; and the consequence was a long continuance in savage, and almost brutal manners. But it has been observed, that where, through an extensive country, the smaller states have united under one general government, civilization has proceeded more rapidly, and the kindly affections have much sooner gained an ascendent than where they still remained under numerous neighboring governments. The reason why one state is more favorable to civil improvement than the other is founded in the constitution of human nature: among small independent states, as among independent individuals, without a common judge, the weak are jealous of the strong — and endeavor by art and cunning to supply their want of power. The strong are ever ready to decide every question by force, according to their own present interest — hence follows a total want of public faith — recriminations — animosities — and open violence — under the idea of reprisals — and the name of foreigner becomes but another name for an enemy. In this situation the minds of men are kept in a constant state of irritation — their turbulent spirits ill brook the restraints of law — the passion of revenge, which, in proportion to the weakness of government becomes necessary for the protection of the individual, is soon inflamed to a degree of enthusiasm. Common danger alone, and that imminently impending, can suspend its baneful influence even among members of the same society: a situation fit only for savages — and in this situation savages have ever existed: but in an extensive government, national prejudices are suppressed — hostilities are removed to a distance — private injuries are redressed by a common judge — the passion of revenge, now no longer necessary for the protection of the individual, is suspended — the people no longer behold an enemy in the inhabitants of each neighboring district — they view all as members of one great family, connected by all the ties of interest, of country, of affinity and blood: thus are the social feelings gratified — and the kindly affections expanded and invigorated.

Vermont, continuing independent, would not be liable to all the inconveniences I have mentioned — but she will be liable to many and great inconveniences. In the vicinity of, and almost encircled by, the united states, now become great and powerful through the means of an energetic system of government, our intercourse with them must be on very unequal, and frequently on very mortifying terms. Whenever our interests clash (and clash they will at some time) with those of the union, it requires very little political sagacity to foretel that every sacrifice must be made on our part. When was it ever known that a powerful nation sacrificed, or even compromised their interest in justice to a weak neighbor, who was unable to make effectual demands? and who shall be a common judge? Nay, such is the constitution of human nature, that men in such cases, were they disposed, are in a great measure incapable of judging with candor and impartiality.

We have experienced the disposition of states whose interests were averse to our own; and well know the consequences: extravagant, and as we deemed them, unjustifiable claims, on their part; animosities, factions, and even bloodshed, among ourselves.

Our vicinity to an extensive province of the british empire, is worthy of consideration. There is not any prospect of an immediate war between the united states and Greatbritain; but from their mutual recriminations relative to the observance of the late treaty; and from the retention of the frontier posts in the hands of the british, contrary to express stipulation; such an event is one day to be apprehended. Should that take place, Vermont would be in a situation much to be regreted.

Our local situation with the united states, and our connexion with many of their inhabitants—cemented by all the ties of blood and kindred affection, would forbid an alliance with Greatbritain. As allies of the united states, we should experience all the resentment of an enemy, whom, by our voluntary alliance, we had made such, and to whose depredations, from our frontier situation, we should be continually exposed. And should we experience in the united states that quick sense of the injuries we should suffer? would they fly to our defence with the same alacrity, with the same national spirit, as they would defend themselves, if attacked in one of their own members? would they attend equally to our interest as to their own, in the settlement of peace, or in finally adjusting the expenditures of the war? The supposition is highly chimerical: nor less chimerical the idea, that by observing a neutral conduct, we may enjoy the blessing of peace, while the flames of war rage on every side. Our country, from its situation, would become a rendezvous, and a thoroughfare to the spies of both nations. Our citizens would frequently be tempted by both to engage in a nefarious correspondence of that kind: every act of friendship, or even of common courtesy, to one party, would excite the jealousy of the other. Their armies, to whom we should not be in a condition to refuse a passage, would think themselves justified on the very least pretext of necessity, in seizing our property for the use of their service. Thus we should be equally misused, equally despised, and equally insulted and plundered by both.

Again, we may view this subject as it relates to the improvement of knowledge, and liberal science. Confined to the narrow limits of Vermont, genius, for want of great occasions, and great objects, will languish in obscurity: the spirit of learning, from which nations have derived more solid glory than all heroic atchievments, and individuals, beyond the common lot of humanity, have been able to contribute to the happiness of millions, in different parts of the globe — will be contracted; and busy itself in small scenes, commensurate to the exigencies of the state, and the narrow limits of our government. In proportion as the views are more confined — more local; the more firmly rivited on the mind are the shackles of local and systematic prejudices. — But received into the bosom of the union, we at once become brethren and fellow-citizens with more than three millions of people: instead of being confined to the narrow limits of Vermont, we become members of an extensive empire: here is a scene opened that will expand the social feelings; — the necessity and facility of mutual intercourse, will eradicate local prejudices; — the channels of information will be opened wide, and far extended; — the spirit of learning will be called forth by every motive of interest and laudable ambition; — genius, exalted by the magnitude of the objects presented, will soar to the heights of science; — our general interests will be the same with those of the union — and represented in the national councils, our local interests will have their due weight. As an inland country, from the encouragement given to arts and manufactures, we shall receive more than a proportional advantage. And in the event of a war, an attack upon us will be felt through every member of the union: national safety — national pride, and national resentment — a resentment, not the petulance of a tribe, but great as the nation offended, will all conspire in our defence — in a word, independent, we must ever remain little, and I might almost say, contemptible; — but united, we become great, from the reflected greatness of the empire with which we unite. . . .

FRIDAY, *january* 13 [7.][1] Three o'clock p.m.

. . . Mr. Buck rose again, and in a lengthy speech observed that it appeared to him there were reasons to be offered against the adoption of the constitution at the present time. Supposing the constitution to be ever so good an one, yet, in order to a fair investigation of the question, as to the expediency of adopting it, perhaps it would be necessary to consider the original cause of all government: he urged that it originated from necessity; that, were it possible for a man to enjoy the blessings of society, security of his person, liberty, and property, without the protection of government, he must be happier in that state than to be under the controul of it; that, in entering into compact and forming government, each individual of the community must necessarily sacrifice such a part of his natural liberty, his interest, and privileges, as to coincide with the common interest of the whole; yet this sacrifice must be in some measure proportionate to the diversity of the interest to be found in the several parts of the community — that the sacrifice of the individuals of a small community must be less than those of a large one, where the interest must be supposed more diverse. He observed, that Vermont, by her local situation, had an uniformity of interest; that there was no mercantile and landed interest found clashing here, and that of the lord and the tenant was not known; the laws, therefore, were simple and suited to the whole; the affairs of government were managed, as it were, under the eye of the people, and the machine was so small that every one could look and see how the wheels moved, and for this reason it was observable, that the people were all politicians. But if Vermont came into the union, the sacrifice she made must be great — her interest must then bend to the interest of the union — where those clashing interests before mentioned were to be found. He said, the blessings

46

resulting to Vermont from her union with an extensive empire, enumerated by the honorable member from Rutland, though very plausible, would not apply to the bulk of the people: some few favorites of fortune, who from circumstances of birth, and advantage of education, might consider themselves fair candidates for some post in government, might be animated by the magnitude of the object, and soar to the height of science; but this number must be but small, while on the other hand, the affairs of government being at such a remove from the eye of the people they could have no knowledge of their transactions, and would naturally degenerate into a state of ignorance. He observed, that all extensive governments had a natural tendency to destroy that equality among the people, which was necessary to keep one part of mankind from oppressing the other; that there was such a thirst for dominion and power implanted in the human breast, that men were ever ready to make use of the advantages they had to tyrannize over others; that as the stimulous to improvement in knowledge, resulting from our union, would operate on a few only, it would serve but to place them as tyrants over an ignorant multitude. — For the truth of these observations, he referred to the present state of the kingdoms of the world, and observed, that the rich, wise, powerful, and great, bear a tyrannical sway, while they view the bulk of mankind in the same light as we do those domestic animals that are subservient to our use; and as to the salutary effects that our union would have on the morals of the people, we should in all probability experience quite the reverse of what was suggested by the worthy member from Rutland — for it was observable, that luxury, debauchery, and licentiousness, were the attendants on power. The court, he said, was the foundation from whence immorality was diffused among a nation: this was so true, that it had become a common saying, that sincerity and honesty were strangers at court; while real virtue and simple honesty were to be found in the cottage. It must therefore be a given point, that Vermont (taking into view the bulk of the people) must be much happier unconnected with any other power, than to be in

47

the union — and nothing but necessity could warrant her accession to the federal constitution; therefore, if it was possible for her to support her independence, it was her wisdom to remain independent. He said there were but two things that could ever render it impossible, or prevent it. He agreed, that in case of war between Great britain and America, it would be impossible. But he urged, that there was no prospect or probability of a war again taking place between those powers; he likewise acknowledged that the local situation of Vermont was such, that it was in the power of congress so to embarrass and hedge her up, as to render it impossible for her to exist; but it was easy to determine whether congress would ever exert this power by considering the state Vermont stood in, with respect to the united states; and what probably would be the motives by which congress would be influenced in her conduct — he said it would be that of her interest. He said it was a just observation, that individuals were generally influenced by their interest; but when applied to political bodies the rule was without an exception: we might therefore fix upon it for certain, that the view which congress had of their interest, would be the helm by which they would invariably steer the federal ship; it remained therefore only to shew, that it could not be for the interest of congress ever to lay any embarrassments on us — and this, when we considered our situation in respect to the union, was very apparent, for, upon the present plan of taxation, which in all probability would not be altered as long as peace remains, we paid, and ever should pay, every whit as much towards the support of the federal government, as though we were in the union, it could therefore, never, unless upon the prospect of an immediate war, be for the interest of congress to take measures to compel us in. — But on the contrary, the moment we were received into the union, our senators, representatives, district judge, &c. must make an additional expense to the federal government — besides, if congress set us upon the same footing with other states, she must assume our expenses of the war; congress must therefore, instead of gaining by our union, be the losers. He observed, that congress had never noticed us, or taken one step that indicated a wish for our union—that all that had been done was in consequence of the movements of Newyork, who had, until congress sat in that state, stood our avowed enemy; and that it was easy to see the motive which caused Newyork so suddenly to change her policy. He said, Newyork viewed the seat of the federal government as an object of greater importance than their claim to Vermont, they had therefore sacrificed that, and were now exerting themselves, to the utmost, to bring Vermont into the union; that thereby they might add another weight to the northern scale. But by the doings of congress, we found that there were a majority in that body who were pursuing an object which clashed with the view of Newyork, and that the same voices which decided that the seat of government should be carried to the Potomac, would, in all probability, decide, that Vermont should not be received until the permanent seat of federal government should be unalterably fixed. Therefore, as the advantage Vermont would receive from the union, would by no means be adequate to the sacrifice she must make—as she had long existed as an independent state, and might long continue so—and as in all probability she would be rejected by congress, if she made application, there could be no necessity or expediency in acceding to the union, or adopting the constitution.

NOTE

[1] This date in the *Gazette* was a blunder of the printer, which was followed in each succeeding date. The convention met on January 6 and dissolved on January 10, 1791.

49

PART II

Forgotten
Founders and
Voices
of
Dissent

Nathaniel Chipman: Vermont's Forgotten Founder

by Samuel B. Hand and P. Jeffrey Potash

Vermont hearts seldom quicken at the mention of Nathaniel Chipman's name. Neither can he be said to occupy a conspicuous place in the state's collective memory. Yet no one can make greater claim to preeminence as architect of Vermont statehood. In 1873, Vermont erected a monument to commemorate his achievements as "a principal founder of the civil institutions of this state, and framer of its fundamental laws,"[1] but even that noble gesture failed to secure Chipman a lofty eminence. His eclipse is a phenomenon worth exploring.

Chipman's origins resemble those of Vermont's better known founding father, Ethan Allen. Born almost a generation apart, both men were raised in the western Connecticut town of Salisbury in Litchfield County and nurtured on the spirit of political independence and economic opportunity. As the eldest sons of frontiersmen who had achieved modest wealth and political recognition, they were groomed by their respective fathers for entry into Yale and admission into the ranks of New England's elite.[2]

Thereafter, the similarities break down. Allen, the older of the two, was obliged to abandon both his studies and his haughty aspirations following the untimely death of his father in 1755. After several frustrating failures to acquire an independent fortune within the increasingly stratified environs of his native Connecticut, he chose to move on to a new frontier, the disputed territory known as the New Hampshire Grants. Arriving in 1770, within three years Allen had gained a position of leadership among the New Hampshire titleholders and assembled the Green Mountain Boys to thwart efforts by New York officials to dispossess them from the Grants.

By contrast, 1773 marked Nathaniel Chipman's entry into Yale College. And as Allen acted out his career as the hero of Fort Ticonderoga and the victim of British imprisonment, Chipman experienced the more tranquil environs of Yale, where he excelled in Hebrew, Greek, and Latin. In the spring of 1777, Chipman's senior year, he left college to obtain an ensign's commission in a Connecticut regiment and his degree was granted in absentia with his class. Joining General Washington's command at Valley Forge, Chipman's letters reflect considerable satisfaction from translating the Latin and Greek texts he carried with him but little of the romance and exhilaration of war described by Allen in his *Narrative*. In June 1778 he did, however, participate in the Battle of Monmouth and was promoted to first lieutenant. [3]

On October 10, 1778, Chipman submitted his resignation to General Washington. Citing financial responsibilities for his parents who "were, the last year, driven from their habitation, plundered . . . and reduced to poverty," Chipman advised Washington that growing debts rendered it "a duty which I owe to myself and others, if possible, to procure a discharge from the service." His decision, he confided to a friend, rested on enlightened self-interest: "I am already in debt, and a continuance in the service, to me affords no other prospect than that of utter ruin. If I resign, unqualified as I am for business, and without friends, at least powerful friends, I shall find myself extremely embarrassed . . . [A]lthough it is a great mortification to me to resign, it is a greater to hold the rank, and not be able to support the character of a gentleman."[4]

Chipman, as had Allen nearly a decade earlier, would seek his fortune on the Vermont frontier. There were, however, significant differences. Chipman would join his family who had already resettled on the Grants, and he planned to practice law, not challenge its authority. "I shall indeed be rara avis in terris, for there is not an attorney in the state," he advised a Yale classmate. "[T]hink what a figure I shall make, when I become the oracle of law to the state of Vermont."[5] His route to Vermont was back through Litchfield County where he studied law for five months. Litchfield, soon to be the site of the nation's first law school, was already a noted breeding ground for lawyers. Admitted to the bar in March 1779, Chipman left immediately for Vermont where he set up practice in Tinmouth.

In fact Chipman became the third rather than the first attorney admitted to the Vermont bar; otherwise his timing proved impeccable.[6] The instabilities rent by war and Vermont's controversial proclamation of independence translated into abundant legal actions and Chipman quickly established a statewide reputation. In 1781, when Rutland County was organized, Chipman was the obvious choice for State's Attorney, a position that provided opportunities for even greater influence. Almost immediately upon taking office, Chipman acceded to a request from his former Salisbury neighbor, Governor Thomas Chittenden, that he assist in the Haldimand Negotiations by assuring George Washington "that the outwardly friendly relations between Vermont and the common enemy did not mean Vermont's abandonment of the Revolutionary cause."[7]

Most Vermont historians generously interpret the Haldimand Negotiations, secret parleys between Vermont and the British to restore Vermont to the British Empire, as an ingenious ploy by Vermont leaders to neutralize the threat of a Canadian invasion while simultaneously pressuring the Continental Congress to admit Vermont into the union. This interpretation is by no means unanimous, and some skeptics have found substantial evidence suggesting that Governor Chittenden along with Ethan and Ira Allen were negotiating in good faith with the British. Chipman's integrity, however, remains unquestioned. These historians depict Chipman, presumably recruited by Chittenden because of his reputation for probity and his loyalty to the American cause, as having been duped into believing the scheme was merely a ruse "on the strength of half and quarter truths orally supplied him."[8]

News of British General Cornwallis's surrender at Yorktown in October of that same year and the subsequent withdrawal of British forces from Vermont's borders eliminated the prospects of invasion and opened the floodgates for a new wave of immigrants. During the decade after 1781, Vermont's population grew at a rate sometimes exceeding ten percent annually. The sheer magnitude of this peaceful invasion initiated a new era in Vermont's political life. Newcomers, occupied with the challenges of transforming forests into farms and villages, refocused legislative attention to stabilizing Vermont's post-war economy.

Chipman was eager to participate in this statemaking. In 1784, he was elected to the legislature as delegate from Tinmouth and joined four other "eminent men" on a committee charged with revising Vermont's statutes. Chipman agreed to serve on condition that he be given "the use, in advance, and finally the ownership, of such books as he should choose from the confiscated library of Charles Phelps," who had run afoul of Vermont authorities by obstinately maintaining his loyalty to New York. The confiscated law library was the finest in the state, and Chipman made considerable and productive use of it during the two years it took the legislative committee to complete the first state code. The volumes Chipman claimed from Phelps's collection provided the basis for a library that served him throughout his long life as a member of the bar and on the bench. Clearly public service and private gain were not incompatible.[9]

Confidence gained from this and other activities now led Chipman to initiate what historian Aleine Austin characterizes as Vermont's "rival leadership." The first episode in a long, intense struggle for political domination was Chipman's public challenge to Governor Chittenden over the betterments issue in October of 1784.

Betterments, precipitated by Vermont's numerous conflicting and faulty land titles, had been debated as early as 1780 and compounded by a Redemption Act that restored property confiscated from Loyalists. Much of the confiscated lands had been turned over to partisans of the Chittenden-Allen faction who had improved the properties through clearing, cultivation, and construction. Governor Chittenden and his protégé and son-in-law, Matthew Lyon, submitted a relief bill to compensate settlers threatened with eviction with full compensation for improvements rendered "at the time when such settlement was begun."[10]

Nathaniel Chipman spearheaded the opposition. Citing legal precedent, he insisted that persons seeking betterments not only had no rightful claims to the property but were themselves technically guilty of trespassing. Joined by like-minded legislator-lawyers and judges, including Isaac Tichenor, Stephen Rowe Bradley and Nathaniel Niles, Chipman succeeded in blocking passage but could not block Chittenden from putting the issue to a non-binding referendum. The referendum vote favored Chittenden. Chipman, however, refused to acquiesce and insisted that Chittenden's proposal be amended to reduce betterments compensation by half. Chittenden agreed and a Betterments Act was finally enacted in 1785.[11]

From Matthew Lyon's vantage point, the battle over betterments constituted nothing less than a "struggle between aristocracy and democracy." Chipman, in collusion with his fellow "law characters," had trampled the natural rights of common men in favor of "their books and their rich clients [who] told them that the common law of England knew nothing of paying betterments for labor."[12] The venomous nature of Lyon's attack reflected a personal and ideological animus towards Chipman, which was compounded by the recognition that Chipman's brash legislative leadership threatened to undermine the powerful stranglehold the Chittenden faction had enjoyed since 1777.

The contest between Chittenden's "principles of natural justice" and Chipman's appeal to common law was clouded by charges that members of the Chittenden faction had abused their authority for personal gain. The Allens were the most obvious targets. While the battle over betterments raged, Chipman spearheaded exposés of Allen excesses. Most noteworthy were charges that they had consciously manipulated state land sales for nonpayment of taxes to bolster their substantial speculative holdings at bargain prices. These activities, declared the *Vermont Journal* of Windsor, threatened to "expose [the] state to hate, ignominy, and disgrace abroad . . . and brand Vermont with [the] name of land-thieves."[13]

Ira Allen became by far the most conspicuous target of the opposition group. In April 1784, the legislature rejected as inappropriate a recommendation made by the Governor and Council to authorize Ira to negotiate a treaty between Vermont and Quebec that would have salvaged his lucrative lumber trade. It refused, the assembly declared, to "tax the inhabitants of the State at large to defray the expense of a treaty, the benefits of which will be partial and confined to a few individuals." Another damaging blow was a 1785 assembly act that annulled all Ira's town surveys. Charging that his slovenly efforts had produced innumerable boundary disputes, the act also prohibited him from undertaking any further surveys in Vermont.[14]

By the winter of 1785, however, debtor relief preempted other concerns. The end of the Revolution and the closing of British and Canadian markets ensnared Vermont, as it did other former colonies, in depression. Demands for debt payment clogged the courts and popular discontent channeled into extra-legal conventions and court riots at which debtors rallied around demands to "stop the courts," "expel the lawyers," and "resist the sheriffs."[15]

Governor Chittenden offered several proposals to the 1786 assembly to defuse the growing excitements. Charging that court costs had so paralyzed the state that "there is hardly any money sufficient to pay for entering the actions, not to mention the debts or lawyers fees," Chittenden proposed a tax on lawsuits. To address the shortage of specie he offered a General Tender Act, permitting farmers to repay debts with produce at an inflated value, and the creation of a state bank authorized to issue scrip as legal tender.[16]

From Chipman's initial response it is difficult to determine whether he was more outraged at Chittenden's debtor relief heresy or his attack upon lawyers. "Attorneys," Chipman versified,

> . . . whose eternal gabble,
> Confounds the inexperienced rabble;
> Who quote down precedents and cases,
> Of ancient date, in ancient phrases;
> Hard lessons taught by deep-read sages
> Whom mankind have revered for ages . . .
> And Tom and John must lose their cause,
> And why? Forsooth, they've broke the laws.
> Then lawyers from the courts expel,
> Cancel our debts, and all is well.[17]

Daniel Chipman reported that the rhyme "was considered at the time [to have] had a very salutary effect," but Nathaniel's more substantial efforts were to rally forces in opposition to Chittenden's legislative proposals. Arguing that no alternatives were fair, the Chipman forces agreed to a referendum to afford "some means by which the proposed measures might be postponed until the passions of the people should have time to cool."[18] During the referendum debate, Chipman's compatriots questioned Chittenden's motives, charging that the plan would enable "the Governor of the State, who . . . is [$]3000 in arrears to the treasury [to] discharge the same [with] paper money." Dire forecasts warned that spiraling inflation would depreciate the notes at a rate of "a thousand to one," bankrupting "every merchant and trader in the state" and worsening the plight of farmers and jeopardizing their mortgaged lands. In sum, Chipman warned, adoption of Chittenden's proposals "must greatly increase and prolong the sufferings of the people."[19] The anti-bank forces scored an impressive referendum victory. By a margin of more than four to one, Vermonters sided with Chipman in opposing both Chittenden's state bank and General Tender Act. In the wake of the referendum vote, Chipman successfully lobbied the enactment of a Specific Tender Act, which obliged "the creditor to receive . . . at their appraised value, such articles of personal property as the debtor had contracted to pay."[20]

Emboldened by these major victories, Chipman next proceeded to reinvigorate the cause for Vermont statehood, stalled since Congress's unceremonious rebuff in April 1782. New York officials, led by Governor George Clinton, had forged an alliance with southern states, warning that a recognition of Vermont's independence would constitute a dangerous precedent legitimizing further frontier secessions. Chipman, however, sensed change was possible.

In September, 1786, the Annapolis Convention issued a call, drafted by Alexander Hamilton, for a convention at Philadelphia in May of the following year to discuss all matters necessary "to render the constitution of the Federal government adequate to the exigencies of the union." Vermont received no invitation but, having achieved considerable notoriety for its role in fanning the fires of democratic revolution in Pennsylvania's Wyoming Valley and Shays' Rebellion in western Massachusetts, was in the consciousness of constitution framers. George Washington himself warned, "considering the proximity of it [Vermont] to

Canada if they were not with us, they might be a thorn in our sides."[21] In March of 1787, Alexander Hamilton had proposed that New York recognize Vermont's independence, warning that he possessed "the strongest evidence" indicating negotiations were again underway between British officials in Canada and those of Vermont. While successful in the assembly, Hamilton's bill was rejected by New York's senate.[22]

Buoyed by events, Chipman, after meeting with Lewis R. Morris and other opponents of the Allens in Tinmouth, wrote Hamilton on July 15, 1788, assuring him that Vermonters would ratify the newly proposed federal Constitution if an amendment were framed guaranteeing that the federal courts would not invalidate New Hampshire titles. Appreciating the need for "compensation" to those holding New York titles, Chipman suggested either some form of assistance from Vermont or, presuming the aggrieved parties preferred land, the substitution of "western lands" provided by "the federal legislature."[23]

Daniel Chipman, who delivered his brother's letter to Hamilton, then attending the New York constitutional ratifying convention in Poughkeepsie, reported that despite the demands of the moment, Hamilton found time to prepare a reply for the next day. Dismissing the likelihood of federal grants of land, his response nonetheless bolstered Chipman's optimism that "this is the favorable moment for effecting" Vermont's entry into the union given the northern need "to find a counterpoise" to Kentucky's bid for independence.[24]

Ethan Allen meanwhile, in a remarkable letter dated July 16, 1788, to Lord Dorchester, Governor of Quebec, was busy soliciting help from the British against what he feared would be a campaign on the part of the framers of the federal constitution "to coerce" Vermont into the union. The majority of Vermonters, he insisted, remained opposed to statehood: "Vermont is locally situated on the Waters of Champlain which communicate with those of St. Lawrence and contiguous to the

Province of Quebec where they must be dependent for trade, business, and intercourse which naturally incline them to the British interests." Lambasting Chipman and others favoring admission into the union as imbibers of "the licentious notion of liberty," Allen called upon Dorchester to supply him and his comrades with arms to prevent the eventuality of statehood. Re-entry into the British empire, Allen concluded, could be readily achieved given that "the leading men of Vermont are not sentimentally attached to a republican form of government."[25]

As the Allens pursued their dreams, Governor Chittenden continued to throw up roadblocks along the drive toward statehood. Seeking to derail Chipman's momentum, Chittenden insisted that Ira Allen be appointed one of the three negotiators to Congress. Allen's hostility to union was manifested by his refusal to serve, and he went instead to confer with Dorchester in Quebec.[26]

Chittenden's strategy went awry, however, owing to the "Woodbridge Affair," a scandal that erupted when the assembly determined that Governor Chittenden had issued a grant to Ira Allen for the town of Woodbridge (present day Highgate) without the consent of the Governor's Council. Reporting that the governor had violated the trust placed in him and had "converted it to private and sinister views," the assembly validated the beliefs of many who charged the Allens were "unjustly making their fortunes out of the whole state."[27]

The ramifications of the scandal became evident during the October 1789 election, when Vermonters for the first time in twelve years failed to provide a popular majority for Chittenden's election as governor. Seizing the opportunity, the assembly replaced Chittenden with his political opponent, Moses Robinson. Shortly thereafter, the assembly appointed six commissioners, led by Nathaniel Chipman and Isaac Tichenor and with Ira Allen the only representative of the Chittenden faction, to meet with counterparts from New York to settle the land dispute.

61

On October 28, 1790, the negotiators agreed upon the figure of $30,000 as compensation for New York titleholders, and New York declared its consent to the admission of Vermont as a state in the union. The settlement made Vermont statehood almost inevitable, and even Ira Allen, who failed to participate in the negotiations, signed the accord. Ira's signing can be said to have signalled the end of significant internal opposition to Vermont statehood. [28]

Events came to a climax in January 1791, when the state of Vermont held a convention at Bennington to ratify the U.S. Constitution. Governor Chittenden and Ira Allen were among the 109 delegates to attend, but were "practically the only representatives of the old guard present . . . The delegates were primarily the more substantial citizenry of Vermont: lawyers, land owners, merchants, office holders [and] ex-army officers. [29]

Nathaniel Chipman opened the convention with an eloquent plea for adoption. The benefits of union rested upon Vermont's capacity to transcend localism. No longer would Vermont need to fear for her security. In breaking out of "the narrow limits of Vermont," he observed, "mutual intercourse will tend to eradicate local prejudices; the channels of information will become wide and far extended; the spirit of learning will be called forth by every motive of interest and laudable ambition . . . genius will soar to the heights of science." [30]

Statehood promised even more tangible rewards than participation in a grand republican experiment, the opportunity to overcome financial and commercial problems that had plagued Vermont's economy throughout its independent era. Though Washington's administration was scarcely two years old, Chipman noted, "They have already provided for funding the national debt; they have in a great measure restored public credit, which, from the weakness of the former government, they found almost in a state of desperation. They have enriched the nation with a very productive revenue." [31]

In conclusion, Chipman enjoined the delegates to embrace the moment. To remain independent, he warned, "we might ever continue little, and, I had almost said, contemptible; united we become great by the reflected greatness of the empire with which we unite." On January 10, 1791, the convention, by a vote of 105 to 4, ratified the Constitution and appointed Chipman and Lewis Morris as commissioners to Congress to secure the enactment of "such act or acts as congress may pass for the purpose of admitting . . . Vermont into the government of the United States." On February 18, George Washington signed such an act into law, and on March 4 Vermont was "received and admitted into the Union, as a new and entire member of the United States of America."[32]

During much of the time Chipman was negotiating with New York and Congress, he was also serving as Vermont's chief justice. Appointed to the supreme court in 1786, the first lawyer to serve, he left after a year of undistinguished service. Daniel attributed this to being "situated as he was on the bench, one of five judges, and he the only lawyer."[33] Returning to the bench in 1789, this time as chief justice and in the company of other lawyers, he remained in office until October 1791 when he was appointed the Judge of the Court of the United States for the District of Vermont. The federal appointment was another example of Chipman's ability to merge public service with personal gain.

In July 1793 Chipman resigned his federal judgeship. While it is difficult to determine the precise reason, Daniel Chipman attributed it to "very little business in the district or circuit court" and scholars concur.[34] It is interesting to observe that during his tenure on the court, Chipman actively lobbied prominent New Yorkers to construct a canal linking Lake Champlain to the Hudson River. Presented to Philip Schuyler as possessing mutual benefits and affording New York the tantalizing opportunity "to command the trade of one hundred thousand people," the canal presumably would have diverted Vermont's trade with Canada to a southerly course and secured even closer political and commercial ties with the union. [35]

Chipman also found time to author two books, both published in 1793. The first, *Reports and Dissertations*, consisted of a brief summary of some twenty-five cases decided by the Vermont Supreme Court during his tenure as chief justice (1789-91). Numbering among the earliest reports published in America, this work underscored Chipman's efforts to systematically introduce precedent in the rule of Vermont law, to accurately recall precedents not only for the wisdom and rationale contributing to "right decisions" but contributing to errors as well. [36]

Chipman's second work published in 1793, *Sketches of the Principles of Government*, constituted an ambitious effort to assemble a "systematic treatise" addressing the distinctive workings of the American system. Although highly praised in its day (political adversary Thomas Jefferson recommended that the *Sketches* be used as a textbook at William and Mary College), the book is now seldom read. [37]

Chipman's resignation from the federal bench and publication of two books in no way marked his retirement from the political battlefield. Indeed, before resigning, he maneuvered the appointment of a Federalist successor over Governor Chittenden's candidate, the then chief justice Samuel Knight. Although Matthew Lyon, Chipman's political nemesis, failed to block Chipman's nominee, he took every opportunity to blacken Chipman's reputation. Writing to New York governor George Clinton, Lyon noted: "So pointed an Enemy as this Chipman is to the Republican Interest [and] what I consider the public Good [,] as well as to myself, I think it my duty to derange as far as is in my power the Measures he interests himself in." [38]

When in 1793 Matthew Lyon ran for United States representative from western Vermont, Chipman, as Vermont's principal spokesman for Federalism, reciprocated by resisting his candidacy. Although Chipman was not himself a candidate, his efforts almost certainly cost Lyon the election. Issues such as Britain's failure to surrender midwestern forts and deteriorating relations with France were essentially jettisoned in favor of mudslinging, with Chipman using two Federalist papers, the *Vermont Gazette*, published in Bennington, and the *Vermont Journal*, published in Windsor, and Lyon writing in his own Rutland paper, the *Farmers' Library*.

Lyon's campaign against "the Aristocratical High federal faction" led him to accuse Chipman of "currying favor with ruling aristocrats . . . in hopes of gaining by it in the next sinecure appointment." Chipman displayed no reluctance in similarly sullying Lyon's motives. "In examining your conduct," he observed, "I will not endeavor to pursue you through all the mazes of your unexampled turpitude. It forms a labyrinth almost inextricable: nor will I attempt to rouse your conscience with the horrors of a guilty conscience: your political conscience is too callous for compunction."[39]

In October 1796 Chipman was once again elected Vermont chief justice and almost immediately embraced the opportunity presented to him in the summer of 1797 to join a legislative committee charged to revise the laws of Vermont. Daniel Chipman observed that Nathaniel was the principal architect of the revisions and alleged that they attracted the attention of jurists from other states who maintained "that they find no other code of statute laws written in a style so distinguished for simplicity, perspicuity, and technical accuracy."[40] In October 1797, even before this task was completed, the Vermont legislature elected Chipman to a full term in the United States Senate.

Much to Chipman's disgust, Matthew Lyon would also be in the Vermont delegation. In 1796 he had won Vermont's western congressional seat. Privately, Chipman prophesied Lyon's impetuous style would backfire. "You cannot," he confided to a colleague, "with all your knowledge of the man easily conceive how incredulous a figure he makes."[41]

Within a few months after taking office Chipman concluded that attacks by Lyon and like-minded Republicans upon the Federalist Adams administration constituted serious threats to national security. American public opinion, roused against France for its refusal to receive a U.S. minister and for setting a $240,000 bribe as a precondition for negotiations, provided the Federalists with opportunities to enact restrictions on Republicans. Two such enactments, the Alien Act and the Sedition Act, advocated by the Adams administration, carried Chipman's strong approval.

Several of the leading Republican publicists were European refugees, and the threat of war with France sharpened hostilities toward aliens. The Alien and Sedition Acts were also advocated by the Adams administration as tools for quashing dissent against its unpopular policies. In support of these acts, Chipman warned that "False and scandalous publications . . . maliciously misrepresenting the motives and proceedings [of Congress]" constituted dangerous "breaches of the privileges of this house" insofar as they placed the membership "under the apprehension of the public contempt."[42]

To further dampen dissent, Congress passed an act imposing a fine of not more than $2,000 and imprisonment not exceeding two years on persons convicted of publishing "any false, scandalous and malicious writing" bringing into disrepute the U.S. government, Congress, or the president. There can be little doubt that Chipman's enthusiasm for the Sedition Act was fueled by a hope to silence Republican dissent in Vermont; five of the eighteen indictments ultimately secured under the act were against Vermonters. The abandon with which Matthew Lyon, the most vituperative of these dissenters, persisted in denunciations of President Adams's "unbounded thirst for ridiculous, pompous, foolish adulation [and] selfish avarice" won him the distinction of early indictment and trial. Found guilty, sentenced to four months in the Vergennes jail cell, and assessed the largest fine recorded under the Sedition Act, Lyon was elevated to the status of Republican martyr and re-elected to Congress while confined to his cell.[43] His success was merely temporary, however, for within a few years Lyon's political and economic fortunes turned and he was driven from the state. Chipman derived little profit from Lyon's exile, for 1801 marked the inauguration of Thomas Jefferson and the Republican party's national ascendancy.

Chipman's efforts during the final two years of his U.S. Senate term focused upon defending the independence and integrity of his cherished judiciary from attack by the Jefferson administration. His single greatest concern was to prevent repeal of the 1801 Judiciary Act. Passage of the act had itself been a blatantly partisan Federalist move and its repeal by the new administration eliminated sixteen newly created federal circuit judgeships, with judges appointed with life tenure. In Chipman's judgement, however, repeal would prove "dangerous to the liberties of the people." Addressing the Senate, Chipman maintained that the constitution provided no rights to abolish a court or to remove a judge "so long as they shall continue to behave well." Any efforts to encroach upon that freedom, he warned, tampered with the logic espoused by the founders and threatened the constitutional balance of powers by inhibiting judges' ability to oppose the legislature "if such a decision be made at the risk of office and salary, of public character and the means of subsistence."[44] The repeal was among Chipman's greatest disappointments. In 1803, at the expiration of his term, he seems to have made no effort to secure reelection nor was his candidacy advocated in the Vermont legislature.

By 1806, however, Chipman returned to the Vermont legislature as the representative from Tinmouth, a post he retained for five of the succeeding six years. In 1813, he served on the popularly elected, thirteen-member Council of Censors.

This council assembled every seven years to examine Vermont's constitution and to call a convention to consider any proposed amendments. Chipman's personal agenda was to make Vermont's frame of government more consistent with the federal model. First and foremost was the conversion of Vermont's unicameral assembly into a bicameral body by transforming the Governor's Council into a senate. A second proposal, designed to provide Vermont's judiciary greater independence from the legislature also was predicated upon the federal model. The intent, Chipman asserted, was to eliminate the "corrupting influence of designing men, who may often promote the election of individuals, in order that themselves, in their turn, may be promoted." Only by protecting an independent judiciary, Chipman concluded, would Vermonters free themselves from "arbitrary judges whose decisions would, in effect, be dictated by their own private passions [and not] by any fixed or known principles of law."[45] The council ultimately proposed twenty-eight interrelated amendments, all of which were rejected by a constitutional convention.

Chipman's last important political act as a Federalist was to caution against Vermont's participation in the Federalist-inspired Hartford Convention. The War of 1812 had been particularly unpopular in Vermont, disrupting commerce and opening state borders to British incursion. Vermont Federalists voiced vehement opposition to it. In November 1813 Federalist governor Martin Chittenden ordered home the state militia stationed in Plattsburgh on the grounds that Vermonters were "exposed to the retaliatory incursions and ravages of an exasperated enemy." The militia refused to return but the comic opera drama tellingly demonstrated the strong disapproval of national policy.[46]

Similar dissatisfactions, experienced throughout New England, led Massachusetts to call for a convention of New England states to discuss "these public grievances and concerns" and to propose amendments to the Constitution. When in October of 1814, the Vermont legislature received an invitation, Nathaniel Chipman rushed to Montpelier from his home in Tinmouth to strongly discourage participation as "a violation of constitutional principles . . . establishing a precedent which might prove injurious to the government." His argument carried the day and Vermont sent only an observer without voting privileges to the Hartford Convention. [47]

Although the convention did not reflect the views of extremist Federalists, the final report did include provisions echoing states' rights doctrine, asserting that it was the duty of the state to interpose itself between the people of the state and the federal constitution, a position that Chipman had long argued against. More significant, the report of the convention was issued almost simultaneously with news of major military victories and the settlement of the war stained the Federalist party with a brush of defeatism. In Vermont, as throughout New England, Federalists suffered extraordinary political losses and the party fell into disrepute. Notwithstanding his efforts to restrain Federalist zealots, Nathaniel Chipman paid the price of defeat along with the rest.

With his political career in shambles, in 1816 Chipman accepted appointment as professor of law at Middlebury College where he remained for three years. Increasing deafness, however, exacted its toll and obliged him to retire to his farm in Tinmouth, where he lived another quarter-century.

In retirement, Chipman remained committed to the causes that had animated him throughout his distinguished career. In 1833, he published a heavily revised edition of his *Sketches*. [48] He jettisoned discussions of natural rights in favor of a detailed examination of current constitutional controversies: President Andrew Jackson's 1832 veto of the Second Bank of the United States, and John Calhoun's nullification doctrine.

In both instances Chipman rejected formulas denying the

judiciary ultimate authority in determining issues of constitutionality. In the former instance, Chipman described Jackson's veto as defying "all the obligations derived from the course of precedents amounting to the requisite evidence of the national judgment and intention" because he specifically repudiated the judicial authority in his veto message. [49]

Disputing Calhoun's argument for nullification, Chipman drew from history to argue that the doctrine was similarly inconsistent with the framers' intent. Recalling his arguments opposing the Kentucky Resolutions almost four decades earlier, and more recently the Hartford Convention, Chipman steadfastly insisted that nullification of federal law was determined by courts, not states. "What the fate of the constitution of the United States would be if a small proportion of the states could expunge parts of it particularly valued by a large majority," Chipman warned, "can have but one answer." [50]

Recognizing, at the age of eighty-one that this would be his last work, Chipman's conclusion to the second edition of his *Principles of Government* reads like an epitaph to his remarkable career. Through his half-century of struggles, serving as guardian of the Constitution and the federalist system, Chipman espoused a cautious faith in the future of the American republic:

> "Let us . . . conceive a rational hope that [this nation] will endure as long as the successive generations of men, attend, with the calmness of philosophy, and the persevering zeal of patriotism, to the enjoyment of its blessings, and the improvement of its principles. To an ardent wish for its perpetual duration, let us add the only means of securing it. Let us endeavor to diffuse, extensively, the principles of useful knowledge, and to impress, indelibly on the minds of the rising generation, the sentiments of liberal virtue, and genuine patriotism." [51]

A decade after the publication of his final work, in 1843, Nathaniel Chipman died at the age of ninety-one.

One can only speculate as to why an individual who so profoundly influenced the course of Vermont events for so many years in so many ways has been largely eclipsed from popular consciousness. Overlooking the earliest histories written in the 1790s by Samuel Williams and Ira Allen on the grounds that both were consciously directed at European audiences, the writing of Vermont history can be said to have begun during the 1830s and 1840s. As the revolutionary generation passed from the scene, the burden of remembering their struggles and accomplishments fell

Monument to Nathaniel Chipman, Tinmouth, Vermont. Photograph by Nelson Jaquay.

both locally and nationally upon a new breed of historians who self-consciously identified themselves as the guardians of civic virtue. Their writings served as the instruments through which the revolutionary spirit and the vision of a revolutionary generation were to be implanted upon succeeding generations who, though not present at the creation, were nevertheless responsible for sustaining the republican experiment.

At the national level, the challenge was realized with George Bancroft's monumental five-volume *History of the United States*. Seeking to prove the thesis that American liberty, born of the revolutionary struggle, was unique in the history of the world, Bancroft employed biography to create a pantheon of founding fathers: paragons of virtue, who had made the necessary sacrifices

71

to bring the vision to fruition. Admittedly, Bancroft was not the first to employ this important genre to pay homage to Revolutionary heroes. Men like Parson Weems, in his 1807 *Life of Washington*, had demonstrated the value both of biography and of artistic license, having invented the famous "cherry tree" tale to impress upon his youthful readers the prophetic quality of Washington's life: the "founding father" destined to lead a people. [52]

Vermont historians embraced the patriotic assignment. Certainly this was so for Zadock Thompson, whose 1842 *History of Vermont* eclipsed all previous and contemporary efforts to portray the history of the state and had a profound effect on all subsequent works of its kind for later generations. [53] Thompson's objective was "to awaken and perpetuate in the breasts of the young, that spirit of patriotism, independence, and self-denial which so nobly animated the hearts of their fathers." To accomplish the task, Thompson borrowed heavily, both from Bancroft's model of biography and from Ira Allen's rather generous portrayal of both his own and his brother Ethan's contributions to the founding of Vermont. [54]

In narrating the story of Ethan Allen as if it were synonymous with that of the early history of the state, Thompson downplayed the significance of both Ethan's supporters and detractors. The former, who numbered among Samuel Williams's "revolutionary generation" — men whose adherence to natural laws had led them to embrace revolt prior to Ethan's appearance on the scene — were portrayed by Thompson as wholly subservient to Allen's leadership. No mention is made in Thompson's history of the repeated efforts of moderate southeasterners to distance themselves from Ethan and his Green Mountain Boys during the first years of the 1770s. Thompson's portrait of the great hero combines elements of Bancroft's revolutionary "founding father" with the newly emerging glorification of the romantic frontier hero (for example, Daniel Boone). [55]

But the question before us relates to Nathaniel Chipman. Fifty years after he steered Vermont's course to statehood, where did he fit within Thompson's first important history of Vermont? The answer, quite simply, is that he did not fit at all. Remarkably, Chipman's name appears only once in Thompson's history: "On the 10th of January, 1791, the legislature of Vermont met at Bennington, and on the 18th, they chose the Hon. Nathaniel Chipman and Lewis R. Morris, Esq., commissioners to attend Congress and negotiate the admission of Vermont into the Union. These commissioners immediately repaired to Philadelphia and laid before the president the proceedings of the convention and legislature of Vermont; and on the 18th of February, 1791 Congress passed an act . . . without debate, and without a dissenting vote, and by it were terminated all the controversies with regard to Vermont."[56]

Few except the most dedicated Vermont historians read Zadock Thompson today. Yet this early history continues to reflect the tone and the intellectual climate that dominate the writing of Vermont history. Statehood was the inexorable culmination of events hatched two decades earlier. Readers are left to conclude that it was change that occurred outside Vermont's borders that finally led Vermont's leaders to agree to the preconditions to statehood. The controversy with New York simply dissolved when New Yorkers realized that Vermont's representation in Congress would bolster "eastern states . . . deprived of their just representation in Congress," this a rather thinly veiled reference on Thompson's part to the problems his generation confronted over the issue of slavery and western expansion.[57]

Thompson's history bears a remarkable similarity to what Frances Fitzgerald has called the "seamless" school texts of the 1950s, which consciously downplayed internal controversies and political rivalries to present an idealized image of consensus.[58] Chipman's eclipse from Vermont's history reflected

Thompson's conscious effort to strike from the historical record the rancor, conflicts, and rivalries of the 1780s. In its place, Thompson substituted an orderly portrait of consensus and consensual politics. Vermonters had unswervingly steered a course toward statehood between 1777 and 1791. Denied entry into the union by vindictive Yorkers and their allies in Congress, Vermont's leaders had been obliged to simply wait until the shortcomings in the American system had been eliminated. The institution of Federalist measures designed to alleviate pressing political and economic problems appeared, Thompson observed, "to be marked with so much wisdom and prudence, as in a great degree, to restore to the people of Vermont that confidence."[59]

Likewise, New York had realized the error of its ways and

Detail of the Chipman monument, Tinmouth, Vermont. Photograph by Nelson Jaquay.

thereby opened the door for Vermont leaders—the very same men who had led the struggle from its inception—to pursue statehood. In this sanitized version, Zadock Thompson succeeded admirably in achieving his civic goal.

Zadock Thompson's rendition of the story became the standard fare for all subsequent generations of Vermonters. Despite no known likeness of Ethan Allen painted from life, his portrait adorns countless state histories, while one larger than life-sized statue dominates the Montpelier statehouse and a second, only slightly less imposing, graces statuary hall in our nation's Capitol. Chipman, also without a portrait from life, [60] captured the admiration of his contemporaries without stirring their imagination. He has come down to us in the figure of a lusterless functionary outshone by men of less learning but greater vision and genius. His monument is an obscure marker along a seldom travelled road in Tinmouth.

With few exceptions — these being academic monographs — Vermont historians have denied Chipman a place as one of Vermont's foremost jurists, authors, political philosophers, and, most importantly, founding fathers. Nathaniel Chipman's banishment recalls Samuel Butler's observation: "God cannot alter the past, but historians can."

NOTES

[1] A description of the monument and its full inscription appear in Abby Maria Hemenway, *The Vermont Historical Gazetteer* (Claremont: Claremont Manufacturing Co., 1877), III, 1157.

[2] On Allen, see Charles A. Jellison, *Ethan Allen: Frontier Rebel* (Syracuse: Syracuse University Press, 1969), 2-3; for Chipman, see Daniel Chipman, *Life of Hon. Nathaniel Chipman, LL.D.* (Boston: C. C. Little & J. Brown, 1846), 9-10; For an excellent description of frontier opportunities in a neighboring town, see Charles A. Grant, *Democracy in the Frontier Town of Kent, Connecticut* (New York: Columbia University Press, 1972).

[3] Chipman, *Life*, 11-12; also see Franklin Bowditch Dexter, *Biographical Sketches of the Graduates of Yale College*, (New York: H. Holt, 1885-1920), III, 660.

[4] Letters to George Washington, October 10, 1778 and to Ebenezer Fitch, October 3, 1778 appear in Chipman, *Life*, 29-32.

[5] To Ebenezer Fitch, March 20, 1779, in Chipman, *Life*, 28-29; also see Dexter, *Biographical Sketches*, III, 660.

[6] The first attorney, Stephen Rowe Bradley, also studied in Litchfield County and was one of the first students of Tapping Reeve. See Jacqueline Calder, letter to Professor Samuel Hand, January 19, 1978, Vermont Historical Society Collections. Ms. Calder, now curator at the Vermont Historical Society, was a candidate for a masters degree at the University of Vermont and an intern at the Litchfield Historical Society at the time the letter was written.

[7] Henry Steele Wardner, "The Haldimand Negotiations," *Vermont History* II (March 1931): 22.

[8] Ibid., 21-3; also see Chilton Williamson, *Vermont in Quandary 1763-1825* (Montpelier, Vt.: Vermont Historical Society, 1949), 90-126; As one would expect, Daniel Chipman defends his brother's involvement on the grounds that the players were "patriots" who "completely duped and deceived" the British. See Chipman, *Life*, 37-61.

[9] E. P. Walton, ed., *Records of the Governor and Council* (Montpelier, Vt: J. & J. M. Poland, 1873-76), III, 81; Abby Maria Hemenway, *Historical Gazetteer*, IV, 324; also see J. Kevin Graffagnino, "'Vermonters Unmasked': Charles Phelps and the Patterns of Dissent in Revolutionary Vermont," *Vermont History* 57 (Summer 1989): 149.

[10] *Records of the Governor and Council*, III, 348-49. For an excellent discussion of the debate, see Aleine Austin, "Vermont Politics in the 1780's: The Emergence of Rival Leadership," *Vermont History* 42 (Spring 1974): 143-4.

[11] *Records of the Governor and Council*, III, 349-51.

[12] Quoted in Austin, "Vermont Politics," 147.

[13] *Vermont Journal* (Windsor), 25 April, 1786.

[14] *Records of the Governor and Council*, III, 397-99. According to Chilton Williamson, it was at this juncture that the Allens "once and for all renounce[d] statehood" and proceeded to engage in frantic efforts to reopen the Haldimand negotiations; see Williamson, *Vermont in Quandary*, 145-161.

[15] *Records of the Governor and Council*, III, 358-66; also see Chipman, *Life*, 18; for a general description of circumstances, see Benjamin Hall, *History of Eastern Vermont* (New York: 1857), 551-52; also Lewis Stilwell, *Migration from Vermont* (Montpelier, Vt.: Vermont Historical Society, 1948), 107.

[16] Thomas Chittenden, "Address to the Freemen of Vermont," August, 1786, *Governor and Council*, III, 359-61; also see Austin, "Vermont Politics," 148.

[17] Chipman, *Life*, 19-20.

[18] Ibid., 67-8.

[19] *Vermont Gazette*, 28 August 1786; 31 August 1786.

[20] Walter H. Crockett, ed., *Journals and Proceedings of the State of Vermont, 1781-1791* (Montpelier, Vt.: Secretary of State, 1928), I, 284-5; also see Chipman, *Life*, 68.

[21] Washington to Weare, July 31, 1782, in John C. Fitzpatrick, ed., *The Writings of George Washington*, (Washington, D. C.: Government Printing Office, 1939), XXIV, 449-50; for an excellent discussion on the constitutional framers' concerns over Vermont, see Peter S. Onuf, *The Origins of the Federal Republic: Jurisdictional Controversies in the United States 1775-1787* (Philadelphia: University of Pennsylvania Press, 1983), 127-148; also see Jellison, *Ethan Allen*, 291-3.

[22] *Records of the Governor and Council*, III, 423-4; also see Williamson, *Vermont in Quandary*, 174-5.

[23] Chipman, *Life*, 74-5. Chipman further contributed to a resolution of title disputes in September 1791 when, acting as chief justice of Vermont's Supreme Court, he ruled in *Paine and Morris vs. Smead* that New York's confirmation grants, issued during the 1770s, were valid insofar as they had been voluntarily agreed upon by former New Hampshire title holders. See Daniel Chipman, *Reports of Cases Argued and Determined in the Supreme Court* (Middlebury: D. Chipman & Son, 1824), 56-63.

[24] Ibid., 81.

[25] Quoted in Williamson, *Vermont in Quandary*, 154-5.

[26] Ibid., 177-8.

[27] *Records of the Governor and Council*, III, 485; *Journals and Proceedings of the General Assembly*, IV, 188.

[28] *Records of the Governor and Council*, III, 430-48; Chipman, *Life*, 81; Williamson, *Vermont in Quandary*, 179.

[29] Chipman, *Life*, 87-8.

[30] Ibid., 93.

[31] Ibid., 88.

[32] *Records of the Governor and Council*, III, 468-86.

[33] Chipman, *Life*, 69.

[34] Ibid., 109. While no figures are available for the Vermont court, one recent scholar observed that with 269 cases tried in New York and 101 in Connecticut between 1789 and 1797 "we do know that there wasn't much business." See Jeffrey Morris, *Federal Justice in the Second Circuit: A History of the U.S. Courts in New York, Connecticut, and Vermont 1787-1987* (New York: Second Circuit Historical Committee, 1987), 15-16.

[35] Chipman, *Life*, 102-5.

[36] Nathaniel Chipman, *Reports and Dissertations* (Rutland: Anthony Haswell, 1793).

[37] According to Roy Honeywell, "Jefferson read the *Sketches* and recommended it, in 1807, together with the European classics and the *Federalist*, to the attention of young Americans. In 1814, he included it in a course of reading for his grandson. Two years later he urged its use as a textbook for William and Mary College." See Roy J. Honeywell, "Nathaniel Chipman: Political Philosopher and Jurist," *New England Quarterly* 5 (1932), 570.

[38] Matthew Lyon to Governor George Clinton, July 13, 1793, University of Vermont Library, Burlington, Vt., Catalogued Manuscript File, Special Collections.

[39] Lyon's attack appears in the *Farmers' Library*, May 13, 1793; Chipman's in the *Vermont Gazette*, September 26, 1794. Chipman also published a long letter against the Democratic-Republican Club in the *Vermont Journal*, September 22, 1794. An excellent work describing the rivalry is Judah Adelson, "The Vermont Democratic-Republican Clubs and the French Revolution, *Vermont History* 32 (January 1964): 3; also see William A. Robinson, *Jeffersonian Democracy in New England* (New York: Greenwood Press, 1968), 10. For a comprehensive discussion of Lyon's behavior, see Aleine Austin, *Matthew Lyon: "New Man" of the Democratic Revolution* (University Park: Pennsylvania State University Press, 1981), 90-2.

[40] Chipman, *Life*, 109; According to Harris Thurber, the 1797 revision was significant insofar as it rejected British common law as its basis, "probably on the basis of the assumption that the statute law of the community was sufficiently developed to sup-

plant the common law adequately for the needs of the community." See Harris Thurber, "The Vermont Judiciary: A Study in Cultural Adaptation," Ph.D. diss., Princeton University, 1955, 44. There seems to be disagreement on Chipman's role. Editor of Vermont State Papers Marlene Wallace maintains that Chipman "served only a few days" on the committee owing to his appointment as senator. See *Records of the General Assembly of Vermont*, Vol. III, Part VIII (1978), 57.

[41] Letter, Nathaniel Chipman to Cephas Smith, Jr., November 24, 1797, Vermont Historical Society, Montpelier, Vt.

[42] Chipman, *Life*, 129.

[43] Quoted in Austin, *Matthew Lyon*, 108-09; see Robinson, *Jeffersonian Democracy*, 22-3.

[44] Chipman, *Life*, 151.

[45] Chipman, *Life*, 185; *Journal of the Council of Censors* (Montpelier, Vt.: Watchman and State Journal Press, 1813), 6; also see Lewis H. Meader, "The Council of Censors in Vermont," *Proceedings of the Vermont Historical Society* (Montpelier: 1898), 121.

[46] On the War of 1812, see Edward Brynn, "Patterns of Dissent: Vermont's Opposition to the War of 1812," *Vermont History* 40 (Winter 1972): 10. For a discussion of Gov. Chittenden, see Walter Crockett, *Vermont, The Green Mountain State* (New York: Century History Co., 1921-23), III, 39-40.

[47] Chipman, *Life*, 110-11; *Records of Governor and Council,* VI, 492; also see Austin Noble, "The Federalist Party in Vermont," unpublished paper, Harvard University, April 1950, 120-1.

[48] Nathaniel Chipman, *Principles of Government: A Treatise on Free Institutions* (Burlington: Edward Smith, 1833).

[49] Ibid., 311.

[50] Ibid., 327-8.

[51] Ibid., 302.

[52] George Bancroft, *History of the United States* (Boston: Little, Brown & Co., 1859-1874), 10 vols. An excellent discussion of the mythicization of Washington appears in Catherine Albanese, *Sons of the Fathers* (Philadelphia: Temple University Press, 1976), 143-181.

[53] J. Kevin Graffagnino, "The Vermont 'Story': Continuity and Change in Vermont Historiography," *Vermont History* 46 (Spring 1978): 83.

[54] Zadock Thompson, *History of the State of Vermont* (Burlington, Vt.: Edward Smith, 1833), 3-4.

[55] An outstanding, though rarely used, source here is Benjamin Hall, *History of Eastern Vermont* (New York: G. P. Putnam, 1858); an excellent discussion on Daniel Boone and the genre of frontier romanticism appears in Henry Nash Smith, *Virgin Land* (Boston: Harvard University Press, 1950), 51-8.

[56] Thompson, *History*, 74-9, 82-3.

[57] Ibid., 82-3.

[58] Frances Fitzgerald, *America Revised* (Boston: Little, Brown & Co., 1979), 10.

[59] Thompson, *History*, 82-3.

[60] A portrait of a young nineteenth-century lawyer held by the Sheldon Museum in Middlebury is sometimes represented as a portrait of Nathaniel Chipman, but this contention has been refuted by recent studies undertaken by portrait specialist Elizabeth Durfee. See letter, Elizabeth Dole Durfee to William E. Wargo, January 30, 1989, copy in Vermont Historical Society Collections.

Anticipating America: Levi Allen and the Case for an Independent Vermont

by Michael A. Bellesiles

 Levi Allen was demented, or at least his wife thought so. In 1802 Nancy Allen apologized for her recently deceased husband to the lieutenant-governor of Lower Canada. Levi, she claimed, "exhibited evident marks of a deranged mind," and as a consequence occasionally said and did "things which he never would have" if he had been "in the full possession of reason." Levi had "uniformly and unequivocally expressed a partiality for the British government," and any of his actions or declarations to the contrary, she asserted, arose "from a mental derangement." The expression of that derangement came in his curious bias towards the notion of an independent Vermont. At key moments in his life, Levi Allen showed a tendency to act in what his wife saw as a romantic fashion to keep Vermont separate from all other jurisdictions. Unable to explain this deviation from the path of pure reason, and Loyalism, Nancy Allen attributed such conduct to a disordered mind.[1] But if Allen's own explanation is to be accepted, his support for Vermont's independence emerged from the purest form of reason: economic self-interest.

Levi Allen's perception of economic advantage led him to favor Vermont's separation from New York and its initial participation in the American Revolution, and then to oppose its full integration into either the British empire or, more significantly, the United States. He opposed Vermont statehood for the most American of reasons, self-interest, even while denying any identification as an American. Allen thus unknowingly anticipated the primary motive force of nineteenth-century America and its central self-perception of individualism.

Clearly it is difficult to define something as elusive as the American character. In 1782 Allen's contemporary, Hector Saint Jean de Crèvecoeur, ventured in *Letters From an American Farmer* to answer the question, "What then is the American, this new man?" Crèvecoeur found his answer in economic attitudes and relations. "[W]e are all tillers of the earth," he proclaimed, animated by a "spirit of industry, which is unfettered and unrestrained, because each person works for himself." Before coming to America, immigrants enjoyed no nationality, for the poor are ever homeless. But in "this great American asylum" they came together, and through their own labor created a society marked by a "pleasing uniformity of decent competence." By their own agency they fashioned "a new mode of living, a new social system," in fact "the most perfect society now existing in the world." This new culture emerged from its enterprise, exemplifying the Latin motto *Ubi panis ibi patria* — "where my bread is earned, there is my country."[2] It is little wonder that when D. H. Lawrence identified Crèvecoeur along with Benjamin Franklin as the key figures in the creation of an autonomous American culture he should write that to "the European, the American is first and foremost a dollar-fiend."[3]

There is no politics in Crèvecoeur's portrait of America, but much subterfuge. Crèvecoeur, as is well known, was no simple American farmer, and he wrote his letters in London, not America. He loved the egalitarian quality of America, which allowed him to remake himself in his own image. Unfortunately for Crèvecoeur, he could not keep his personal opinions private. Hating war, he refused to take sides in the Revolution. As a consequence the patriots hounded him and burned his farm, while the British threw him in prison.[4] Crèvecoeur came up hard against the wall of Revolutionary America's hostility to neutrality, as would Levi Allen.

The Revolutionary generation discovered, and modern historians have rediscovered, the uniqueness of American character in the relation of the individual to the state and society, most specifically in widespread land ownership and a high level of commitment to the common good. Historians have labelled this emphasis on the citizen's political responsibility and its agrarian roots "republicanism." Drawing on the classical traditions of the polis and civic virtue, republicanism demands vigilance and self-sacrifice. The republican citizen is freed from dependence on others by the ownership of property and is thus able to think and act independently and to recognize the true interests of the commonwealth. The good republican citizen must be ready to subsume his personal interest to the needs of the community and his personal prejudices to the corporate values.[5] Levi Allen's brother Ethan voiced these key republican themes in all his writings and attempted, though not always with perfect fidelity, to live up to these standards.[6]

For the last three decades historians have debated extensively the nature and meaning, and effective duration, of republicanism and have reached no consensus.[7] Linda Kerber has written that "'Republicanism' has become so all-embracing as to absorb comfortably its own contradictions"; while Michael Johnson compared it to the contemporary theory of ether, a substance that fills all empty spaces between what is known.[8] Republicanism has been found permeating working-class consciousness up into the twentieth century, transferred to women in the early nineteenth century, influencing the founding of the Republican party, and underpinning Southern defenses of slavery and states' rights.[9] Other historians have seen republicanism transformed into Jeffersonian agrarianism *and* its supposed opposite, liberal commercialism.[10]

81

There is a general agreement, though, that in their under-standing of political participation, the Revolutionary genera-tion kept stumbling over the problem of self-interest. Good republicans insisted on the primacy of the community over selfish concerns. Yet within the republican paradigm there lay a powerful contradiction and eventual negation. Throughout the 1780s and 1790s, American patriots struggled to reconcile the differing im-pulses of economic advancement and political virtue. By the second decade of the nineteenth century an insistence on civic virtue would appear either quaintly anachronistic or merely rhetorical as the new nation pursued its unrestrained economic growth. [11] In the last years of the eighteenth century Levi Allen anticipated much of this emerging culture of Smithian self-interest. He would pay a heavy price for being a generation ahead of his time.

By his own account, Levi Allen lived his whole life in the shadow of one or another of his brothers, Heman, Ira, and especially Ethan. His relationship with his brothers often deter-mined Levi's decisions. At the age of fifteen, Levi became angry with Ethan, the "dictator of the younger brethren," and "in a mif walked off." Levi discovered quickly, as he put it in his third-person autobiography, that he "could live without the assistance of his good mother, and more so without that of his arbitrary brother." Lacking a "Scholastic or Scientific" education, Allen found his "wild Gander education Obtained flying" sufficient for his purposes. Motivated by "Volatile Ideas" of success in this world, Allen sought business opportunities as he traveled across the northern frontier in the last decade of British rule. He final-ly discovered his calling in the remote outpost of Detroit. [12]

Though his father "had early taught him that next to religion landed Property was the most Substantial," Levi Allen found trade much more exciting. Land was for farmers, or speculators with excess capital, and Levi was neither. Trade served the ambitions of those with little capital, offering a route out of the cycles of the farm, which Levi found extremely boring. Following a chance encounter with some Indians in the Taconic hills east of Saratoga, Allen became an Indian trader. These Iroquois bartered fur for ammunition and introduced Allen to a number of other Indians who would enter into similar exchanges. In the ensuing years Allen developed an abiding respect and affection for the Iroquois and Abenakis, establishing connections that would prove very useful for himself, his family, and the state to which they devoted themselves. [13]

His initial successes in the Indian trade made Levi a convert to the emerging entrepreneurial ethos actively promoted by Benjamin Franklin and other urban theoreticians. For a youth with a "vigerous body and enterprising mind," Allen wrote, "the world . . . will open fast enough, full as fast as he is prepared for it." Albany merchants granted Allen credit "on no other Recommendation but the pushing industry he observed in the course of Supplying the Indian hunters." The young entrepreneur should rely on "what he doth know is true being derived from nature and a moral" education, and "be religiously Punctual, not in order to go to heaven, but to live happily on Earth." Allen sounds like an early American Babbitt as he extols the virtues of sound work habits and good character, assuring graduates of the school of hard knocks that with the assistance of the "two Sisters, Temperance & Frugality, a Fortune might soon be Obtained." "Economy Industry and Steady perseverance on a well laid plan will soon put a man above Such abject Necessity, & make plenty of Friends when one doth not want them." [14]

Like Ben Franklin, though, Allen realized that a discontinuity existed between his hopes for opportunity and the economic structures of his society, appreciating that luck often played a greater role than effort. [15] Allen understood the conditional nature of his entrepreneurial values, learning the hard way that established orders resented those who presumed to attain equality of opportunity. Just as ministers attacked those who thought for themselves, Allen wrote, so "Nothing appears more redicalous to men of business" than an ambitious youth of humble background who thinks that hard work and honesty should bring success. Everywhere he went, Allen found a perpetuation of the status quo; the elite held the advantage in every exchange and used the power of the law to keep newcomers out. Even on the frontier around Detroit, "a new Trader Stood no Chance." Some Indian friends warned Allen of a murder plot by "those in the employ of the great Traders" who resented his competition. He escaped thanks to the aid of "the *Faithful Indians*." Allen concluded that the "Christians have not so much to boast over the American Indians as they Vainly attribute to themselves."[16]

By the time he turned twenty, in 1766, Levi had become a formidable salesman. Like many other would-be manipulators of a market economy, he convinced himself of his own infallible reason in economic matters. His self-confidence proved unwarranted. After what he thought to be several seasons of profitable trading with the Indians, Levi found himself "double in debt, which is the never failing consequences of Punctuality, Joined to honest frugal Industry."

Allen's early experiences taught him the need to act in concert with others. He found his natural allies in his family. The other Allens also chafed at an economic system that seemed designed to keep them in their place. In the normal course of events, the Allen siblings would have established themselves on farms smaller than their father's and would have worked for decades trying to acquire enough land to see their children into a secure adulthood. The Allens hoped to circumvent this traditional structure by purchasing illegal land grants in the Green Mountains.

Since the New Hampshire deeds had been declared worthless by the Privy Council in 1764, the shrewd and the foolish could acquire title to hundreds of acres very cheaply. The Allens seemed particularly adventurous, buying worthless deeds to thousands of acres of land, and even organizing a land company to try and draw more settlers into the Green Mountains. The sellers expressed relief at getting rid of their valueless paper; the Allens expressed a surprising confidence that they could, through some political alchemy, transform this paper into gold.

The Allens never actually transmuted their paper into precious metals, but they convinced others to accept it as such, which proved almost as valuable. The path of the Allens, their cousins, in-laws, neighbors, and assorted allies to the creation of an independent Vermont is well known; what is less appreciated is the route the new state took into the American union. [17]

The key moment in the twenty-year struggle for the legitimacy of the one-time New Hampshire Grants came on May 10, 1775, when Ethan Allen led the Green Mountain Boys into Fort Ticonderoga and out of the British Empire. By seizing military control of Lake Champlain, Allen cleverly linked the struggle of the inhabitants of the New Hampshire Grants against the Royal Province of New York with the larger struggle of the American colonists against a perceived British tyranny. Present at this "perfect dawn" of freedom, as Ethan Allen hailed it, Levi Allen offered a different vision of this victory: "From this unhappy Period Allen dates his Damnation!"

This disparity of opinion actually reflects well the ambiguity of the war for the Allens. At one and the same time, the Revolution constituted a family tragedy and their greatest triumph. Ethan Allen fell from glory to ignominy, suffering one of the most brutal captivities of the war; Remember Baker, Heman, Heber, and Zimri Allen all died in these years; Levi was discovered a Loyalist and read out of the family; only Ira seemed to emerge unscathed, battling and conniving to keep the self-created state of Vermont afloat in a sea of troubles.

Levi Allen thought the war accomplished nothing that could

not have been more efficiently resolved in peace. As a firm believer in the pacific powers of free trade, Allen found all wars inherently stupid and wasteful, the Revolution only demonstrated his point. [18] After the war he wrote a British official that, while a perception of self-interest had made him "Truly & uniformly loyal," he conceived the British "the greatest Fools" for not appreciating that both nations would eventually gain from American independence. [19]

Nonetheless, Allen played an active role in the campaigns of 1775 around Lake Champlain. Ethan Allen included Levi on his list of prospective officers for the Continental Green Mountain regiment. But then "the old Farmers on the New Hampshire Grants" met at Dorset on July 26, 1775 and violated Congressional orders by appointing officers for the Green Mountain Boys rather than allowing their free election. Ethan Allen, denied a commission in the regiment he created, swallowed his pride and went to work on General Schuyler's staff. Levi Allen followed the example of other former officers of the Green Mountain Boys like Remember Baker, Robert Cochran, and Peleg Sunderland, and refused to serve in this new regiment. [20]

Levi Allen had initially joined in the revolutionary struggle, certain that vigorous action would convince both New York and Great Britain of the foolishness of their attempted tyrannies and of the commitment of the Grants settlers to keep their lands. From such a realization would flow profits for the Allens and a peaceful resolution to the imperial crisis. But despite the "reasonableness" and "absolute necessity" for both sides to reach "an accommodation. . . . Pride madness and folly presided over the Councils, and a war was carried on in which neither party had anything to gain and much to loos." Over the next eight years Allen continued to argue that if the two sides would just listen to reason and appreciate where their true interests lay, they would end their unprofitable war. Instead, "all the Devils in Hell were let loos," and "a heated Zeal" took hold, "moderation alone was highly criminal, All Virtue collectively centered in Whigism and the reverse . . . in the least Suspison of Toryism." The war turned "brother against brother, Friend against Friend, and neighbour agt. neighbour."[21]

"Brother against brother" held particular meaning for Levi Allen. From October 1775 until early 1778, Levi dedicated himself to a single cause: effecting the release of his brother Ethan from a cruel imprisonment. Levi moved restlessly about North America seeking information from British prisoners, annoying American officers and members of Congress, supplying his brother and other American prisoners with basic necessities, and recruiting supporters for his efforts to make an exchange for Ethan Allen the Continental Army's top priority. In May 1778, Levi finally succeeded, and Ethan Allen returned in triumph to Vermont. [22]

But along the way Levi Allen's bitterness with the new government of the United States grew. Levi failed to discern much difference between the two imperial systems of the United States and Great Britain; greed and corruption dominated both, entrenched elites monopolized opportunities in each. Levi saw no reason to commit himself excitedly to either cause. Instead, he tried to convince his brothers to simply pursue their self-interest without necessary reference to a foolish political conflict among competing elites. [23]

Ethan Allen had suffered too much for the cause of American independence to accept such logic. Emerging from captivity with a black and white conception of the world, and the democratic state of Vermont incarnated good, Ethan could not tolerate a member of his own family remaining neutral. He shared with most other patriots a conviction that neutrality served as a cover for Loyalism, as any true American and republican would not hesitate to commit himself to the cause. Ethan's curse on Levi summed up his judgment, and captured well Levi's character: "Damn his luke-warm soul!"[24]

As the *Narrative* of his captivity demonstrated so well, Ethan

Allen identified himself with Vermont and equated the independence of Vermont and the United States. This equation helped to keep Vermont alive over the next decade, despite the opposition of New York, the Continental Congress, and, occasionally, Great Britain. It also justified bringing charges of Loyalism against his own brother before Vermont's court of sequestration. Ethan charged Levi with conspiring with "inimical persons" to monopolize "the necessaries of life" and "endeavoring to lessen the credit of the continental currency." It infuriated Ethan to discover that his brother owned land in Vermont yet refused to live there, taking up residence in, of all places, a heavily Loyalist area of Dutchess County, New York. Aggravating the situation, Levi had bought a slave, a further repudiation of everything Vermont and Ethan Allen represented. Ethan expressed his anger by failing to mention Levi in his *Narrative*, despite all that his younger brother had done to liberate him. [25]

Final evidence of Levi's betrayal of both country and family came with Levi's refusal to accept Continental currency from his brothers. Levi argued rationally that Continental money kept losing its value; Ethan saw only a denial of the legitimacy of the new government and a rejection of the traditional economic process. Among family and neighbors, anything should be acceptable in exchange; the participants in a trade agreed upon a value, even for money. But that new economic theorist, Adam Smith, influenced Levi Allen. Smith argued that money served as an objective measurement of reality, its market exchange value correctly reflecting its worth. Such arguments, which Levi copied into his notebooks, eluded Ethan Allen. [26] Where Levi Allen saw economic rationality, Ethan Allen saw a sophistic justification for Toryism. [27]

But Levi Allen was no ideological Loyalist. No theory of hierarchy, no fear of disorder drove him to join the British in 1778. Like a great many of those Americans who supported the Crown during the Revolution, Allen did so temporarily in hopes

88

of profiting from the confusions of war and attempted to swing from side to side with the pendulum of monetary fortune. Any area occupied by the British created marked opportunities for profiteering. New York City under the British proved especially notable for its economic energy and corruption. Levi Allen initially entered the city searching for Ethan, but the temptation to trade with the British for specie overwhelmed any hesitation he may have felt about conducting business with his brother's captors. [28]

Yet pursuing his self-interest left Levi Allen little defense when others did exactly the same to his detriment. Levi consistently discovered that the British system was based on connection and birth. [29] Denied an acceptable status by birth, Allen spent years trying to cultivate powerful connections, occasionally with success. Nonetheless, he found the British elite all too willing to jettison its lackeys when necessary. After accepting a British offer to found a community in Florida near the war's end, Allen learned that the Peace of Paris in 1783 turned that region back to Spain. Thus was a "disgraceful war ended by a more infamous Peace." After making "considerable Progress at my own expense" in settling East Florida, "peace . . . put an end to my Prospects." Levi put his losses at £1500, "not by Harrycanes, or Other convulsions in *nature*, but by an out right robery of those in Power."

In looking back at the Revolution, Levi Allen saw only personal disaster. He had lost "his whole capital, and three years attentive Industerous labour under the Torred Zone," as well as having been separated for too long from his "Virtuous perfectly agreeable wife child friends relations, native Country."[30] The experience reinforced his tendency to strike out on his own and look skeptically at the conventions of his peers.

Nonetheless, underneath Allen's carefully cultivated veneer of hardened individualism lurked a sentimental soul. Two possibly contradictory issues obsessed Levi Allen: determining self-interest and establishing trust. [31] The heartless commercial world Allen helped to create had little room for trust, the contract would come to replace an individual's word. Levi warned Ira Allen to be "Extremely cautious who you trust[,] times was never more uncertain nor common faith & honesty less regarded." As a good businessman, Levi complained constantly about the capriciousness of the market, but found it offering the only valid measurement of an individual's worth. Levi thought himself "too well acquainted with the world to let every damnd Rogue & fool too take advantage of me," but felt the need for harmony at home. He relied on his brothers to look after his affairs and his wife to manage his household. In return for Nancy Allen's promise to "Omit Crying finding fault & provisying Evil" Levi swore to "Omit Destilled Liquor Swearing & Staying Out late at nights, (a fair Bargain)." Levi Allen anticipated the nineteenth-century transformation of the American family into "a haven in a heartless world" by his personal efforts to find surety within his own family. [32]

When Ethan and Ira Allen charged Levi with Loyalism, Levi responded with a barrage of personal articles in the *Connecticut Courant*, reproducing family letters that revealed the Allens' warm feelings for one another. Levi put forth a curious defense, his intended audience not the people of New England, but Ethan Allen. Levi tried to remind his brother of how much they cared for each other. Instead of attacking Ethan for denying his own brother justice, Levi printed protestations of affection. But Ethan proved obdurate, refusing to read the articles and rebuffing efforts by Levi to meet. Levi even challenged Ethan to a duel in hopes of forcing a personal confrontation. Ethan proclaimed Levi mad and refused to meet him, either to talk or fight — at first. [33]

With the war over, Levi, bitter over his treatment by the British, returned to Vermont. It took only one meeting with Ethan for Levi to be accepted back into the family. Ethan welcomed Levi's rehabilitation with great warmth, but did not always agree with him that trade rose above morality. When the British General Haldimand proposed a little scheme to make some money on the side by trading salt and other items to New York by way of Vermont, Ethan applauded the idea, but asked that the British avoid Vermont's territory. Levi could not believe that Ethan would pass up such profitable opportunities. [34]

Over the next decade, Levi Allen served as Vermont's unofficial ambassador to Canada and Britain, arranging numerous political and business deals, with his main goal the removal of all trade barriers. Free trade held real attractions for a cash poor economy, and the situation offered many opportunities for his family. The Allens, like most Vermonters, had little of the hard currency required by customs agents to pay duties or bribes before goods crossed the border. Eliminating the duties would, as Levi wrote his brothers, give them all a fighting chance to compete in the Montreal markets. Levi opened a store in St. Jean on the upper end of Lake Champlain and worked with his brothers, who owned vast quantities of land in the region, to orient Vermont economically towards Montreal rather than Albany. [35]

Following Adam Smith's lead, Allen believed free trade would bring greater profits and economic certainty. When a Canadian customs official seized some beaver hats Levi sought to sell in Vermont, Levi responded angrily that a businessman could not keep track of all these British regulations: "if Commerce is at the Option of and depends Intirely on the Capricious humor of a Drunken Custom house Officer, It follows of Course property is Very uncertain." Allen complained that the British did not enforce their commercial laws with anything approaching consistency, thus proving that it was better to have none. [36] The British showed every sign of agreeing with Allen, and Governor Carleton removed most restrictions on trade between Canada and Vermont in April 1787. [37]

Attempting to establish the Allens as the commercial link between Vermont and Canada, Levi saw little advantage in joining the United States. "If Vermont Joins the foedral Union," Levi wrote Ira Allen, "it will never again be in their power to Obtain the favours in Commerce now only to be asked for."[38] This perception of economic self-interest determined his opposition to Vermont's ratification of the U.S. Constitution. Just as Levi had never been an intellectually dedicated Loyalist, so his battle to keep Vermont out of the union contained no element of the anti-federalist critique of a strong central government or an extended republic. Levi Allen's guiding light was not Montesquieu, but Adam Smith. His position is simply stated: Vermont stood to gain more by remaining independent than by joining the United States.

Ethan Allen shared this perception, at least when negotiating for free trade agreements with the British. He told Carleton in 1788 that most Vermonters feared that joining the union would "ruin their commerce." Emerging from the Revolution without debts, Vermont risked "insolvency" if it shared responsibility for the rest of America's debts. Far better to continue neutral, maintaining "a friendly intercourse and commerce" with the rest of the world.[39]

Building on these economic fears, Levi Allen advised the British government that "Commerce was the 'opening Wedge' by which G. Britain could work upon & command Vermont." He made this suggestion in hopes that the government might help put together a ship full of "Cargo suited to the market," which he would then take to St. Jean and from there sell in Vermont. Such an enterprise would demonstrate "the Commercial Advantages" of an economic connection with England, "strengthen . . . his Family interest & Connections, & prevent Vermont from listening to the overtures of Congress." Allen confidently predicted that the argument of "goods coming thro' Canada directly from the Manufacturers in England and sold cheap in Vermont would have opened the Eyes of the People, more than all the wise learned men of Europe would have done by Logical Orations." Levi Allen would, of course, keep the profits of this venture for "his Services." John Graves Simcoe, the new governor of Upper Canada, accepted these arguments, providing Levi with credit and helping him receive an annual compensation as a Loyalist.[40]

While Levi Allen's opposition to the ratification of the U.S. Constitution responded to specific local conditions, other Antifederalists employed the same logic — their states stood to gain more from being outside the union. Arguments similar to Allen's appeared in the writings of opponents of the Constitution in every state. For instance in Massachusetts, "Agrippa" wrote that "It is vain to tell us that we ought to overlook local interest. It is only by protecting local concerns, that the interest of the whole is preserved." Both sides used the language of Adam Smith, but the Antifederalists demonstrated greater intellectual consistency in arguing the virtues of free trade. "Agrippa," writing that "when business is unshackled, it will find out that channel which is most friendly to its course," expressed a common fear that the proposed central government would regulate the economy to the benefit of one class, region, or interest group.[41]

Levi Allen asked Vermonters what guarantee the Constitution offered that the central government would not close their border with Canada. As an independent nation, Vermont held a balance of power, political and economic, between British Canada and the United States. Each side would attempt to woo the mountain republic, and Vermont would be in a position to name its price, which Allen confidently predicted would include free trade. As Levi wrote Ira Allen, remaining autonomous would bring every advantage "to Vermont, & our Family in Particular." But if it joined the U.S., Vermont would become but a remote backwater of an expanding empire, of no consequence to the controlling powers of the new nation in New York, and subject to national tariffs. Given the enormous commercial success that traditionally agricultural Switzerland enjoyed when it became neutral a generation later, there is reason to believe that Levi Allen may have been correct in his analysis that Vermont's true interest lay in continued independence. [42] But Allen missed two important counter-impulses working against his efforts: that other parties within Vermont held different interests and the strength of the emotional identification of many Vermonters as Americans. [43]

The main support for a quick ratification of the U.S. Constitution came from a powerful group in the southwestern part of the state. Led by the conservative Nathaniel Chipman, this faction, most of whose members would join the Federalist party, saw its business interests directed towards Albany and New York and its political interests tied to the new federal government. Chipman came to Vermont to exercise his considerable ambition, fully expecting a meteoric ascent to political power. Caught in a loathsome democracy, which he worked to limit, Chipman found his path blocked by the persistent domination of Vermont politics by the Chittenden/Allen faction. The Chipman faction gained control of the state only once in the two decades following independence, and then by stealing it. In the November 1789 election, Chittenden won again, but fell 170 votes short of the necessary fifty percent majority, throwing the election into the state assembly. The assembly ignored the wishes of the voters and appointed Moses Robinson governor, even though he had received only a quarter of the popular votes cast. At the next election the voters turned out to reverse this decision, returning Chittenden to the governorship every year thereafter until his death in 1797. [44]

Most historians have argued that the brief interlude of the Robinson governorship set the stage for the ratification of the Constitution, giving credit to Nathaniel Chipman for engineering a major nationalist victory. [45] Levi Allen shared this view, telling the British government that Vermont's ratification of the U.S. Constitution was an accident. [46] While it is true that the

Chipman faction stood to gain from the patronage of the federal government, Chipman's role in the ratification—and much else—is often overrated. The self-interest of most Vermonters, including Ira Allen, demanded the ratification of the Constitution.

For twenty years the settlers of the Green Mountains fought to secure their land titles. The constant goal of the Allens, who tied their interest closely to that of the other holders of New Hampshire Grants, remained the acknowledgment of the legitimacy of those grants. From 1777 through 1790, Vermont's government continually requested and expected admission into the United States as an equal partner. Despite several solemn promises, Congress consistently drew back from union at the last minute because of the heated opposition of New York. But after Ethan Allen held Vermont aloof from Shays' Rebellion in early 1787, the New York legislature dropped its opposition to Vermont statehood, as long as Vermont reimbursed those New Yorkers who lost their lands in the region. Over the next several years representatives of the two states worked out the details that culminated in the treaty of 1790, and New York vacated its claims to the Green Mountains upon Vermont's admission into the union. [47]

Given this context, ratification of the Constitution seemed almost a formality. At last the Vermonters gained the end they had sought for twenty years—of course they accepted the deal. Thomas Chittenden returned to the governorship in October 1790, just in time to recommend the acceptance of the treaty and ratification of the U.S. Constitution. The Vermont assembly approved the treaty on October 25, 1790, voting the same day to call a "convention to deliberate upon and *agree to* the constitution of the United States." [48]

There hardly seemed any issues worthy of debate at the convention, which met in early January 1791. [49] After electing Chittenden president, the convention listened to Nathaniel Chipman's long-winded argument in favor of joining the union so that Vermont might share in the power and glory of the United States. Chipman of Rutland saw that "instead of being confined to the narrow limits of Vermont, we become members of an extensive empire." Most members of the convention seemed content to enjoy the narrow limits of their farms, Daniel Buck of Norwich speaking for many in holding that "the blessings resulting to Vermont from her union with an extensive empire . . . would not apply to the bulk of the people: some few favorites of fortune" would reap the benefits. Interest, not empire, demanded their attention.

Benjamin Greene of Windsor agreed that economic interest lay at the heart of the debate. But where others feared that Vermont's interests "must then bend to the interest of the union," Greene found the two mutual, insisting that pot and pearl ashes cried out for union.

But many representatives still did not trust New York. They suspected a trap to entice Vermont into the union so that the federal courts and U.S. Army could take away their lands. Benjamin Emmons of Woodstock drew the convention's attention to the core issue before them: would their land titles be safe under the federal judiciary? Emmons compared "Our present transaction . . . to the act of Adam in eating the forbidden fruit" in that they were "acting for future generations." He therefore requested a postponement until October to allow the people a chance to consider whether they would eat of that fruit. Emmons thought the people "feel fearful lest some trap should be found hidden by a fair disguise."

Chipman responded that "the delegates are virtually the people themselves" and should act as such. He called on the classical tradition in perceiving rationality and virtue as confined to the aristocracy, rather than natural or genetic. But this elitist formulation did not satisfy many. Ira Allen of Colchester, who as one of the biggest landowners in the state had as much to gain as anyone from ratification, provided the necessary amendment. Allen simply premised Vermont's ratification on the U.S. government keeping its part of the bargain. Since Congress had reneged several times in the past, the convention's approval of this amendment demonstrates a reasonable suspicion. Debate apparently ended with this amendment and the convention approved the Constitution by an overwhelming majority of 105 to 4. [50]

Angry with Ira for supporting statehood, Levi Allen criticized his brother for not recognizing "Your real Interest," accusing Ira of being blinded by fears that he would lose his lands bordering on Canada. [51] But it was Levi who did not understand: Ira Allen's interests lay elsewhere. While it is true that Ira Allen devoted a lot of energy to establishing trade connections between Vermont and Canada, his premier economic activities revolved around land. Whether farming the land or selling it, the economic future of Ira's family depended on the validation of his land titles. Ira's idealization of land ownership replicated the dominant republican opinion of his time. Land guaranteed personal independence and economic autonomy, supporting a well-ordered republic and individual liberties. [52] Levi confidently expected to "splice" land speculation "into the mercantile line"—using land titles as capital to acquire credit for use in trade. [53] For years Levi tried to draw Ira away from the land and into trade, giving unasked-for lessons in business management and correct investment procedures: "for Gods Sake make no Ingagements in purchasing land that will Interfear with Trade." But until the late 1790s, Ira contentedly stayed in Vermont and built up a portfolio of land titles. [54]

Levi found it "distasteful" that Vermont joined the United States, but self-interest led him to compromise and accommodate himself to the new reality. His land holdings and trade connections demanded his return to and continued involvement in Vermont's political and economic life. Allen hoped that the people of Vermont would realize their error and reverse their decision. The building of a customs house on the Vermont / Canada border by the U.S. government seemed an evident provocation, and Allen predicted that it would shortly "suffer desolation by accidental fire as there are many very careless People in Vermont." But when it came right down to it, Allen, like opponents of the Constitution throughout America, accepted defeat and got on with the routines of life under the new national government. On November 14, 1791, with Vermont in the union and trade restrictions in place, Levi Allen abandoned St. Jean and returned to Vermont.[55]

Except in family relations, Levi Allen's loyalty proved fungible, tied to the best offer or temporary advantage. When the Vermont government appointed him to negotiate with Great Britain in 1789, he insisted that he acted for the benefit of Vermont and referred to himself as a Vermonter. Seeking Canadian lands in 1792, he insisted to the government of Canada that he had negotiated those same treaties for the benefit of Quebec and Great Britain and maintained that Quebec was his home.[56] Generally Levi insisted that he acted "for the Good of Vermont and every individual thereof now alive or to be born." Any Vermonter who opposed his efforts to establish free trade with England "Aught to be damned & die like a toad under a harrow." He did admit, however, that what was good for Vermont was good for his business as well.[57]

In trade, Levi could be a hard-headed pragmatist. Levi advised Ira that in its negotiations with Britain Vermont must ask for more than it actually wanted, such as shipbuilding rights. "You may laugh at the Idea of Ship building," Levi reminded Ira, but "what may not be wanted Just now may be some futer day, and not so Easily Obtained, if Obtained at all."[58] Constantly searching for an angle, Levi became involved in the machinations of the would-be bishop of Vermont, Samuel Peters.

Levi advised Ira that if Peters succeeded in his claim to the glebe rights of the Church of England and the Society for the Propagation of the Bible granted in the New Hampshire titles, the Allens stood a good chance of purchasing these lands cheaply from the Church. Failing that arrangement, Levi suggested that Vermont "appropriate Said land for the use of the State." Yet even in the midst of such grandiose plans, Levi remained concerned enough over expenses to ask Ira to "write in a Small close fine hand to Save postage."[59]

Levi Allen thought himself a citizen of the world, yet continually revealed himself a provincial American. As an American businessman in London, Allen found himself in a labyrinth of mumbled excuses, subtle hints, and necessary connections of which he was not a part. As he complained to Nancy and Ira, "Every thing here is conducted by an Indirect method." His every effort seemed obstructed by some unknown "piece of Court deception" as he was ushered from one official to another, all of whom disclaimed responsibility and sent him on to the next office. Sir Charles Middleton in the Naval Office "gave me smoothe words in round flowing periods" and immediately forgot Allen existed. If he could approach these officials "with plenty of cash," then maybe they would listen, but otherwise he found that "people here are too well bread to Speak much truth." "The method of doing business in this polite place," Levi wrote, "is all a Joke." When he arrived, he foolishly thought that the "lowest offer" would win the contract. But "No contract is ever Obtained here without able friends . . . [and] a member of Parliament" who must be brought into the enterprise and "git Something handsome to purchase Votes."[60]

If Levi Allen often felt contempt for the petty emotionalism of his fellow Americans, he expressed a deeper loathing for the British. They had "barter'd their Sincerity" for style and sold their national economy to a spoiled elite. With remarkable accuracy, Allen predicted in May 1789 that the British would soon be at war, since the elite would reap enormous profits from the ensuing military contracts. [61] Levi thought that a renewed conflict might serve Vermont well and would certainly lead to a free trade agreement as the Vermonters would be in a good position to provision the British troops in Canada. [62] With American optimism, Levi insisted that "its a folly to be cast down." He assured Nancy that he was in "higher Spirits & Shall try hard to make some contract." If he could "only git the wheels agoing Shall do something cleaver yet." He held firm to his "great expectations"; he would have been well advised to have listened to his wife and stayed in Vermont or St. Jean. [63]

The best-laid plans of the rational businessman, even if he knew his markets and planned properly for the distribution of his goods, were crushed easily by the vagaries of nature and the machinations of well-connected competitors. A combination of bad weather, "unavoidable Procrastinations," the impressment of his ship's crew by the British Navy, and "obstructions thrown in my way by the Merchants in this Country who supply Canada" ended Allen's grand schemes. In addition he felt a keen "Anxiety . . . being asked every day whether my Brother [Ethan] is really dead, the most unfortunate questions in the power of men or demons to ask." Stunning confirmation came in a letter from Ira. It did not seem possible that Ethan could have died so soon. The world, Levi wrote Nancy and Ira, had "turned her Rough Side" towards him, and he longed to return home and live his last years quietly with his family. [64] "If the great atlantick suffers me to cross it again Safe," he promised Nancy that he would "go immediately to St. Albans & Settle down contented & Sing Oh be easy." To Ira he wrote "I may comfort myself that as I have lost 15 years of the Prime of life, that I have not so much now to lose, — for Gods Sake, Vermont the Family & all *Friends* to our Israel let me not die of disappointment." [65]

In many ways Levi Allen represents the deracinated individualist of America's emerging capitalist order. Certainly a

Loyalist, Allen never shifted from his first loyalty, to himself. His break with the past is reflected in his willingness to sue those in debt to him without the usual grants of extension. [66] Like most people who proclaim their adherence to self-interest, Levi Allen worked on the assumption that everyone else operated by the same lights but lied about it. Whenever he heard someone loudly proclaiming a disinterested love of country, he expected to receive a bill. For Allen, all the patriotism of the Revolutionary period functioned as a smoke screen for real economic motivations. The core consistency in all Levi Allen's formulations remained self-interest: "For Interest is the strongest tie in nature, and when the same is mutual it will of course be Perminant."[67]

But Levi Allen spoke too soon. A good American before the Americans formulated their national character, Levi Allen expressed values and made plans that would have flourished in the enterprising environment of the 1820s or 1830s. His promotion of free trade, his ideas for limited corporations and a canal system to link Lake Champlain with the Richelieu Valley and beyond, his sense that commerce, especially international trade, offered enormous rewards and that money begets money, and most especially his continuing emphasis on self-interest over abstract notions of the common good would have found ready acceptance just a few decades in the future. But in the late eighteenth century such attitudes led to Allen's ostracism by community, friends, and even family, and, eventually, to economic ruin.

The degree to which commercialism formed an integral part of American republicanism divided Allen's contemporaries, as it continues to divide historians. One reason may be the hesitance of even the most committed eighteenth-century supporter of the free market to proclaim the pre-eminence of individual self-interest. As J. E. Crowley has written of the debates of 1785 and 1786 over the Bank of North America, "the most striking feature of their arguments was their forthright assertion that selfishness was not socially dangerous." But the promoters of self-interest, such as Robert Morris, the great financier of the American Confederation, did not abandon the rhetoric of republicanism, clinging self-consciously to the justification of communal service. Like Levi Allen, supporters of the new capitalist ethos maintained that pursuing one's self-interest redounded to the benefit of the entire polity. The strength of the Federalists in the Constitutional debates would come from their ability to merge both strands of American political culture: the dominant one of republicanism with the emerging ideology of capitalist liberalism. A strong central government would have the power to set commercial policy, even while calling forth a republican empire that would protect the people's virtues from a hostile world. [68]

In terms of economic theory, Levi Allen had all the makings of a federalist and nationalist. But like so many other opponents of the Constitution, Allen perceived a choice between liberty and power, a strong central government attaining the latter by limiting the former. For Allen the liberty that mattered was economic. Where nationalists like Morris, operating in the centers of power in Philadelphia and New York City, saw their interest best served by a strong national government, Allen saw his interest promoted by and serving an independent Vermont guided by the principles of free trade. [69]

Arguments for free trade also aroused suspicion. Levi Allen, like so many others, learned his appreciation for free trade in the crucible of war. Many Americans agreed reluctantly with Tom Paine's hesitant admission that "trade flourishes best, when it is free." [70] By 1779 Congress felt compelled to adopt a private contract system, finding a number of merchants quite willing to make a profit off the Revolution. [71] Yet American patriots remained ambivalent over what they had wrought, for they felt that excessive pursuit of self-interest undermined the corporate good and the spirit of self-sacrifice republicans promoted. [72]

102

Republicanism found it difficult to free itself from the constraints of mercantilism and the need for the state to hold economic authority. Even leading merchants supported various forms of restraint on trade, hoping thereby to protect their own commercial advantages without the uncertainties of open competition. Free trade continued to be perceived as self-serving — as it was — right through the nineteenth century. Free trade had initially been raised as an issue in Colonial America by smugglers, and some of the stigma remained after the Revolution.[73] Since Levi Allen's activities were perceived by some as akin to smuggling, it is not surprising that most Vermonters rejected his preference for free trade and saw little problem with coming under the Constitution's umbrella of legislative commercial power.

Given the intellectual climate of Revolutionary America it is not difficult to understand why many people saw Levi Allen as mad, or at best eccentric. Throughout the eighteenth century greed appeared a personal failing, a sign of mental weakness, if not instability. To place one's own economic interest above that of the common good could only indicate a diseased mind.[74] Thus patriots often attacked Loyalists as self-interested lunatics, thrusting a dagger into their mother's bosom in return for British pounds. Likewise, war profiteers could easily be compared to mad dogs or some other dangerous animal. No rational persons could fail to perceive their duty to the community that sustained them.[75] Ethan Allen had made such charges in his immensely popular *Narrative* when he described the unnecessary deaths of hundreds of American prisoners from malnutrition and mistreatment to "the hellish delight and triumph of the tories." Allen reported seeing "tories exulting over the dead bodies of their murdered countrymen," and when reproached, refused to acknowledge themselves Americans. Allen reduced the Tories to "the most mean spirited, cowardly, deceitful, and destructive animal[s] in God's creation." Certainly "legions of infernal devils . . . are impatiently ready to receive" these Loyalist monsters "into the most exquisite agonies of the hottest regions of hell fire."[76] It was a short step for Ethan to see his own brother as crazed, refusing to duel Levi and contemptuously dismissing him as unworthy of discourse with rational people.

But was Levi Allen deranged, as Nancy Allen charged? It is worth noting that she made this accusation to serve her self-interest, to win a land grant Levi had initiated. William Harrington better understood his friend Levi when he labelled him "exantrick" but rational, at least until the last few months of his life.[77] Allen did not fit precisely in the intellectual milieu of frontier Vermont. But the reason that he did not is vital. Allen anticipated later developments in America, particularly the dominance of an ideology of self-interest.

During the Revolution and immediately thereafter, individual greed appeared to pose a threat to the survival of the new American states, including Vermont. In the years after the passage of the U.S. Constitution, private acquisitiveness and selfishness faded as perceived threats to political survival, opening the way for the triumph of liberal economic theories. Writing George Washington in 1784, Thomas Jefferson refused to speculate "whether commerce contributes to the happiness of mankind," but thought it clear that "All the world is becoming commercial." The U.S. must adjust to this fact and "in our own defence endeavor to share as large a portion as we can of this modern source of wealth and power."[78] Jefferson's rhetoric continued to hold up the ideal of a perfect agrarian republic, but once president, he found himself seduced by the image of empire and a vision of continental prosperity.

For a few decades at the end of the eighteenth century, republicanism and liberalism formed competing ideologies in America, but in the early nineteenth century the anti-commercial component of republicanism gave way before American economic expansion.[79] There were those like Nathaniel Chipman who hoped that economic growth would actually foster republicanism, but they missed the point entirely.[80] Adam Smith hoped that society would abandon its evaluation of people by civic involvement, which he felt too often led to war and other destructive efforts to attain glory, and instead base its collective judgments of worth on economic activity, a more productive criteria. Smith's view took hold in America more strongly than anywhere else in the world. Joyce Appleby has described "what was truly revolutionary in the liberal world view: the replacement of the economy for the polity as the fundamental social system."[81] As Malcolm Rohrbough pointed out, Jefferson's Louisiana Purchase guaranteed the triumph of the free enterprise system on the frontier, shifting the vision of frontier communities outward, towards national and international markets.[82] This market orientation had formed the heart of Levi Allen's vision for Vermont. His error, his derangement, had come in being ahead of his time.

Throughout his life Allen felt "Amasingly Ambitious to do Something cleaver," yet kept finding that "So many little Stumbling Blocks are in the way."[83] Like Robert Morris, Levi Allen built a paper empire, practiced all the self-interested capitalist virtues recommended by the most modern thinkers in Europe, and died a bankrupt. Despite Allen's years of effort in London to crack the hard protective shell of privilege, he returned to America a poorer man, hoping to spend his last years at home in peace. But his long absence in pursuit of self-interest had destroyed his business in St. Jean, and Allen spent the 1790s trying to recover what he had lost.[84] Levi Allen died in 1801 while imprisoned for debt in the Burlington jail. The law stated that whoever claimed a jailed debtor's body claimed his debts as well. Levi's friends and family understood their self-interest well, leaving the corpse to be buried in an unmarked grave in the jailyard.[85]

NOTES

The author wishes to thank J. Kevin Graffagnino, D. Gregory Sanford, and Michael Sherman for their intelligent commentary, Ondis Eardensohn and Dosia Sanford for their hospitality and good company, and the National Endowment for the Humanities for its support of his research.

[1] Nancy Allen to Robert Milnes, Feb. 10, 1802, Public Archives of Canada (Ottawa) [hereafter PAC], Lower Canada Land Papers, R.G. 1, L3, vol. 30: 15933-34.

[2] J. Hector St. Jean de Crèvecoeur, *Letters From an American Farmer* (New York: New American Library, 1963), 60-63.

[3] D.H. Lawrence, *Studies in Classic American Literature* (New York: Thomas Selzer, 1923), 33.

[4] Albert E. Stone, "Foreword," Crèvecoeur, *Letters*, xi-xii.

[5] For the classic statements of republican ideology see J. G. A. Pocock, *The Machiavellian Moment: Florentine Political Thought and the Atlantic Republican Tradition* (Princeton: Princeton University Press, 1975); Gordon S. Wood, *The Creation of the American Republic, 1776-1787* (Chapel Hill: University of North Carolina Press, 1969); John M. Murrin, "The Great Inversion, or Court versus Country: A Comparison of the Revolution Settlements in England (1688-1721) and America (1776-1816)," in Pocock, ed., *Three British Revolutions: 1641, 1688, 1776* (Princeton: Princeton University Press, 1975), 368-453.

[6] See especially Ethan Allen, *A Vindication of the Opposition of the Inhabitants of Vermont to the Government of New-York*, (Bennington, Vt.: Spooner, 1779), reprinted in E. P. Walton, ed., *Records of the Council of Safety and Governor and Council of the State of Vermont* (Montpelier, Vt.: J.&J.M. Poland, 1873-1880) 1:444-517; Ethan Allen, *The Narrative of Colonel Ethan Allen* (New York: Heritage, 1968).

[7] For the state of the debate, see Lance Banning, "Jeffersonian Ideology Revisited: Liberal and Classical Ideas in the New American Republic," *William and Mary Quarterly* 43 (1986): 3-19; Joyce Appleby, "Republicanism in Old and New Contexts," ibid., 20-34.

[8] Linda Kerber, The Republican Ideology of the Revolutionary Generation," *American Quarterly* 37 (1985): 480; Michael Johnson, "Comments," Annual Conference of the Organization of American Historians, 1985.

[9] Eric Foner, *Free Soil, Free Labor, Free Men: The Ideology of the Republican Party Before the Civil War* (New York: Oxford University Press, 1970); Sean Wilentz, *Chants Democratic: New York City and the Rise of the American Working Class, 1788-1850* (New York: Oxford University Press, 1984); Linda Kerber, *Women of the Republic: Intellect and Ideology in Revolutionary America* (Chapel Hill: University of North Carolina Press, 1980); Lacy K. Ford, *Origins of Southern Radicalism: The South Carolina Upcountry, 1800-1860* (New York: Oxford University Press, 1988). For a rejection of republicanism's persistence, see John P. Diggins, "Republicanism and Progressivism," *American Quarterly* 37 (1985): 572-98.

[10] Lance Banning, *The Jeffersonian Persuasion: Evolution of a Party Ideology* (Ithaca, N.Y.: Cornell University Press, 1978); Drew R. McCoy, *The Elusive Republic: Political Economy in Jeffersonian America* (Chapel Hill: University of North Carolina Press, 1980); Joyce Appleby, *Capitalism and the New Social Order: The Republican Vision of the 1790s* (New York: New York University Press, 1984); Eric Foner, *Tom Paine and Revolutionary America* (New York: Oxford University Press, 1976).

[11] Steven Watts, *The Republic Reborn: The War of 1812 and the Making of Liberal America* (Baltimore: Johns Hopkins University Press, 1987). Daniel W. Howe, *The Political Culture of the American Whigs* (Chicago: University of Chicago Press, 1979) notes that both Whigs and Democrats employed classical republican rhetoric to opposite ends.

[12] Levi Allen, "Autobiography," unpaginated, in Levi Allen's Daybook (badly burned), Levi Allen Papers, Henry Stevens Collection, Vermont State Archives, Montpelier [hereafter LAP]. Quote on education from Levi to Nancy Allen, March 28, 1795, Allen Family Papers, Wilbur Collection, Bailey / Howe Library, University of Vermont, Burlington, Vt. [hereafter AFP].

[13] L. Allen, "Autobiography"; E. Allen to Caughnawagas, May 24, 1775, to Noah Lee, May 21, 1775, and to Eliphalet Dyer and Silas Deane, July 3, 1775, Ethan Allen Papers, Stevens

Collection, Vermont State Archives, Montpelier, Vt.; Allen to the Continental Congress, May 29, 1775, Peter Force, ed., *American Archives* (Washington, D.C., 1839), 4th series, 2: 713-14, 732-34. In general see Colin G. Calloway, *The Western Abenakis of Vermont, 1600-1800: War, Migration, and the Survival of an Indian People* (Norman: University of Oklahoma Press, 1990); Michael A. Bellesiles, *Revolutionary Outlaws: Ethan Allen and the Struggle for Independence on the Early American Frontier* (forthcoming), ch. 6.

[14] L. Allen, "Autobiography"; Levi to Ira Allen, Sept. 20, 1788, LAP; Levi to Nancy Allen, March 28, 1795, AFP. See also Crèvecoeur, *Letters*, 64. On the economic attitudes of the day see J. E. Crowley, *This Sheba, Self: The Conceptualization of Economic Life in Eighteenth-Century America* (Baltimore: Johns Hopkins University Press, 1974); Benjamin Franklin, *Autobiography* (New Haven: Yale University Press, 1964).

[15] Franklin, *Autobiography*, 77-108, 121-25.

[16] Allen's emphasis; L. Allen, "Autobiography." The savagery of European-American traders in comparison to the conduct of the Native Americans disturbed many contemporary observers. See, for instance, Benjamin Franklin, "The Futility of Educating the Indians" (1753) in *The Annals of America* (Chicago: Encyclopaedia Britannica, 1976), 1:497-98; "Red Jacket and the Missionary" (1809) in Wilcomb Washburn, ed., *The Indian and the White Man* (Garden City, N.Y.: Doubleday, 1964), 209-14; John Heckewelder (1819), *History, Manners, and Customs of the Indian Nations* (New York: Arno Press, 1971), ch. 6 and 23.

[17] See Matt B. Jones, *Vermont in the Making, 1750-1777* (Cambridge, Ma.: Harvard University Press, 1939); Chilton Williamson, *Vermont in Quandary: 1763-1825* (Montpelier: Vermont Historical Society, 1949), ch. 1-5; Michael A. Bellesiles, "The Establishment of Legal Structures on the Frontier: The Case of Revolutionary Vermont," *Journal of American History* 73 (1987), 895-915.

[18] Other Tories shared this view. See, for instance, Samuel Seabury, *A View of the Controversy Between Great-Britain and Her Colonies* (New York: James Rivington, 1774) [generally known as "Letters of a Westchester Farmer"].

[19] Levi Allen to Simcoe, May, 1790, AFP.

[20] Walton, *Records* 1:6-10; James B. Wilbur, *Ira Allen, Founder of Vermont* (Boston: Houghton, Mifflin, 1928) 1:67-68; Allen to Trumbull, Aug. 3, 1775, in Peter Force, ed., *American Archives* (Washington, D.C.: U.S. Congress, 1837-1853) ser. 4, vol. 3:17-18; John E. Goodrich, comp., *Rolls of the Soldiers in the Revolutionary War, 1775-1783* (Rutland, Vt.: Tuttle & Co., 1904), 816; Ira Allen, *The Natural and Political History of the State of Vermont* (London: J. W. Myers, 1798), 62-63; B. J. Lossing, *The Life and Times of Philip Schuyler* (New York: Sheldon and Co., 1873), 1:365-66.

[21] Allen's arguments here are very similar to those of Charles Inglis, whose *The True Interest of America Impartially Stated* (Philadelphia: James Humphreys, Jr., 1776) circulated widely and was very popular with Loyalists. Robert M. Calhoon, *The Loyalists in Revolutionary America, 1760-1781* (New York: Harcourt Brace Jovanovich, 1973), 205-7.

[22] *Connecticut Courant*, 30 March 1779; Force, *Archives*, ser. 5, vol. 1: 498, 1587, 2: 1133, 1225, 3: 412, 416; L. Allen to Washington, Jan. 27, 1776, LAP; Levi to Nancy Allen, March 28, 1795, AFP.

[23] L. Allen, "Autobiography"; *Connecticut Courant*, 30 March 1779.

[24] Abby M. Hemenway, ed., *The Vermont Historical Gazetteer* (Burlington, Vt.: pub. by the author, 1868-1891) 1:562; Levi Allen, "Autobiography." On the difficulty of remaining neutral see John Shy, *A People Numerous and Armed: Reflections on the Military Struggle for American Independence* (New York: Oxford University Press, 1976), 215-22; Charles Royster, *A Revolutionary People at War: The Continental Army and American Character, 1775-1783* (Chapel Hill: University of North Carolina Press, 1979), 281-82; Catherine S. Craig, ed., *The Price of Loyalty: Tory Writings from the Revolutionary Era* (New York: McGraw-Hill, 1973), 34-5, 52-4, 60-8, 77-86.

[25] *Ethan and Ira Allen v. Levi Allen*, 1779, Rutland County Court Records, 98, and Vermont Superior Court Records, 1: 4; *Connecticut Courant*, 15 Dec. 1778.

[26] William Slade, comp., *Vermont State Papers* (Middlebury, Vt.: J. W. Copeland, 1823), 563; *Connecticut Courant*, 16 June 1777, 9 Feb., 2 March, 30 March, 3 Aug. 1779; L. Allen to Nathaniel Taylor, Aug. 2, 1797, AFP. There is more than just a coincidence of views

between Smith and Levi Allen. Allen's notebook contains transcriptions from the *Westminster Magazine*. But given the badly burned condition of the notebook, it is difficult to know when and where quotations begin, and there is only one reference to Smith, which may even be to another Smith. There are at least four passages that may be muddled quotations from Smith by either Allen or some third author, and three others that appear to be paraphrases — though again there is always the chance that such language was simply in the air. For example, Allen wrote that "the rich enjoy parading their riches," while Smith wrote "With the greater part of rich people, the chief enjoyment of riches consists in the parade of riches." Allen, "Autobiography"; Adam Smith, *An Inquiry into the Nature and Causes of the Wealth of Nations* (orig. 1776; New York: Modern Library, 1937), 172, see also 13-14, 324-29, 423, 674.

[27] Smith, *Wealth of Nations*, 276-80, 398-418. Ethan Allen's economic attitudes may be said to have been traditional and Lockean. See John Locke, "Some Considerations of the Consequences of lowering the Interest, and Raising the Value of Money," and "Further Considerations concerning raising the Value of Money," in *The Works of John Locke* (London: C. and J. Rivington, 1824), vol. 4.

[28] L. Allen, "Autobiography"; Philip Ranlet, *The New York Loyalists* (Knoxville, Tenn.: University of Tennessee Press, 1986), ch. 5; Ronald Hoffman, *A Spirit of Dissension: Economics, Politics, and the Revolution in Maryland* (Baltimore: Johns Hopkins University Press, 1973); Robert M. Dructor, "The New York Commercial Community: The Revolutionary Experience," Ph.D. diss. (University of Pennsylvania, 1975); Jacob E. Cooke, *Tench Coxe and the Early Republic* (Chapel Hill, N.C.: University of North Carolina Press, 1978), ch. 2-3; Edward Papenfuse, *In Pursuit of Profit: The Annapolis Merchants in the Era of the American Revolution* (Baltimore: Johns Hopkins University Press, 1973); Thomas M. Doerflinger, *A Vigorous Spirit of Enterprise: Merchants and Economic Development in Revolutionary Philadelphia* (New York: Norton, 1986), ch. 5; Bernard Mason, "Entrepreneurial Activity: New York during the American Revolution," *Business History Review* 40 (1966): 190-212.

[29] Again, Levi Allen's experience suggests similarities with Ben Franklin's youth. During his years in London, Franklin found hard work wasted before the inertia of the British economic structure. Franklin, *Autobiography*, 92-106.

[30] L. Allen, "Autobiography"; L. Allen to H. Motz, May 8, 1788, Levi to Nancy Allen, March 28, 1795, undated fragment by L. Allen, AFP; Wilbur H. Siebert, *Loyalists in East Florida, 1774 to 1785,* 2 vols. (DeLand, Fla.: Florida State Historical Society, 1929); Paul Smith, *Loyalists and Redcoats: A Study in British Revolutionary Policy* (Chapel Hill, N.C.: University of North Carolina Press, 1964); Wallace Brown, *The Good Americans: The Loyalists in the American Revolution* (New York: William Morrow & Co., 1969), ch. 6-8.

[31] Levi Allen's Daybook is filled with quotations and poems on these two issues, LAP.

[32] Levi to Ira Allen, undated (c. Spring, 1786), Aug. 26, 1786, Oct. 11, 1788, Feb. 15, 21, 1789, LAP; Levi Allen to Fraser and Young, Aug. 20, Aug. 21, 1786, Levi to Ira Allen, Nov. 11, 1788, AFP. On the establishment of separate spheres and the bourgeois family in nineteenth-century America, see Kerber, *Women of the Republic*; Mary P. Ryan, *Cradle of the Middle Class: The Family in Oneida County, New York, 1790-1865* (New York: Cambridge University Press, 1981).

[33] *Ethan and Ira Allen v. Levi Allen*, 1779, Rutland County Court Records, 98, and Vermont Superior Court Records, 1: 4; *Connecticut Courant*, 24 Nov. 1778, 2 and 30 March, 3 Aug. 1779; Hemenway, *Vermont Gazetteer*, 1: 562; Levi Allen, "Autobiography."

[34] Haldimand to Allen, Nov. 29, 1782, and reply, Dec. 20, 1782, PAC, ser. B (Haldimand Papers) 175: 300-03, 178: 11; Vermont Historical Society *Collections* (Montpelier, Vt.: VHS, 1870-1871) 2:293-94. On British officers seeking a profit through contacts with the Allens, see PAC, B, 175: 82, 174, 185, 177-2: 673, 681; Wilbur, *Ira Allen*, 1: 411-12.

[35] Levi to Ira Allen, Sept. 12, 1784, Dec. 19, 1787, Nov. 11, 1788, Levi to Betsey Allen, Dec. 7, 1784, Ira to Levi Allen, undated (c. 1785), Levi Allen Memorandum Book, AFP; L. Allen to Lord Dorchester (Sir Guy Carleton), Aug. 5, 1795, L. Allen to Nathaniel Taylor, July 16, 1797, LAP; Ira Allen to Haldimand, Sept. 10, 1784, PAC, B, 174: 278; petition of Jan. 1, 1785, Mary G. Nye, ed., *Petitions for Grants of Land* (Brattleboro, Vt.: Vermont Printing Co., 1939 [vol. 5 of *State Papers of Vermont*]), 354; Walton, *Records* 3: 113, 399-401,

409-10. On Levi Allen's role as trade emissary for Vermont, see B. F. Cockerham, "Levi Allen (1746-1801): Opportunism and the Problem of Allegiance," M.A. thesis (University of Vermont, 1965), ch. 5-8. On free trade ideas in eighteenth-century America see Cathy Matson, "Fair Trade, Free Trade: Economic Ideas and Opportunities in Eighteenth-Century New York City," Ph.D. diss. (Columbia University, 1985).

[36] L. Allen to Major Matthews, March 19, to Thomas Ainslie, April 19, 1787, AFP. See also Smith, *Wealth of Nations*, 466-71, 549-51, 636-37, 832-33.

[37] Proclamation of Lord Dorchester, April 18, 1787, PAC, Ser. Q (Canadian State Papers) 28: 9-11, 38-39; L. Allen to Chittenden, April 29, 1787, AFP.

[38] Levi to Ira Allen, May 24, 1789, quoted in Cockerham, "Levi Allen," 142, original in Historical Society of Pennsylvania.

[39] Ethan Allen to Lord Dorchester, July 16, 1788, L. Allen to Dundas, Aug. 9, 1791, PAC, Q 36: 448-454, 45: 701; Levi to Ira Allen, May 24, 1789, LAP.

[40] L. Allen to Simcoe, May, 1790, L. Allen Memorandum Book for 1792, AFP; L. Allen to Simcoe, Nov. 19, 1791, Simcoe to Dundas, Aug. 2, 1791, PAC, Q 278: 55-59, 259-70.

[41] Letters of Agrippa (probably James Winthrop), published in the *Massachusetts Gazette*, Nov. 1787 to Feb. 1788; reprinted in Herbert J. Storing, *The Complete Anti-Federalist* (Chicago: University of Chicago Press, 1981), 4:81-82. See also the opinions of Edmund Randolph (Virginia), 2:86-98; the "Federal Farmer," 2:214-357; "an Old Whig" (Pennsylvania), 3:17-52; "Deliberator" (Pennsylvania), 3:176-93; "A Farmer" (New Hampshire), 4:204-16; Rawlins Lowndes (South Carolina), 5:148-59; the Albany Antifederal Committee (New York), 6:122-27.

[42] Gordon A. Craig, *The Triumph of Liberalism: Zurich in the Golden Age, 1830-1869* (New York: Charles Scribner's Sons, 1988).

[43] Levi to Ira Allen, Aug. 20, 1791, L. Allen, Memorandum Book, AFP; L. Allen to Simcoe, Nov. 19, 1791, PAC, Q 278: 55-59.

[44] Vermont *Gazette*, 2 Nov. 1789, 18 Oct. 1790. On Chipman see Daniel Chipman, *The Life of the Honorable Nathaniel Chipman, LL.D.* (Boston: Little and Brown, 1846); Alein Austin, "Vermont Politics in the 1780's: Emergence of Rival Leadership," *Vermont History* 42 (1974):140-54; Hemenway, *Vermont Historical Gazetteer* 3:1154-59.

[45] Williamson, *Vermont in Quandary*, is largely responsible for this perception. In a single paragraph Williamson gives the impression that the Chittenden / Allen faction opposed statehood through the adroit use of biased interpretation based on an introductory piece of misinformation: "So outraged was a majority of Vermonters at the public disclosure of this [the Woodbridge] scandal that, in the October election of 1789, Chittenden was defeated by the opposing candidate, Moses Robinson" (179). This statement is entirely false.

[46] L. Allen to Dundas, Aug. 9, 1791, PAC, Q 54: 701-04.

[47] Walton, *Records* 3: 421-63.

[48] Emphasis added, Walton, *Records* 3: 464. In both his Thanksgiving Proclamation of Oct. 14 and his inaugural speech of October 20, Chittenden called for quick action to finally bring Vermont into the union. *Vermont Gazette*, 1 Nov. 1790.

[49] The newspapers were equally free of controversy on the matter, approval seeming a foregone conclusion. The editor of the *Vermont Gazette* announced on Dec. 6, 1790 — before the convention met — that in light of the probable "speedy accession of Vermont" to the Union he was postponing the publication of his *Laws of Vermont* so that he could include the U.S. Constitution and relevant national laws.

[50] Walton, *Records* 3:469-81. "The Act and Resolutions of the Convention," passed on Jan. 10, 1791, approved the Constitution based on Vermont's agreement with New York, "In full faith and assurance that the same will stand approved and ratified by Congress." Ibid., 480. For Chipman's political theories see his "Constitutionalist" articles in the *Vermont Gazette*, 18 and 25 Sept., 2 Oct. 1783; and Nathaniel Chipman, *Principles of Government: A Treatise on Free Institutions* (orig. 1833; New York: DeCapo Press, 1970).

[51] Levi to Ira Allen, Aug. 20, 1791, AFP; L. Allen to Simcoe, Nov. 19, 1791, PAC, Q 278: 55-59.

[52] Alan Macfarlane, *The Origins of English Individualism* (New York: Cambridge University Press, 1979).

[53] L. Allen to S. Peters, Sept. 5, 1790, AFP.

[54] Levi to Ira Allen, Sept. 12, 1784, AFP; Levi to Ira Allen, undated (c. Spring, 1786), Aug. 18, Aug. 26, 1786, Nov. 22, 1787, Dec. 19, 1787, Sept. 20, 1788, Feb. 21, 1789, LAP.

[55] L. Allen to Dundas, Aug. 9, 1791, PAC, Q 54: 702; L. Allen to Peters, June 8, 1791, L. Allen to Simcoe, July 24, 1791, L. Allen Memorandum Book for 1792, AFP.

[56] L. Allen to Governor Clarke, March 16, 1792, PAC, S 125: Barford file.

[57] Levi to Ira Allen, May 24, 1789, quoted in Cockerham, "Levi Allen," 143, original in Historical Society of Pennsylvania; Levi to Ira Allen, May 24, 1789, LAP; Simcoe to Dundas, Aug. 2, 1791, PAC, Q 278: 260-62.

[58] Levi to Ira Allen, May 24, 1789, quoted in Cockerham, "Levi Allen," 143, original in Historical Society of Pennsylvania.

[59] Ira Allen followed the latter approach, attempting to use the glebe rights to support his pet project for a University of Vermont. Levi to Ira Allen, May 24, 1789 (two letters), LAP; C. R. Batchelder, ed., *The Documentary History of the Protestant Episcopal Church in the Diocese of Vermont* (Claremont, N.H.: Claremont Manufacturing Co., 1870), 6-103.

[60] Levi to Nancy and Ira Allen, May 3, and 24, 1789, LAP; Levi to Nancy Allen, April 29, 1789, AFP.

[61] Levi to Nancy and Ira Allen, May 3, and 24, 1789, April 12, 1790, LAP.

[62] Levi to Ira Allen, May 22, 1789, LAP; Williamson, *Vermont in Quandary*, 162-4.

[63] Levi to Nancy and Ira Allen, May 3, and 24, 1789, LAP; Levi to Nancy Allen, April 29, 1789, AFP.

[64] Levi "to all the survivors of the Allen family if any," Aug. 2, 1789, Levi to Ira and Nancy Allen, July 22, Nov. 29, 1790, Feb. 15, 1791, LAP; Levi to Ira Allen, May 3, Nov. 21, 1789, L. Allen to S. Peters, Sept. 5, 1790, June 9, 1791, AFP; L. Allen to Dundas, Aug. 9, 1791, PAC, Q 54: 698-99.

[65] Levi to Nancy Allen, April 29, 1789, AFP; Levi to Ira Allen, July 22, 1790, LAP.

[66] L. Allen to "Mr. Thingumbob," Jan. 27, 1788, AFP; L. Allen's notice, Dec. 19, 1787, Levi to Ira Allen, Nov. 22, 1787, LAP.

[67] L. Allen to Simcoe, July 24, 1791, AFP. See Smith, *Wealth of Nations*, 14, 423.

[68] See especially the Federalist Papers 6, 23, 37, 39, 48, 49, 84, in Michael Kammen, *The Origins of the American Constitution: A Documentary History* (New York: Penguin, 1986), 134-40, 169-86, 193-202, 234-44; Tench Coxe, "An Enquiry into the Principles on which a Commercial System for the United States should be founded," *American Museum* 1 (June, 1787): 499; William Barton, *The True Interest of the United States, and Particularly of Pennsylvania* (Philadelphia, 1786); Peter S. Onuf, *The Origins of the Federal Republic: Jurisdictional Controversies in the United States, 1775-1787* (Philadelphia: University of Pennsylvania Press, 1983).

[69] Crowley, *This Sheba, Self*, 153, see generally 147-57; Barton, *True Interest*; John Witherspoon, *Essay on Money as a Medium of Commerce* (Philadelphia, 1786).

[70] Thomas Paine, *The Crisis* (Garden City, N.Y.: Doubleday, 1973), 178.

[71] E. Wayne Carp, *To Starve the Army at Pleasure: Continental Army Administration and American Political Culture, 1775-1783* (Chapel Hill: University of North Carolina Press, 1984), ch. 2-3; Robert A. East, *Business Enterprise in the American Revolutionary Era* (New York: Columbia University Press, 1938), 30-65, 190-96; Hoffman, *Spirit of Dissension*, ch. 2.

[72] Royster, *A Revolutionary People*, 186-207; Cathy Matson and Peter Onuf, "Toward a Republican Empire: Interest and Ideology in Revolutionary America," *American Quarterly* 37 (1985): 496-531; Benjamin Rush, "On the Defects of the Confederation," in Dagobert D. Runes, ed., *The Selected Writings of Benjamin Rush* (New York: Philosophical Library, 1947), 26-31.

[73] East, *Business Enterprise*, ch. 9 and 12; Cal Winslow, "Sussex Smugglers," in E. P. Thompson, et al., *Albion's Fatal Tree: Crime and Society in Eighteenth-Century England* (New York: Pantheon, 1975), 119-66; Matson, "Fair Trade, Free Trade," ch. 6.

[74] Crowley, *This Sheba, Self*, esp. ch. 4; Albert O. Hirschman, *The Passions and the Interests: Political Arguments for Capitalism before Its Triumph* (Princeton: Princeton University Press, 1977).

[75] See, for instance, the letter from "An Enemy to Tories," *New Hampshire Gazette* (Portsmouth), 12 Jan. 1777. In general see Brown, *Good Americans*, ch. 3 and 5. On war profiteers see Carp, *To Starve the Army*, ch. 3 and 5; Royster, *A Revolutionary People*, ch. 5 and 7.

[76] Allen, *Narrative*, 66, 79-81, 107.

[77] Harrington to Simcoe, PAC, Series S (Correspondence), 49: 79.

[78] Jefferson to Washington, March 15, 1784, *The Papers of Thomas Jefferson*, ed. Julian Boyd, 23 vols. to date (Princeton: Princeton University Press, 1953-1990) 7: 25-27.

[79] Matson and Onuf, "Toward a Republican Empire"; James Oakes, "From Republicanism to Liberalism: Ideological Change and the Crisis of the Old South," *American Quarterly* 37 (1985): 551-71.

[80] Speech of Chipman at Constitutional Convention, Walton, *Records* 3: 468-72; Chipman, *Principles of Government*, esp. 39-54, 254-60; John E. Kasson, *Civilizing the Machine* (New York: Penguin Books, 1977). On the failure of republicanism to address key issues in post-Revolutionary America see John P. Diggins, *The Lost Soul of American Politics: Virtue, Self-Interest, and the Foundations of Liberalism* (New York: Basic Books, 1985); Isaac Kramnick, "Republican Revisionism Revisited," *American Historical Review* 87 (1982): 629-64.

[81] Appleby, "Republicanism and Ideology," *American Quarterly* 37 (1985): 470.

[82] Malcolm J. Rohrbough, *The Trans-Appalachian Frontier: People, Societies, and Institutions, 1775-1850* (New York: Oxford University Press, 1978), 91.

[83] Levi to Ira Allen, Aug. 17, 1788, LAP.

[84] Nancy to Ira Allen, June 29, 1787, Levi to Ira Allen, May 3, 1789, LAP. On Morris see Clarence L. Ver Steeg, *Robert Morris: Revolutionary Financier* (Philadelphia: University of Pennsylvania Press, 1954); Barbara Ann Chernow, "Robert Morris: Land Speculator, 1790-1801," Ph.D. diss. (Columbia University, 1974).

[85] Wilbur, *Ira Allen* 2: 311.

PART III

·

A
More Perfect
Union

Adjusting To Union: An Assessment of Statehood, 1791-1816

by Paul S. Gillies

"May we never experience a less happy moment than the present under the federal government."[1] *Toast to Vermont statehood, at Rutland, March, 1791.*

 On the evening of Friday, January 7, 1791, following a full day of debate at the Constitutional Convention in Bennington called to ratify the U.S. Constitution and pave the final mile to the statehood of Vermont, Daniel Buck had an epiphany. As he explained on the floor of the convention the following morning, he had studied the U.S. Constitution more closely the night before and "obtained conviction that the danger of losing the sovereignty of the separate states, by entering the union, was not so great as he had imagined; the cession of power to congress was not so great as he had conceived it to be, and the rights of the state sovereignties more guarded."[2]

Daniel Buck was one of the few men at the convention who expressed his reservations about Vermont's running full tilt into union. His midnight conversion removed the last serious opposition to ratification. By a vote of 105 to 4 on the following Monday morning, the convention voted to join the union and be bound to the government of the United States forever.

As Vermont celebrates the bicentennial of admission, Vermonters enjoy the luxury of looking back over two centuries of statehood and assessing how worthwhile the risk really was. The years of independence, from January 16, 1777, to March 4, 1791, are now regarded as the golden years of Vermont history. The hardwon fight for geographic identity from the State of New York commingles with the heroic battles fought by Vermonters to end the Revolutionary War, leaving only warm memories of a determined people struggling to find peace and security at home in the face of aggressive forces from outside the state. Statehood seems, in the light and shadow of the 1990s, to have been both the goal and the end of independence, and these conflicting feelings make Vermonters uncertain about how fervent their celebration of the bicentennial ought to be.

If Vermonters in 1791 had any doubts beyond Daniel Buck's reservations and those of a few others such as Levi Allen, the record does not show them. Statehood came with cannons, parades, high-toned toasts, and unmitigated joy in the Green Mountains, and no wonder. The end of the conflict with New York brought a secure and well-defined western border and an end to the threat of conflicting New York titles to Vermont land. The northern border of Vermont became the northern border of the United States, and intrusions into Vermont became offenses against the sovereignty of the union. Vermont finally had an official voice in Congress. Vermonters expected that union would bring prosperity. Vermont would have clear and legal access to the ocean and international markets, its economy stabilized by the sound credit of a national currency. Its population would increase, and life among the Green Mountains would be peaceful and fruitful.

The hope that accompanied admission was not entirely justified by the experience of the following few years. Vermonters underestimated the difficulty they would have with the transition. The imprint of independence was too strong to allow easy

115

compliance with the dictates of a central government. Just as the celebration of statehood now seems ambiguous, so the transition of the first generation following admission appears awkward and difficult. Statehood was not at all like independence. It meant sacrifice. It meant learning how to be one among many.

To see how Vermont adjusted to its new role as the fourteenth state, we should look at three themes. The first is the cost of settling up with the past. The end of the fight with New York was expensive, and it took some years to pay off the debt. The question of what to do with the debt left by the Revolutionary War was another hurdle for Vermont. There were no admission fees for Vermont in 1791, but there lingered a question about whether the new state ought to bear its proportionate share of the burden of conducting the war with Great Britain.

The second theme is legal in nature. Vermont legislatures since 1778 had enacted their own laws, based on common sense and revolutionary zeal. By 1791, Vermont was already on its second constitution. Conforming to federal law would require further sacrifices. The U.S. Constitution, adopted in 1789 and ratified by Vermont as a condition of statehood, was more than a yardstick. Vermonters viewed it with talismanic reverence, as a gospel and an icon. The idea of the federal constitution would change Vermont jurisprudence forever.

The third theme is jurisdictional. Vermont was a border state, but the Canadian line was unsettled, both politically and geographically. Collisions along the border would bring Vermont into direct confrontation with the government of the United States. Caught between the need to protect itself from invasion and to conform to national foreign policy, Vermonters would learn painful lessons in self-control.

The tension in the first twenty-five years of Vermont life following admission was between instinct and discipline, between revolutionary fervor and national identity, between independence and statehood. Absolute capitulation was unacceptable. There would be sacrifices to be sure, but this was Vermont. Nothing would come easily.

SETTLING UP

The immediate cost of statehood was thirty thousand dollars, to be paid to the State of New York by June 1, 1794, to extinguish the claims of New York to lands in Vermont.[3] The agreement between the commissioners of New York and Vermont provided that upon payment of this money "all rights and titles to land within the State of Vermont, under grants from the government of the late colony of New York or from the State of New York ... should cease."[4] The only exceptions were confirmatory grants made by New York on land originally granted by New Hampshire. To raise money to pay this debt, the legislature assessed a one-half penny per acre tax on all lands except those sequestered for public, pious, and charitable uses on November 3, 1791.[5]

This was not the first statewide property tax in Vermont history. The first revenues raised by Vermont came from the confiscation and sale of Tory estates. The first tax on all property in the state was enacted in 1780, when the legislature ordered the towns to raise 72,700 pounds of beef; 36,389 pounds of salt pork, "without Bone, except Back bone and Ribs"; 218,309 pounds of wheat flour; 3,068 bushels of rye; and 6,125 pounds of Indian corn, all for the support of Vermont troops in the Revolutionary War.[6] In 1781, the Vermont legislature first authorized town taxes to build houses of public worship, school houses and bridges, up to two pence per acre.[7] There were further statewide property taxes in 1781, 1783, 1785, 1787, 1788, and 1789 to raise provisions for the troops and to defray the debts of the state and the cost of maintaining its government.

Constables of Vermont towns had to pay the tax assessed

117

on the New York debt to the state treasury by January 1, 1794.[8] Collections in hard times were not easy. Gold, silver, and currency were scarce, and the legislature failed to meet the deadline for payment to New York. When proprietors' clerks refused to give up their books and records to town clerks, thus preventing the selectmen from assessing against land in the town, the General Assembly intervened in 1792, ordering them to do so within a month on penalty of personal liability for taxes on lands described in those records.[9] That same day, the law was changed a second time to clarify the responsibilities of the state treasurer, because of disparities in the organization of some towns. As amended, the law named the towns to be taxed and directed the sheriffs of the various counties to deliver the tax warrants to town constables, who would in turn collect the tax.[10] The following year the General Assembly again amended the law to encourage collections and strengthen the ability of collectors to sell lands for delinquent taxes.[11] Ironically, some of the same land freed from New York claims by the New York-Vermont agreement was sold to raise the thirty thousand dollars owed to New York for its release of those claims.

By the date the debt was due to New York, Vermont had garnered little more than twenty-five thousand dollars from its citizens. In 1794, New York agreed to extend the time for payment. The money that had been collected was held in a vault in Rutland. Early on May 7, 1794, Samuel Mattocks, Vermont State Treasurer, left Rutland carrying the booty. One box of gold coins burst as he climbed the hill before the Clarendon meetinghouse, and money rolled down the road. Daylight still hours off, Mattocks had to ask local citizens for torches and help in picking up the loose coins.[12]

In 1798, the legislature ordered the remaining debt paid from the one cent per acre state property tax of 1797.[13] Mattocks reported in 1799 that of the $36,766 he had collected that year, $4,798 was earmarked for the State of New York.[14]

118

Finally, in October of 1799 Governor Isaac Tichenor proudly announced that "[b]y the wise and prudent arrangement of the last and preceding Legislatures, the debts that were contracted in support of our revolutionary war, and for extinguishing the claims of a neighboring state, are now happily discharged. . . ."[15]

Once the debt was paid, the claims of those who had lost land and money to Vermont were settled by New York commissioners. The commissioners' report showed an allocation of the thirty thousand dollars among seventy-six claimants, including $948.23 paid to the Hon. Jonathan Hunt, who had served as Vermont's lieutenant governor in 1794 and 1795, and as a member of the Constitutional Convention of 1791 that ratified the U.S. Constitution.[16]

Even before the debt to New York was paid, the question of land titles in Vermont had been settled. The New York-Vermont agreement had nullified all grants, charters, and patents of New York to Vermont land, other than grants made by New York confirming title originally granted by New Hampshire in Vermont. The final step in the settlement of land titles in Vermont was left to Nathaniel Chipman, Judge of the Vermont Supreme Court, who decided the case of *Paine and Morris v. Smead* in 1791.[17]

William Smead had applied through an agent for confirmation of his New Hampshire charter of the town of Windsor from the governor of New York in 1771, and a New York charter was granted the following year. The proprietors agreed to sell three thousand acres in Windsor to pay for the New York charter. Smead's son and heir claimed a hundred-acre parcel of the three thousand, arguing that the New York letters-patent were invalid. Judge Chipman answered that argument, writing "[F]rom the acceptance and long acquiescence of the New-Hampshire proprietors, under this grant, it should seem,

119

that the acceptance and acquiescence alone, which must have involved almost the whole property of the land in town, would be construed a waiver of the former grant, and a confirmation of the latter."[18] Chilton Williamson wrote that this case "validated all confirmatory patents which had been generally accepted by the confirmees and ended all disputes over New York land titles."[19] Daniel Chipman, in his biography of his brother Nathaniel, quoted an unnamed eminent jurist who practiced before the supreme court at the time as saying, "Judge Chipman was the first among our judges, who rose so far above the prejudices of the times in Vermont, against the State of New York, as to give such effect to the confirmation charters, as effectually to secure the rights of the grantees under them, consistently with the rights of the New Hampshire grantees."[20]

The last great debt Vermont faced before its leaders could finally attend to the business of statehood was settling its share of the Revolutionary War expense. In 1779, Ethan Allen and Jonas Fay had written Congress, proposing union of Vermont with the United States. In the letter, Allen and Fay confirmed that Vermonters "stand ready, in conjunction with their fellow brethren in the United States, to pay their equal proportion of the expenses of the present just war with Great Britain."[21] In 1782, Vermont's agents to Congress, appointed to attempt a settlement of the question of statehood, were given instructions that included "a condition not on any account to be dispensed with, that this State be admitted free from the arrears of the Continental Debt already assumed, this State discharging its own debts — and if this should be rejected by those with whom you are to treat, you will endeavor to obtain the conditions on which this State may be admitted and lay the same as soon as may [be] before your Constitutents."[22] At the convention held at Bennington on January 10, 1791, to ratify the U.S. Constitution, the members recommended "that as soon as this State shall be received into the Union the Legislature do take the most effectual measures to procure an equitable adjustment of the expenditures of this State during the late War between Great Britain & the United States."[23]

The cost of the Revolutionary War was enormous. On August 5, 1790, Congress enacted a law that apportioned the debt among the thirteen states. Debtor states were obliged to pay; creditor states were entitled to make claims for reimbursement from the federal government. Apportionment of cost was based on population, using the standard for apportioning representatives and direct taxes described in Article I, Section 9 of the U.S. Constitution.[24] Whether this law applied to Vermont was an open question.[25]

The Vermont legislature assumed the law did apply to Vermont. On November 3, 1791, the day Vermont ratified the Bill of Rights, the General Assembly appointed three commissioners to collect and arrange the bills for expenditures of Vermont during the war.[26] The claims of Vermont seemed promising to the legislature, based on the state's commitment of men and supplies. The commissioners failed to submit any claims, however; no record of any report or claim to the Congress can be found, even after Congress amended the law to authorize an extension of the time for submitting the claims to December of 1793.[27] Vermont's contributions were neither assessed nor recovered. Nor did Vermont ever pay any expenses of the United States from the late war.

Vermont's Revolutionary War debts became an issue in 1841. The Vermont General Assembly appointed Henry Stevens, the president of the Vermont Historical and Antiquarian Society, to look into the claims and opportunities missed during the first years of statehood. Stevens's work collecting and copying early records of Vermont became the nucleus of the State Papers of Vermont and subsequently the State Archives. He concluded that ". . . [W]e have an equitable, just and well founded claim against the United States for a sum exceeding five hundred thousand dollars, exclusive of interest, exclusive of property destroyed by their enemy, exclusive of military stores, — more than three hundred cannon, tons of balls, barrels of flints, tons of powder, two hundred batteaux, and one sloop, containing provisions and military stores, delivered for the benefit of the Colonies. Again, for all these services we have received no compensation."[28]

On October 16, 1848, a legislative committee of three reviewed Stevens's conclusions in a report to Governor William Slade. The commissioners found that Vermont's decision not to submit claims to the Congress in 1791-3 was based on the awareness that the balance would not be in Vermont's favor. The committee thought Vermont would have to show expenditures amounting to $1,800,000 during the war to qualify for a balance against the United States. To those who argued that Vermont's total expenditures should be repaid, without consideration of what other states had spent, the committee issued a stiff lecture on patriotism:

> This view of the case presents Vermont in the light of a foreign ally, rendering aid to the General Government for compensation, and excludes the idea that our people had any common interest with the people of the other States in the revolutionary struggle. Admitting that this view of the case should be adopted by Congress, of which there seems not the slightest probability, the undersigned conceive it would be degrading to the State to accept of compensation upon such terms. An admission that the people of Vermont did not feel a common sympathy with those of other States, and derive a common benefit from the result of the war, would not only be a contradiction of all history, but would involve a sacrifice of the character of our people for patriotism, for which dollars and cents, however numerous, could be but a poor compensation.[29]

The story of Vermont's relationship with the federal government, as reflected in the question of what the U.S. owed it, is not complete without a look at the war debt of 1812. Vermont had paid its first federal tax in 1798, amounting to $46,864.18 (and seven mills). [30] Like the money needed to meet the New York debt, the money needed to pay the United States took some time to collect, but in due course it was raised. In 1813, Congress assessed a second direct tax to pay for the War of 1812, this time apportioning to Vermont a bill of $98,343.71. [31] In 1815, the Congress assessed another war tax against the states. Now the bill amounted to $196,687.42. [32] While the war taxes were apportioned in the manner specified by the federal constitution, the war had an unequal impact on the states. Vermont's own contributions were proportionately greater than those of many other states, since much of the war was fought along its border and on Lake Champlain.

In 1931, the Vermont General Assembly resolved to try a new tack in obtaining reimbursement for the sums of money spent by Vermont in the War of 1812. Earlier efforts had failed. Governor Stanley Wilson was directed to contract "for the services of such special counsel or agent of the state as he may choose and on such terms as shall appear to the Governor for the public welfare, provided the same shall be by contingent fees with no expense to the State of Vermont, unless a part or a whole of said claim shall be recovered from the Government of the United States of America." [33] Wilson already had his agents in mind — a Washington attorney who specialized in these matters named De Knight and Probate Judge Charles I. Button of Middlebury. Judge Button in turn contacted Mary Greene Nye, who was working in the Secretary of State's Office as a researcher and compiler of the State Papers. Together they were successful in convincing the Comptroller General and the Congress to appropriate nearly $93,000 to Vermont in 1941 in settlement of the debt the United States owed Vermont for the War of 1812. [34]

In the sesquicentennial year of 1941, the legislature adopted a budget of $1,078,445.50. The 1812 money amounted to 8.6 percent of that total.

CHANGES IN VERMONT LAW

Not all the adjustments Vermont made to join the United States or to conform to its laws were unexpected or unwelcome. Vermont was so anxious for statehood it willingly made some concessions to the federal constitution prior to statehood, and after statehood the state continued to conform.

In 1786, to implement the state constitution's prohibition against slavery in Vermont, the General Assembly passed an act "to prevent the sale and transportation of negroes and mulattoes out of this state." The act prohibited "the sale of any subject of this State" or the conveyance of "any subject out of this State with intent to hold or sell such person as a Slave." In 1797, the General Assembly repealed this act, believing that it violated the U.S. Constitution. Judge Royall Tyler described its repeal as one of the small sacrifices of "our local sentiments and feelings" that Vermont had to make to join the union, but felt that its loss was far outweighed by the blessings of statehood. He also suggested that the repeal was unnecessary. [35]

The repeal was based on a misreading of the federal constitution. Vermont's law had prohibited the sale and transportation of former slaves who were *subjects* of Vermont. The Fugitive Slave Clause of the U.S. Constitution applied to slaves temporarily residing in non-slave states. Vermont overreacted to the demands of statehood and in doing so turned its back on one of its most fundamental principles.

The 1791 convention, called to ratify the U.S. Constitution in Vermont, recommended the modification of "the several laws commonly called *tender acts* as shall be least obnoxious to the constitution of the United States & least prejudicial to the citizens of this & the United States, where contracts are subject to the operation of these Laws."[36] Tender acts allowed citizens to pay debts and taxes in produce and other personal property. They were needed in an economy that relied on goods and produce as a medium of exchange. Less than three weeks later, the Vermont legislature amended those laws by limiting their application to contracts made prior to June 1, 1791.[37]

The convention of 1791 also hoped that statehood could come without damage to the Betterment Act of 1785.[38] Vermont had adopted its first act to protect the rights of the early settlers in 1781. The act allowed those who had improved lands without good title to recover the cost of those improvements before they could be ejected from their homesteads. Later versions of that act in 1783 suspended all trials of land titles for a year for the same purpose. In 1785, the assembly reactivated land trials and provided settlers the right to recover one-half of the rise in value of the lands.[39] Expressly exempted from the act that repealed nearly all Vermont law passed before 1787,[40] the last betterment act died quietly in the changes that came with Nathaniel Chipman's wholesale revision of Vermont laws in 1797.[41]

The first opportunity Vermont had to amend its own constitution after statehood came in 1792-3. The third Council of Censors proposed amendments, and the Constitutional Convention of 1793 adopted many of the council's recommendations. There was no longer a need to appoint a delegate to Congress, and that section was repealed. Article XXI of the 1786 Vermont constitution was amended to eliminate the guarantee of a right of all people to "form a new state in vacant countries, or in such countries as they can purchase, whenever they think that thereby they can promote their own happiness"[42] to avoid any confusion about the necessary loyalty of Vermonters and their continuing commitment to the union. Reacting to the sensitivity of the First Amendment to the U.S. Constitution toward mixing of church and state, the convention abolished the test that required all legislators to "own and profess the protestant religion."[43] An amendment to the section on the Vermont militia provided that the men would "be trained and armed for its defence, under such regulations, restrictions and exceptions as Congress, agreeably to the Constitution of the United States, and the Legislature of this State shall direct."[44] Persons holding offices of profit or trust under the authority of Congress would be ineligible to appointments in the legislature or the executive or judicial branches of Vermont. [45]

In these alterations to the Vermont constitution, Vermont contoured its highest law to the U.S. Constitution. The creation of a constitutional incompatibility between the holding of a federal and state office at the same time helped ensure that Vermont would not become simply an agency of the federal government. The changes to the oath of office for legislators, the deletion of the authority to form new states, and the recognition that the Vermont militia would be regulated as the U.S. Constitution provided show Vermont's eagerness to change the fundamental law of Vermont for the sake of consistency with federal standards.

The Constitution of the United States was as important to Vermonters' commitment to the union as any other single emblem of statehood, but for many years its effects in Vermont were principally symbolic. The Vermont judiciary took its own time in finding a place for the federal constitution and laws in its jurisprudence. [46]

The authority of the judiciary to declare an act of the legislature invalid because it violated the Vermont or U.S. constitution is not for us a radical idea. We accept the practice as a well-established part of constitutional life, but this was not always the case. In the early years of statehood, the Vermont courts avoided challenging legislative authority. The Vermont Council of Censors was the principal reviewer of legislative acts.[47] The Vermont Constitution of 1777 was silent on the powers of the judiciary in relation to legislative acts, but in Chapter II, Section XLIV, it created a Council of Censors "to recommend to the legislature the repealing of such laws as appear to them to have been enacted contrary to the constitution." The power to recommend did not include the authority to force repeal or amendment of legislative acts, but in most cases the legislature responded to the council's concerns. In the years following 1785, for instance, the General Assembly repealed or amended fifteen of the twenty-five acts judged by the council to be unconstitutional. Of the legislative acts left untouched by the legislature, the majority were private acts.

The practice of awarding individual citizens special privileges by private act was an integral part of legislative practice. Citizens routinely petitioned for a new trial, for the right to introduce evidence rejected by the courts, for authority to grant prisoners the liberties of the jailyard even when they refused or were unable to take a poor debtor's oath, or to suspend citizens from prosecution for debts for a period of years. Every council from 1785 through 1827 complained about such private acts.

In 1785, the council condemned "the practice of legislating for individuals. . . . If a subject feels himself aggrieved, and thinks the law incompetent to give him redress, he immediately applies to the Assembly; and too often, laws are suddenly passed upon such application, to relieve in particular cases, which introduce confusion into the general system, or are afterwards discovered to be wholly unnecessary."[48] The council worried that the practice would destroy the power assigned by the Vermont constitution to the judicial branch.

A critical shift in the orientation of the Council of Censors occurred in 1813, when for the first time it concluded that an act of the General Assembly preventing trade with Canada was unconstitutional, because it appropriated powers granted the United States by the federal constitution.[49] The council also objected to a legislative act suspending civil process against the persons and property of officers and soldiers in the service of the state, believing it would impair the judicial power of the United States, the obligation of contracts, and other rights guaranteed by the federal constitution. [50] The federal constitution finally became a force of its own, restraining the Vermont legislature from intemperate acts that would grant special privileges to Vermonters above other citizens of the United States.

Vermont courts awakened to the power of the U.S. Constitution about the same time. Although the Vermont Supreme Court heard arguments against the legislative practice of granting new trials to petitioners as "gross interferences by the legislative with the judicial power" as early as 1802, [51] not until 1814 did the court actually strike down a legislative act, and then only when the court's own authority was challenged by the legislature. In its decision, the court concluded that "The act [directing a deposition rejected as inadmissible by a court to be read in any future trial] is most clearly unconstitutional and void. It is an attempt of the legislature to make a judicial decision in a particular case; but the constitution of this State, prohibits the legislature from the exercise of any judicial powers." [52]

That same year the Vermont Supreme Court first applied the U.S. Constitution to a Vermont case. In a fight over whether the sheriff should be held liable for the escape of a prisoner, the court reviewed a private act releasing a man named Moses Sage from imprisonment and freeing him from arrest on all counts for a term of three years beginning January 1, 1812. Rather than repealing the private act, Chief Judge Nathaniel Chipman, on behalf of the court, concluded that the private act could not be extended to apply to suits on Sage's jail bond, since that "would have been a palpable violation of the constitution of the United States, which renders null and void every act, even of a State legislature, made in violation of any express provisions of that constitution." To read the Vermont act as eliminating a right to sue to collect the jail bond would impair contracts, "and, certainly, the Court ought anxiously to avoid any construction of a law, which implies in the legislature, either an ignorance of their powers and duties, or a design to violate the national constitution."[53]

The Council of Censors' constitutional mission to maintain vigilant watch over the separation of powers was fulfilled by the judicial activism shown by the *Starr* and *Dupy* cases. The federal constitution had changed the jurisprudence of Vermont. The supreme power of the legislative branch over all things governmental was doomed.

THE BORDER

Despite the fervor of Vermont patriotism after 1791, the strong affection for George Washington, and reverence for the U.S. Constitution, Vermont had difficulties adjusting to the preemptive power of the federal government. The old habits of self-defense and of forging foreign policy based on its own needs were not easily forgotten. The border between Canada and Vermont was the site of many collisions between British and American and American and Vermont — authority. Part of the problem was a continuing dispute over the location of the line.

In June of 1792, Gov. Thomas Chittenden learned that a Vermont deputy sheriff and two others had been arrested by British forces at Alburgh, eight or nine miles inside Vermont, and then brought over the Canadian border for questioning. Chittenden believed this violated the Treaty of Paris of 1783, and he wrote Canada's acting governor Alured Clarke in Quebec to request an "explanation of this unprecedented conduct and unprovoked insult upon the government of Vermont."[54] Chittenden also wrote President Washington to apprise him of the situation.

Clarke wrote Washington to say he had ordered an investiga-

129

tion of the incident. In a separate letter, Clarke promised Chittenden he would present his findings to the president of the United States, who had authority for these matters, rather than sending the report to Governor Chittenden. "I am to presume," wrote Clarke, "that a similar Deference will be held by yourself, towards the Power, to which the State you Govern is reputed to be Subordinate."[55]

After reading Clarke's letter, Chittenden wrote Washington a letter of explanation. "[A]s I was Sensible that the Conduct of this garrison might Involve questions of national Importance and desarve a national discursion I took the earliest opportunity of transmitting to your Excellency the Information I had recieved upon the subject but as the Injury was more immediately felt by the Citizens of this State I consider my Self Justifiable in requesting from the Commanding officer at Quebec an Explanation of so new and unprecedented abuses."[56]

One explanation for the incident was uncertainty about the location of the northern border of Vermont. Until well into the 1790s, Alburgh was claimed by New York, Vermont, and Britain. Throwing down the gauntlet, some of the residents of Alburgh decided in June of 1792 to organize as a Vermont town.[57] Two Vermont justices of the peace—Samuel Mott and Benjamin Marvin—began active enforcement of the Vermont law in Alburgh. In May of 1792, Mott ordered the seizure of the property of two Canadians—Patrick Conroy (Convoy, in some accounts) and Minard Yeomans—to cover the costs of a suit against Conroy for his actions in Alburgh as a justice of the peace under British authority.[58]

Enos Wood, Deputy Sheriff and Constable of the State of Vermont, took Conroy's cattle to Grand Isle on June 8, where Wood, his companions, and eight of the ten cattle[59] were captured by British soldiers from the garrison at Point-au-Fer. Wood was taken to St. Johns and not released until he could provide ample security for his liberty. Four days later, Conroy and a party of soldiers seized Benjamin Marvin, the Alburgh justice, and took him before the commandant at Point-au-Fer. Now Marvin's authority to act as a justice was questioned before British authority. Marvin was allowed to leave after promising not to act as a justice for ten days.

The tension along the border did not abate. Vermonters objected to the presence of the British garrison at Point-au-Fer, which they claimed had been built on American soil, and to the garrison at Dutchman's Point in North Hero, since it was clearly on Vermont soil.

The focus of the Alburgh controversy eventually shifted toward the behavior of Gov. Thomas Chittenden. U.S. Secretary of State Thomas Jefferson wrote Chittenden twice during the summer of 1792, asking him to maintain the peace in Alburgh until federal authorities could work out an agreement with the British by way of negotiation. Jefferson explained that ". . . it would be truly unfortunate if any premature measures on the part of your state should furnish a pretext for suspending the negotiations,"[60] and he rebuked the governor for encouraging Vermont officials to enforce Vermont law in a disputed area. A committee of the Vermont General Assembly concluded that Chittenden had conducted himself "with that degree of spirit and propriety which ought to mark the conduct of the Chief Magistrate of a free and independent State."[61]

That was Jefferson's point: by acting like the head of a free and independent state Chittenden ignored his responsibility as a governor of one of the states in the union to conduct foreign relations through the federal government. The governor's support for Vermont officials in Alburgh made a tense situation worse and embarrassed the United States, which needed to demonstrate to the world its control over its member states as well as its integrity in foreign relations.

The border heated up again in 1794, and there was talk of war between Great Britain and the United States. In Ohio, Lord

Dorchester, the British governor of Canada, in an angry speech to "a council of hostile Indians" alleged further outrages, infringements, and encroachments of the Vermonters against British authority. "[T]he unrepressed and continued aggression of the State of Vermont" would lead to war, he warned. [62] When pressed by Secretary of State Edmund Randolph for an explanation, Chittenden protested that Vermonters had done more than their share of keeping the peace, although he acknowledged one incident during the winter of 1794 in which four armed men "in the common dress of the citizens of this state" were arrested at Alburgh for assaulting an inhabitant of that town. The men were convicted of breaking the peace and fined. Although they were British subjects, Chittenden found no reason to believe they were acting under British authority, since they were without credentials.

Vermont was not alone in creating tension along the border. British batteaux patrolled Lake Champlain, disrupting established trade routes. Alburgh resident Royal Corbin told how "I am not suffered to pass Southward to Isle-la-Motte—because they alledge I am within their lines, & [must] apply to the Ship, for liberty. Neither am I allowed to pass to or from, St. John's, altho' within their lines—So I am deprived of every advantage a citizen of every State ought to enjoy."[63] In August, Corbin suffered the loss of nearly forty bushels of salt and a puncheon of rum after a British batteau seized his boat at gunpoint. There were reports of troops gathered at Montreal and of a new twelve-gun brig at Point-au-Fer. In May Major General Ira Allen's Grand Isle regiment surrounded the garrison at Dutchman's Point, but later withdrew without incident.[64] That same month Congress authorized eighty thousand troops from the militia of the various states to serve in case of an emergency. War seemed likely.[65]

To avoid further trouble, Washington sent John Jay on a mission to London, where in November of 1794, Jay and British authorities agreed to substitute the "firm and perpetual Peace" of the Treaty of Paris of 1783[66] for "a firm inviolable and universal Peace, and a true and sincere Friendship."[67] The treaty was finally approved by the Senate in June of 1795 and proclaimed by President Washington on February 29, 1796. It required the British to relinquish all forts in U.S. territory by June 11, 1796, and gave British subjects residing in Vermont the option of U.S. citizenship. The Treaty of 1794 also allowed "[a]ll Goods and Merchandise whose Importation into His Majesty's said Territories in America [to] freely, for the purpose of Commerce, be carried . . . by the Citizens of the United States . . ."[68]

Vermont reacted to the Jay Treaty with alarm. While the Federalists on the east side of the mountains generally favored the treaty, many Vermonters on the west side of the mountains were troubled by the secrecy with which it was ratified in the U.S. Senate. They saw the treaty as a virtual pact with the British, at a time when relations between Vermont and Britain were strained, when memories of the late war were still fresh, and as an offense to France, the country that had been so friendly to the United States during the Revolution.[69] Jay was burned in effigy in Rutland County.[70] In Bennington, on September 30, 1795, a county convention condemned the negotiation of the Jay Treaty without senatorial advice. A Shaftsbury town meeting resolved by a vote of 224 to 0 that the treaty, if ratified, "will be derogatory to the honor and dignity of the United States and very detrimental to the interest thereof."[71]

The Jay Treaty is the first example of political resistance to federal policy in Vermont. Party spirit began to flourish in the Green Mountains. National and international perspectives, rather than more parochial matters, began to dominate political debate. Politically, as well as geographically, Vermont was feeling the pull of national and international influences.

No single figure in Vermont politics represents this shift better than Matthew Lyon, who was elected U.S. representative from the Western District in 1796.[72] When he arrived in Washington, Lyon made a strong impression in Congress with

133

a well-publicized incident of "gross indecency": Lyon spat in the face of Connecticut representative Roger Griswold. This precipitated fourteen days of debate in the House of Representatives on whether Lyon should be expelled from the body. Escaping that judgment, Lyon soon found himself in deeper trouble when he fought a duel with fireplace tongs on the floor of the House with Griswold, after Griswold battered Lyon with a heavy cane. [73]

Then, in June of 1798, Lyon published a letter to the editor in *Spooner's Vermont Journal*, criticizing President John Adams.

> . . . [W]hen I see every consideration of the public welfare swallowed up in a continual grasp for power, in an unbounded thirst for ridiculous pomp, foolish adulation, or selfish avarice; when I shall behold men of real merit daily turned out of office for no other cause but independence of sentiment; when I shall see men of firmness, merit, years, abilities, and experience, discarded on their application for office, for fear they possess that independence, and men of meanness preferred for the ease with which they take up and advocate opinions, the consequence of which they know little of: when I shall see the sacred name of religion employed as a State engine to make mankind hate and persecute one another, I shall not be their humble advocate."

This statement became the substance of Count I in the indictment against Lyon for violating the Sedition Act. [74] Lyon was tried, convicted, and sentenced to four months in prison and to pay the costs of prosecution and a thousand dollar fine.

Lyon's defiance was open and unrepentant, and when the September election resulted in no choice for U.S. representative because of a lack of a majority, the voters of the Western District compounded the political tension in the runoff by re-electing Lyon to Congress while he sat in the Vergennes jail. [75] The parade of Antifederalist supporters that followed Lyon from his release

Fight between Matthew Lyon, wielding the fire tongs, and Roger Griswold of Connecticut on the floor of the U.S. House of Representatives, Philadelphia, February 15, 1798. Vermont Historical Society.

at Vergennes to Middlebury was twelve miles long.[76] Vermonters were learning to enjoy a new kind of independence within the federal system, based on the freedom to complain openly about the actions of the federal government and even the president of the United States.

The ceremony attending the dedication of the first Vermont State House in October of 1808 was marred by the presence of federal troops inside the building. The State House was too small for all who wanted to attend the festivities, and some contributors to the building of the capitol who were left outside objected so loudly that the troops were ordered to withdraw.[77] Coming nine months after the passage of the land embargo of March 12, 1808, and after open defiance of federal law, the ejection of federal

135

troops from the State House was emblematic of the discomfort Vermonters felt with the growing federal presence. Many Vermonters would have been just as happy ejecting the federal government from Vermont altogether in 1808. They were not pleased with the federal order closing the border to international trade.

In the late 1790s, many Vermonters moved to Canada because it offered inexpensive land. Vermont seemed crowded to these pioneers. To them the border was an indistinct, imaginary line, and trade with Vermont, unregulated for so many years, was assumed a right of all U.S. citizens on both sides of the border.

Vermont had closed its borders to Canada on its own before becoming a state. Its first embargo prohibited the sale of wheat, rye, Indian corn, flour or meal to any nonresident, with the exception of stores bound for the colonial armies. The embargo was imposed by the Council of Safety on January 14, 1778,[78] apparently out of fear that provisions needed by the army would not be available and that scarce resources would drive up prices. In 1779 Governor Chittenden responded to legislative pressure to forbid the export of wheat and wheat flour "except such as is necessary to procure sale and other necessaries for the use of any private family."[79] The resolution recognized the authority of the governor to lift the embargo whenever it was no longer necessary. In 1780 the legislature expanded the list of provisions governed by the embargo.[80] It renewed the embargo in 1781.[81]

In March of 1789, Governor Chittenden reacted to the crop failure of 1788 and the resulting famine by proposing an embargo on wheat and other grains, and the Governor and Council imposed it by ordinance. The ordinance authorized law enforcement officers to stop sleighs, carts, wagons, and carriages for inspection and gave justices of the peace or two selectmen the right to hold summary trials to determine whether someone had violated the ordinance.[82] That same year Congress imposed the first duty on goods, wares, and merchandise imported into the United States,[83] an act expressly applied to Vermont when it entered the union in March 1791.[84]

The first federal embargo affecting Vermont after statehood was a non-importation act, imposed in 1806, at President Jefferson's urging as an attempt to keep the United States neutral in the war between England and France.[85] Vermonters most felt the pain of embargo through the "Land Embargo" act of March 1808, which ordered the suspension of all commerce across the border. When Jabez Penniman, the Collector of the Vermont District, received word of the land embargo on April 1, 1808, he confided in a letter to the Secretary of the Treasury that it would be impossible to administer the law without military force.

Jefferson asked Vermont governor Israel Smith for help, and in May Smith ordered a regiment of militia from Franklin County to oversee the enforcement on Lake Champlain. A few weeks later, Rutland County militia were also ordered north to help, insulting Franklin County officials with the suggestion that their own militia could not or would not enforce the law. In July citizens of Franklin County signed a petition, declaring "that if military aid should be called, and the troops should kill a person in attempting to enforce the laws, the inhabitants would immediately RISE and drive them from their stations." The inhabitants on Lake Champlain declared they would never submit to the enforcement of the embargo law.[86]

In August a band of smugglers on board the *Black Snake* were attacked on the Winooski River by a party of the Vermont militia. Two of the smugglers and Capt. Jonathan Ormsby of Burlington were killed in the ensuing battle. The surviving smugglers were promptly arrested and tried and one was executed, but a federal prosecution against three others for high treason resulted in a jury verdict for acquittal. Samuel Mott of Alburgh, who had participated in the border troubles of 1792 as a Vermont justice of the peace, was among the smugglers and eventually received fifty lashes for his part in the battle. [87]

In October 1808, Isaac Tichenor was swept back into the governor's office in a reaction to Jefferson's embargo. In his inaugural address, Tichenor took a conciliatory tone: "While . . . we regret the stain upon the character of a respectable portion of our citizens, in consequence of the conduct of a few, who had violated a law of the general government, suspending our commerce by an embargo without limitation, we sincerely regret that the law was not accompanied with that evidence of national necessity or utility which at once would have commanded obedience and respect." He deplored the need for military force to enforce the law, but he spoke to Vermonters of the need to obey the law. "Nothing could be more erroneous, dangerous, and inconsistent with republican principles, than an avowed or hostile opposition to the law. Our duty and our interest as citizens are undoubtedly to obey the laws of our country, and to avoid and discountenance every measure that tends to impair the majesty of the laws, the authority of the government, or the sacred regard which is due to the federal constitution."[88] In the legislative response to the governor's speech — a tradition in Vermont from 1778 to 1816[89] — the Federalists called the embargo "the only practicable measure that could have averted the dangers and horrors of a war with one or more of the contending nations of Europe."[90]

Tichenor visited Franklin County in February of 1809. According to the account of John Henry, a Vermonter who spied for Canada's commander-in-chief James Craig during these years, Tichenor

> is now visiting the towns in the northern section of [Vermont]; and makes no secret of his determination, as commander in chief of the militia, to refuse obedience to any

command from the federal government, which can tend to interrupt the good understanding that prevails between the citizens of Vermont and his majesty's subjects in Canada. It is farther intimated, that in case of a war he will use his influence to preserve this state *neutral*, and resist, with all the force he can command, any attempt to make it a party. I need not add, that, if these resolutions are carried into effect, the state of Vermont may be considered as an ally of Great Britain.[91]

E. P. Walton, among others, doubted that Tichenor's words amounted to treason, believing instead that his recommendations were more political than conspiratorial. Nonetheless, the allegations soon became a scandal in themselves, after Henry sold his correspondence with Craig to the federal government for fifty thousand dollars, and the perceived disloyalty of a Vermont governor became public knowledge in Washington.[92]

In 1809 Vermonters defeated Tichenor and elected Democratic-Republican Jonas Galusha in reaction to accusations about Tichenor's attitude toward enforcement of the embargo.[93] While many Vermonters had disliked the embargo, they were clearly uncomfortable with the public image of disloyalty by their leaders. The thought of separatism brought Vermonters back from the brink of open hostility to the embargo.

While the embargo had made every policy seem political, the War of 1812, and particularly the battle of Plattsburgh, united Vermonters in a common cause and eventually dissolved political differences. Two months before the outset of the war, Congress authorized the president to call out 100,000 militia, of which Vermont was expected to muster three thousand men. On May 1, 1812, Governor Jonas Galusha issued general orders to that effect, and Vermont militia were promptly on the march to Plattsburgh to serve under federal authority.[94]

The Vermont General Assembly adopted two acts during

139

1812 that demonstrated a lack of understanding about the role a state could play in times of international troubles. The first was an act prohibiting entry into Canada without a permit from the governor. The second suspended civil process against the officers and soldiers of the Vermont militia in order to protect them from suits during their service. When the Council of Censors met in 1813, both acts were roundly condemned for violating the U.S. Constitution. [95] The legislature repealed both acts in November 1813. [96]

In October 1813 Governor Martin Chittenden admitted personal reservations about the use of the militia for the defense of other states, except for cases expressly required by the federal constitution, namely, to execute the laws of the union, suppress insurrection, and repel invasions. Chittenden believed the framers of the U.S. Constitution never expected militia to become a national army for the purpose of invading foreign countries. [97]

In November 1813 many Vermont militia were ordered to Plattsburgh, leaving the state defenseless. Chittenden ordered Vermont troops at Plattsburgh to return to Vermont to protect their home state from the expected invasion of the British. The officers of the militia refused, explaining

> that when we are ordered into the service of the United States, it becomes our duty, when required, to march to the defence of any section of the Union. We are not of that class who believe that our duties as citizens or soldiers are circumscribed within the narrow limits of the Town or State in which we reside, but that we are under a paramount obligation to our common country, to the great confederation of States. We further conceive that, while we are in actual service, and during the period for which we were ordered into service, your Excellency's power over us as Governor of the State of Vermont, is suspended. [98]

140

In January 1814 there was talk in the U.S. House of Representatives of instructing the U.S. Attorney General to prosecute Chittenden for violating the federal law that prohibited attempts to entice soldiers in the pay of the United States to desert, but the resolution was tabled before any formal vote was taken.[99]

In November 1814 Plattsburgh was again at risk of a large British invasion. Thousands of Vermonters left their farms and headed for the lake. They were not militia, most of them, but volunteers. They traveled on foot, on horseback, and in wagons, not because the federal government ordered them to do so, but out of a sincere commitment to protect the union from British invasion. For the first time since Thomas Chittenden had left the governorship, Vermonters were united. From a hill in St. Albans, Vermonters who did not make it to Plattsburgh watched the naval battle fought off the shores of that city on a Sunday morning.[100] In September 1815, Martin Chittenden, the last Federalist governor of Vermont, lost to Jonas Galusha in the general election. The Federal era was over.

After the War of 1812 came depression.[101] The Canadian market was no longer as profitable or promising as it had been before the war. In 1816 Vermont suffered the worst weather in its history. There were frosts every month of the year and most crops failed.[102] The years ahead would see Vermonters emigrating in large numbers to the west. The boldness of independence that marked the early years of Vermont's statehood waned.

Simultaneously, the high political passions of the previous years cooled. For the next decade, according to Vermont historian David Ludlum, there was "a practical unanimity in politics while the people just 'turned within' to an age of intensive self-cultivation."[103] The northern border ceased to be a military problem. After the Treaty of 1817, the United States and Britain were allowed only one armed vessel each, not exceeding

"Battle of Plattsburgh and victory on Lake Champlain, in which 14,000 British myrmidons were defeated and put to flight by 5,000 Yankees and Green Mountain Boys, on the memorable eleventh of Sept. 1814." Broadside, Windsor (Vt.), 1815. Vermont Historical Society.

one hundred tons and armed with one eighteen-pound cannon, on Lake Champlain. [104] The legal boundary of the United States and Canada was finally and firmly established by the Webster-Ashburton Treaty of 1842. [105]

In 1822 a canal linking Lake Champlain with the St. Lawrence River was completed, and a healthy timber trade with Canada began anew. [106] The Champlain Canal, connecting Vermont with the Hudson River, was completed in 1823. [107] Trade routes were open, and Vermonters got on with their business.

The tension between statehood and independence continued unabated throughout Vermont's history. [108] When their support has been needed, as in wartime, Vermonters have been good soldiers, willing to make sacrifices for the sake of the United States. When the federal government proposed a parkway along the spine of the Green Mountains [109] or the development of hydropower in Vermont on the scale of the Tennessee Valley Authority, [110] Vermonters refused to comply and then celebrated their unwillingness to capitulate to Washington's wishes in the name of independence.

That independent spirit is part of the mythology and the character of Vermont. It is an independence that stops short of disloyalty to the union. There is always talk of secession, founded on the proof that Vermont once managed its own affairs, outside the family of the United States, but secession is too easy an answer to the dilemma of the statehood of Vermont. Vermonters paid dearly for statehood and the struggle to achieve it did not end on March 4, 1791.

NOTES

[1] *Records of the Governor and Council*, III, ed. E. P. Walton (Montpelier: J. and J. M. Poland, 1875), 483 (hereafter *G.&C.*).

[2] "The Vermont Convention of 1791," Appendix I, *G.&C.* III, 476.

[3] *G.&C.* III, 462-3.

[4] "An Act Directing the Payment of Thirty Thousand Dollars to the State of New York, and Declaring What Shall Be the Boundary Between the State of Vermont and State of New York; and Declaring Certain Grants Therein Mentioned, Extinguished," *Laws of Vermont 1785-1791*, ed. John A. Williams, *State Papers of Vermont* XIV (Montpelier: Secretary of State, 1966), 532-4 (hereafter SP).

[5] "An Act for the Purpose of Raising Thirty-Thousand Dollars," *Laws of Vermont* 1791-1795, ed. John A. Williams, SP XV (Montpelier: Secretary of State, 1967), 49-50.

[6] "An Act for the Purpose of Procuring Provision for the Troops, to be Employed in the Service of This State for the Year Ensuing," November 3, 1780, *Laws of Vermont 1777-1780*, ed. Allen Soule, SP XII (Montpelier: Secretary of State, 1964), 212-17.

[7] "An Act Enabling the Inhabitants of the Several Towns to Tax the Lands, Within Their Respective Towns, for Certain Cases Therein Mentioned," *Laws of Vermont* 1781-1784, ed. John A. Williams, SP XIII (Montpelier: Secretary of State, 1965), 61-2.

[8] "An Act for the Purpose of Raising Thirty Thousand Dollars," SP XV, 49-52.

[9] "An Act in Addition to an Act Entitled 'An Act for Raising 30,000 Dollars,'" *SP* XV, 133.

[10] "An Act in Addition to an Act Entitled 'An Act for the Purpose of Raising Thirty Thousand Dollars,'" SP XV, 133-4.

[11] "An Act in Alteration of, and in Addition to an Act Entitled 'An Act for the Purpose of Raising [Thirty] Thousand Dollars,'" SP XV, 184-86.

[12] Abiel Moore Caverly, *History of the Town of Pittsford, Vermont* (Rutland: Tuttle, 1872), 308.

[13] "An Act Making Appropriations for the Support of Government for the Present Session, and from Thence until the Session of Assembly in October, 1799," Sec. 3, SP XVI, 345.

[14] *Journals and Proceedings of the General Assembly*, 1797-1799, ed. Marlene Wallace, SP III, Part VIII (Montpelier: Secretary of State, 1978), 590-1.

[15] Walter Hill Crockett, *Vermont, The Green Mountain State* (New York: Century History, 1921), Vol. II, 484. *G.&C.* VI, 511.

[16] See *G.&C.* III, 101-2; Benjamin Hall, *History of Eastern Vermont*, Vol. 2 (Albany: J. Munsell, 1865), 562-5, 761-2.

[17] 1 D. Chip. 56 (1791).

[18] Ibid., 58.

[19] Chilton Williamson, *Vermont in Quandary 1763-1825* (Montpelier: Vermont Historical Society, 1949), 191.

[20] Daniel Chipman, *The Life of Hon. Nathaniel Chipman, LL.D.* (Boston: Little and Brown, 1846), 101-2.

[21] Letter dated July 1, 1779 to the Hon. the Congress from Ethan Allen and Jonas Fay, *G.&C.* II, 169.

[22] Crockett III, 243.

[23] *G.&C.* III, 482.

[24] ". . . [T]he rule for apportioning to the states the aggregate of the balances . . . shall be the same that is prescribed by the constitution of the United States, for the apportionment of representation and direct taxes, and according to the first enumeration which shall be made." "An Act to provide more effectually for the settlement of the Accounts between the United States and the individual States," Chapter XXXVIII (August 5, 1790), *The Public Statutes at Large of the United States of America*, ed. Richard

Peters (Boston: Little and Brown, 1845), Vol. 1, 178-80 (hereafter Public Statutes). Article I, § 2 of the U.S. Constitution provides, "Representatives and direct Taxes shall be apportioned among the several States which may be included within this Union, according to their respective Numbers, which shall be determined by adding to the whole Number of free Persons, including those bound to Service for a Term of Years, and excluding Indians not taxed, three fifths of all other Persons."

[25] "An Act for the admission of the State of Vermont into this Union," (February 18, 1791), Public Statutes, Vol. 1, 191. This was a simple act of admission to the United States. On March 2, 1791, the Congress adopted, "An Act giving effect to the laws of the United States within the state of Vermont," which was a more comprehensive legislative recognition of Vermont. Public Statutes, Vol. I, 197-8. This act provided that "from and after the third day of March next, all the laws of the United States, which are not locally inapplicable, ought to have, and shall have, the same force and effect within the state of Vermont, as elsewhere within the United States."

[26] SP III, 88. Ira Allen, Benjamin Green, and Isaac Tichenor were members of this committee.

[27] "Report of Henry Stevens on Revolutionary Claims of Vermont upon the United States," *Laws of 1842*, Appendix, 80-1. Stevens explained that the commissioners' failure to complete their report was related to bad record-keeping (no one could assemble the proper vouchers), as well as the delay in settling the accounts of State Treasurer Ira Allen until October of 1792.

[28] Ibid., 90.

[29] "Report of Committee Appointed to Examine the Matter of Revolutionary Claims &c. Upon Application of Henry Stevens," *Laws of 1848*, 236. Charles Paine, Hiland Hall, and Isaac F. Redfield served on this committee.

[30] Public Statutes, Vol. I, 597-64.

[31] Public Statutes, Vol. III, 53.

[32] Ibid., 576.

[33] *Laws of 1931*, 284-5.

[34] *Report of the Committee of the Judiciary*, U.S. House of Representatives, July 15, 1941, Report No. 953.

[35] *Selectmen of Windsor v. Jacob*, 2 Tyler 192 (1802).

[36] G.&C. III, 481-2.

[37] "An Act to suspend operation of an act entitled, 'An Act to compel the fulfilment of contracts according to the intent of the parties,'" (January 25, 1791), *Laws of Vermont 1785-91*, SP XIV, 563. Since Vermont entered the union on March 4, 1791, this June 1, 1791 effective date provided nearly three months of overlap between statehood and the last betterment act.

[38] G.&C. III, 481.

[39] Ibid., 352-5.

[40] "An Act to repeal the several statutes therein mentioned or described," (March 10, 1787), SP XIV, 337-9.

[41] This is my assumption since the 1785 Betterment Act is not included in Nathaniel Chipman's 1797 compilation. Curiously, the act is not mentioned among the laws expressly repealed through the 1797 compilation process. "An Act repealing certain acts therein-mentioned," *Laws of the State of Vermont 1797* (Rutland: Josiah Fay, 1798), 599-615.

[42] *Slade's State Papers*, (Middlebury: J. W. Copeland, 1823), 519.

[43] Ibid., 523-4.

[44] *Vermont Constitution of 1793*, Chapter II, Section 22, SP XV, 171.

[45] Ibid., 172.

[46] The first reported application of federal law to a Vermont Supreme Court case

was *Jacques v. Griswold*, 2 Tyler 235 (1802). The case turned on the court's recognition of the 1791 "Act giving effect to the laws of the United States within the State of Vermont" and another federal law relating to customs duties.

⁴⁷ See Glenn Howland, "The Roots of the Doctrine of Judicial Review in Vermont," (Unpublished thesis, Vermont Law School, 1988).

⁴⁸ *Address, Vermont Council of Censors* (1785), *Slade's State Papers*, 542.

⁴⁹ *Journal*, October 20, 1813, *Council of Censors* 1813.

⁵⁰ Ibid., 168-9.

⁵¹ *Pearl v. Allen*, 2 Tyler 311 (1802).

⁵² *Dupy qui tam v. Wickwire*, 1 D. Chip. 237, 238 (1814). The *Wickwire* case did not stop the legislature from adopting private acts. The practice continued for another decade. The Vermont Supreme Court, however, was not willing to ignore the point. In 1824, the court struck down an 1823 act that authorized an appeal beyond the statutory deadline. *Bates v. Kimball*, Adm., 2 D. Chip. 77 (1824). ("That which distinguishes a Judicial, from a Legislative act, is, that the *one* is a determination of what the existing law is, in relation to a particular thing already done or happened; while the *other* is a predetermination of what the law shall be for the regulation and government of all future cases falling within its provisions. . . . [The act] is not a law, but a sentence or decree. . . .") The following year, the court confirmed the ruling in a case involving a legislative act authorizing the extension of commissioners' terms, to justify an appeal from a probate court decision involving the submission of claims against an estate. "[T]he act . . . is unconstitutional and void, as being an exercise of power by the legislature, properly belonging to the judiciary, and as being in the nature of a sentence or decrees, rather than a law, wholly retrospective in its operation and taking away a vested right." *Staniford v. Barry*, Adm., Brayton 315, 316 (1825). That same year the court struck down an 1819 act freeing Eli Barnard from imprisonment and arrest on any civil process for five years. It conferred "a privilege, not extended to other citizens in like circumstances; and [took] from the creditor rights, enjoyed by other citizens, in like circumstances." *Ward v. Barnard*, 1 Aikens 121, 123 (1825). The court decisions of the 1820s took their toll. The last private act, at least denominated as such, was enacted in 1825. The legislature continued to authorize administrators and executors to sell assets of estates, to restore citizens their legal rights after their conviction for felonies or to grant them rights although they were not citizens, but there were no new trials granted, no appeals expended, or civil actions suspended after that date.

⁵³ *Starr v. Robinson*, 1 D. Chip. 257, 261 (1814). Daniel Chipman, in his essay in the first volume of court reports officially printed in Vermont, remarked that these changes in the Vermont judiciary were the direct result of the impact of the federal constitution on Vermont's understanding of the role of the courts. Looking back to the first Council of Censors, and its frustration at the legislative appropriation of judicial powers through the adoption of private acts, Chipman wrote:

> The powers thus exercised by the Legislature with the approbation of a majority of the people, naturally confirmed the idea, that the power of the Legislature was unlimited and supreme. No idea was entertained that the Judiciary had any power to enquire into the constitutionality of acts of the Legislature, or pronounce them void for any cause, or even to question their validity. Indeed, the framers of the Constitution could never have intended to confer on the Courts the power of pronouncing an act of the Legislature void of any cause, when they provided for an annual election of the Judges by the same Legislature who were to pass the laws.
>
> This was in the year 1786, before the adoption of the Constitution of the United States, and before it was ascertained that in a Republican Government, to secure the people in the full enjoyment of their civil rights, it is indispensible that the

powers of the Legislature be limited, and that practically they cannot be limited but by an independent Judiciary, without which, declarations of rights and limitation of powers become a dead letter.

Daniel Chipman, "Preface," *Reports of Cases Argued and Determined in the Supreme Court of the State of Vermont* (Middlebury: D. Chipman & Son, 1824), 22-24.

[54] *G.&C.* IV, 458-9.

[55] Ibid., 460.

[56] Note on spelling: Governor Chittenden was not well educated. Most of his correspondence was free of the kinds of errors found in this letter to Washington, revealing perhaps the companionship of an editor. Here his haste in responding to Washington left him no time to improve the quality of his writing. Where misspellings occur, they are those of the original text; the author and editor are aware of them and have preserved them without the intrusions of [sic] throughout the text.

[57] The hostilities on the border were clearly promoted by Thomas Chittenden, who in a letter to the officers of Alburgh, May 16, 1792, wrote, "Would those people chuse to be under the British government, they must move within its limits, otherwise they ought to submit to the government of the State in which they live." *G.&C.* IV, 464.

[58] Conroy had been the subject of a bounty in 1791. Vermonters had been promised a reward of one peck of potatoes for his capture. *G.&C.* IV, 470.

[59] Two of the cattle were lost in the crossing to Grand Isle.

[60] *G.&C.* IV, 463.

[61] If Chittenden's real offense was acting independently in corresponding with a foreign power, rather than turning to the federal government for its diplomatic services, Governor Isaac Tichenor in 1808 was also guilty. Tichenor, acting on the request of the General Assembly, wrote to Sir James Craig, governor of Canada, for his help in stopping a band of counterfeiters who were residing near the Vermont border and "preying upon the property of the good citizens of this and the United States" by passing false bank notes in Vermont. Tichenor sent Josiah Dunham to Montreal to meet with Craig, who was willing to help but found a lack of law restraining him from taking action. Quickly, the provincial parliament responded, and the counterfeiters were arrested. *G.&C.* V, 502-5.

[62] Dorchester quoted by George Hammand in a letter to Edmund Randolph, the U.S. Secretary of State, May 22, 1794. *G.&C.* IV, 475.

[63] Letter from Royal Corbin to Governor Chittenden, May [Aug.] 1794, *G.&C.* IV, 473.

[64] James Wilbur, *Ira Allen, Founder of Vermont 1751-1814* (Boston and New York: Houghton Mifflin, 1928), vol. II, 59. The garrison at Dutchman's Point in North Hero was established in 1781. Ibid., vol. I, 257.

[65] These troops were never called into active service. *G.&C.* IV, 482.

[66] *Treaties and Other International Acts of the United States*, ed. Hunter Miller (Washington: Government Printing Office, 1934), vol. 4, 155.

[67] Ibid., 245.

[68] Ibid., 246. The border itself remained a problem. In 1804 Governor Isaac Tichenor reported to the General Assembly that the boundary, in the eyes of several credible persons, was some distance south of the true 45th parallel, set by the Treaty of 1783. If this were true, many acres of land believed to be in Canada actually belonged to Vermont. The following year Tichenor hired the Rev. Samuel Williams to "ascertain by celestial navigation" the location of the line. Williams was obliged to construct his own quadrant for the mission with the help of a blacksmith in Newport.

Williams's report to Tichenor concluded that Vermont was entitled to land equal to more than seventeen townships. Later studies by British and American surveyors showed Williams in error. In 1818, surveyors appointed by the United States and Britain found that the unfinished American Fort Montgomery in Rouses Point, New York, later known as Fort Blunder, was in Canada, if the 45th parallel was the actual line. This report was kept confidential to avoid trouble. The Webster-Ashburton Treaty of 1842 finally settled the line by establishing the border as "the old line of boundary surveyed and marked by Valentine and Collins previously to the year 1774, as the 45th. degree of north latitude, and which has been known and understood to be the line of actual division between the States of New York and Vermont on one side, and the British Province of Canada on the other. . . ." This returned Fort Blunder to American soil. *Treaties*, vol. 4, 364-5.

[69] Jonathan Daniels, *Ordeal of Ambition* (Garden City, New York: Doubleday, 1970), 177.

[70] Crockett II, 541.

[71] Crockett II, 542.

[72] *Vermont Elections 1789-1989*, ed. Christie Carter, *State Papers of Vermont XXI* (Montpelier: Secretary of State, 1989), 172-7.

[73] Aleine Austin, *Matthew Lyon: "New Man" of the Democratic Revolution* (University Park and London: Pennsylvania State University Press, 1981), 96-103. Neither Lyon nor Griswold was expelled for this fight.

[74] Ibid., 109. Not all Vermonters were opposed to the Sedition laws. In the assembly's response to the Kentucky resolutions in 1799, a majority of House members explained that "If we possessed the power you assumed, to censure the acts of the General Government, we could not consistently construe the Sedition bill unconstitutional; because our own constitution guards the freedom of speech and the press in terms as explicit as that of the United States, yet long before the existence of the Federal Constitution, we enacted laws which are still in force against sedition, inflicting severer penalties than this act of Congress." *G.&C.* IV, 527. Presumably this refers to the Vermont law on defaming civil authority, adopted March 9, 1787, which provided "That whosoever shall defame any Court of Justice, or any sentence or proceedings thereof, or any of the Magistrates, Judges, or Justices, of any such Court in respect of any Act or sentence therein passed, and be thereof legally convicted before the Supreme Court in this State, shall be punished for the same by Fine, imprisonment, Disfranchisement or Banishment, as the quality & measure of the offence in the opinion of the Court before which the trial is had, shall deserve." *Laws of Vermont 1785-1791*, SP XIV, 334.

[75] Ibid., 124-5.

[76] Crockett II, 560-1.

[77] Crockett III, 18.

[78] *Assembly Journals 1778*, SP III (Part I), 40.

[79] Ibid., 97.

[80] "An Act to prevent the transporting provisions out of this state," (March 15, 1780), SP XII, ed. Allen Soule (Montpelier: Secretary of State, 1964), 191-2, 199-200.

[81] "An Act to prevent the transportation of provisions out of this State," (June 27, 1781), SP XIII, ed. John A. Williams (Montpelier: Secretary of State, 1965), 53-4.

[82] *G.&C.* III, 181-3.

[83] *Public Statutes*, Vol. I, 28-9.

[84] "An Act giving effect to the laws of the United States within the state of Vermont," (March 2, 1791), § 7, Ibid., 198.

[85] Crockett III, 3.

[86] *G.&C.* V., 472-5.

[87] Mott was pardoned by Governor Jonas Galusha on October 15, 1817. *G.&C.* V., 476fn. The others had been pardoned in earlier years.

[88] *G.&C.* V, 396-7.

[89] In 1817 a motion to raise a committee to draft a response failed for lack of a majority and the custom was abandoned. *G.&C.* VI, 434.

148

[90] *G.&C.* V, 399.

[91] Letter from John Henry to James Craig, February 14, 1809, *G.&C.* V, 483-4.

[92] Henry lost $49,000 of his booty after being defrauded in the purchase of a French estate. *G.&C.* V, 478-9fn.

[93] Williamson, 263.

[94] *G.&C.* VI, 466-9.

[95] *Journal, Council of Censors* October 21, 1813, MS, Office of the Secretary of State, Montpelier, Vt., 168f.

[96] *G.&C.* VI, 470-1.

[97] Ibid., 420.

[98] Ibid., 491-4. See also Crockett III, 81-5.

[99] Ibid., 494-6.

[100] Crockett III, 96-105.

[101] Ibid., 129.

[102] Zadock Thompson, *Natural History of Vermont* (Burlington: Z. Thompson, 1852), 20.

[103] David Ludlum, *Social Ferment in Vermont, 1791-1850* (New York: Columbia University Press, 1939), 86.

[104] *Treaties* 2, 644-54.

[105] That did not, however, end all invasions of Canada from the United States. In 1837, L. J. Papineau led two hundred men across the border in a failed invasion, and in 1867 and 1870 the Fenians tried the same thing with the same lack of success.

[106] Williamson, 281.

[107] *G.&C.* V, 475.

[108] G. G. Benedict reports on "the most extensive case of discipline that ever occurred in the history of the Second Vermont Regiment," during the Civil War, while stationed in Virginia in July of 1861. "When the order to fall in was given on the evening of September 28th, Lieutenant Phillips of Company F and a detail of about 100 men, who had just come in from picket duty, acting on the theory that volunteers were not obliged to regard orders which did not seem to them reasonable, ignored the command and remained in their tents." For this breach, a regimental court martial was held against all 150 men in the company. Privates were fined and sent to the guardhouse; most officers were reduced in rank; the captain was suspended; and Lieutenant Phillips was dismissed from the service. G. G. Benedict, *Vermont in the Civil War, A History* (Burlington: Free Press, 1886), Vol. 1, 75.

[109] Frank Bryan, *Yankee Politics in Rural Vermont* (Hanover: University Press of New England, 1974).

[110] George Aiken, *Speaking From Vermont* (New York: Frederick A. Stokes, 1938).

Vermont and the Union

by Peter S. Onuf

 In late August 1787, hot, tired, and increasingly irritable delegates at the Constitutional Convention in Philadelphia sought to put the finishing touches on a new federal constitution to save the tottering American union from complete collapse. Of course, the independent republic of Vermont was not part of this union, and though many Vermonters were deeply interested in the outcome, they were not directly represented in these crucial deliberations.

As on previous occasions, Vermont could rely on friendly support from neighboring New England states: New England would welcome an additional vote in Congress. Besides, many prominent New England politicians had speculative and personal reasons to uphold the independence of this booming frontier state. But this time Vermont's traditional allies were joined by a sizable number of delegates from other sections. As a result, the convention eventually agreed to language incorporated into Article IV, Section III, that would finally make possible the new state's long-delayed admission to the union. Many of the themes surrounding the convention are ones I have treated at length in my books, *Origins of the Federal Republic* and *Statehood and Union*.[1] Still, the sequence of proposals and votes that led to the happy result of Vermont's admission is worth recounting.

By August 29, delegates had been through a lengthy and bitter debate about whether or not to admit new states on terms of full equality. This is documented, for example, in James Madison's notes on the debates included in the four volumes of *Records of the Federal Convention of 1787*.[2] The *Records* show that conservative Easterners feared the proliferation of new states would leave them at the mercy of semi-savage Westerners, but Gouverneur Morris of Pennsylvania then offered a brilliantly evasive formula: "New States *may* be admitted by the Legislature into this Union."[3] Breathing a collective sigh of relief, the convention accepted this wording without debate. However, Morris suggested the proviso should go on to read that "no new State shall be erected within the limits of any of the present States, without the consent of the Legislature of such State, as well as of the Gen[era]l Legislature." This apparently innocuous proposal proved to be a bombshell, and for the next two days the frazzled delegates reargued the great jurisdictional controversies that had crippled the Confederation. The fate of Vermont appeared to hang in the balance.

The delegates' vehement response undoubtedly took the urbane Morris by surprise. Frayed nerves may provide an explanation, or perhaps the irascible Marylander Luther Martin — soon to become a leading opponent of the new constitution — had been lying in wait for just such an opportunity.

> Nothing he said would so alarm the limited [or small, landless] States [without western claims] as to make the consent of the large States claiming the Western lands, necessary to the establishment of new States within their limits. It is proposed to guarantee the States. Shall Vermont be reduced by force in favor of the States claiming it?[4]

Responding to Martin's eloquence — and perhaps temporarily sharing his assessment of large-state motives — five "small" states (Connecticut, New Hampshire, Maryland, Delaware, and New Jersey) — voted against Morris's proposal. All — except Connecticut — were already familiar allies in the old western lands controversy. Here, as Martin intimated, was yet another sinister Yorker plot to crush Vermont. In less hyperbolic language, William Samuel Johnson of Connecticut agreed. As the clause stood, he feared "Vermont would be subjected to N[ew] York."

John Dickinson and other small-state delegates dwelled on the "impropriety of requiring" them "to secure the large [states, like New York] in their extensive claims of territory."[5]

The Continental Congress had been too weak to do more than pass resolutions against frontier separatists, but a stronger central government presumably could deploy its power effectively. Just as the small states had sought some constitutional guarantee for their continued existence—secured through the famous Connecticut compromise providing equal representation in the Senate—this coalition of landless states now sought to protect unrecognized new states like Vermont, Franklin (later to become Tennessee), and Kentucky from a powerful national government acting at the behest of the large states.

Morris may well have wondered where all these eloquent advocates for "dismembering" the large states and supporting frontier self-determination had been for the last several years. Were they unaware that New York (in 1782), Virginia (1784), Massachusetts (1785), and Connecticut (1786) had already relinquished their vast claims northwest of the Ohio River? Had not Virginia made it clear through a series of legislative acts required by his proposal that it was prepared to recognize Kentucky's independence? Earlier, as one of New York's leading politicians, Morris himself had supported Vermont's claims. He thought the adverse reaction to his proposal, premised as it seemed to be on the supposedly irresistible ambition of the large states, was simply perverse. Indeed, he had thought "that the small States would be pleased with the regulation, as it holds up the idea of dismembering the large States."

Certainly, small-state rhetoric exaggerated the hidden dangers of the Morris proposal. Subsequent efforts by the Maryland delegates to reopen the western lands struggle by asserting Congress's independent claims to the unceded lands fizzled. After all, large as well as small states could threaten to bolt the convention. Morris sensibly warned that if the small states were aiming their proposals at one or two states—say North Carolina or Georgia—the "gentlem[e]n from these would pretty quickly leave us."[6] And however desirable it was to promote greater equality among the states, the union could not possibly survive if the territorial integrity of its members was not secured. Morris's colleague from Pennsylvania, James Wilson, "knew of nothing that would give greater or juster alarm than the doctrine, that a political society is to be torne asunder without its own consent."[7]

Delegates from all the states—even Maryland—did not really want to tamper with the hard-won settlement of the western lands dispute, which had gone a long way toward cutting the larger states down to size and opening the West to national development. Meeting at New York only a few weeks earlier, Congress had capped three years of deliberation on western policy with the famous Northwest Ordinance, pledging that the region under national jurisdiction eventually would be divided into new states and admitted to the union on an "equal footing." Perhaps the Constitutional Convention should leave well enough alone: Wilson and Roger Sherman of Connecticut suggested that the Morris proposal was "unnecessary"; it went without saying that "the Union cannot dismember a State without its consent."[8] But the very force of this logic brought the Vermont problem into even sharper focus: neither Congress nor New York had worked out a satisfactory accommodation with the new state. Thus, while Edward Rutledge of South Carolina could dismiss small-state rhetoric about having to march across the mountains to quash Franklin or Kentucky, he acknowledged that "the case of Vermont" would have to be "particularly provided for."[9]

In the end, a few artfully chosen words resolved the issue and so paved the way for the renegade state's admission. In the crudest and most transparent reference to Vermont, Sherman proposed that Congress be granted the power "to admit other States." By a fairly straight sectional vote (with South Carolina,

153

paying off its debts on the slave-trade concession, joining the northern bloc), Sherman's motion was narrowly defeated on August 30.[10] But Johnson and Morris quickly put together a winning formula, stipulating, respectively, that the clause applied to states "hereafter formed" — no one had any doubt that Vermont was already quite definitively "formed" — and that the territorial guarantee would only apply to areas within the "jurisdiction" of the old states and not to those within their "limits" or claimed boundaries.[11] Again, Vermont perfectly fit the bill. Although, harking back to a 1764 British Privy Council decision, New York could argue that the Connecticut River was indeed its eastern boundary, the state had not even pretended to exercise jurisdiction in the region since 1782. With this carefully crafted language, the framers rejected New York's claims and removed the important obstacles to Vermont's admission.

Beyond the obvious local significance of the federal constitution's new-state provision, why does it warrant such extended consideration? I would agree with Morris that the delegates worked themselves into gratuitous rhetorical frenzy, both on the western lands question and on Vermont. Always excepting Martin, the delegates were, in fact, in basic accord on jurisdictional issues. But this does not mean that these issues were not fundamentally important; the delegates recognized that a few false steps on the new-state question would have disastrous implications for the union. After all, the delegates agreed, the union was wobbling on its last legs. The failure of the Confederation to admit Vermont — and thus to perfect the *union* between this new state and its neighbors — was a standing warning to Americans of the dangers of "disunion." More than anything else in the preconstitutional period, the Vermont problem illuminated the most critical defects in the Articles of Confederation.

Historians have emphasized the difficulty of revising the Articles. Even more than the explicit reservation of undelegated powers, the voting provisions made the Confederation "imbecilic." First, all states—large and small—had one vote, thus making it possible for a small group of small states to obstruct policy. This possibility was exaggerated both by the requirement that nine states had to agree on any important question, and by the all too frequent failure of the states to keep up their representation. Finally, any substantive modification of congressional power—for instance, to establish national commercial policy—required unanimous agreement by all the state legislatures. Although Article XI invited Canada to join the union and permitted nine states to admit any other "colony," the admission of any new "state," including Vermont, would probably have depended on unanimous endorsement by the thirteen states.

The constitutional issue was never seriously broached. Except for one quickly retracted offer to recognize Vermont at a time when America's wartime prospects seemed particularly grim, Congress was never willing to act. The political obstacles to "dismembering" any one of the states proved decisive. Congress naturally was reluctant to offend the crucially important state of New York. Furthermore, all the states had an interest in discouraging similar challenges to their territorial integrity. But it did not follow that Congress would offer any real assistance to New York or any other state facing a separatist challenge. When New York called on Congress to quash the Vermonters, the shoe was on the other foot, and states that openly or covertly supported the new state's independence could easily veto any effective measures. Before acting, congressmen claimed, it was necessary to review all conflicting state claims—New Hampshire and, briefly, Massachusetts advanced claims of their own—or perhaps it would be prudent to wait for the end of the war. But scheduled hearings on Vermont were repeatedly postponed and eventually abandoned. Meanwhile, the war dragged on.

The resulting impasse dramatically revealed Congress's impotence under the Articles. Of course, any number of equally illuminating instances could be discussed, but failure to respond to the demands of territorial expansion was fundamental. If the union could not accommodate new states like Vermont — the most durable of self-proclaimed new states of the Revolutionary era — then its very survival was in jeopardy.

Let us take a closer look at the "Vermont problem." As we do so, you should recognize some of the themes Federalists later developed in describing the "crisis" of American politics that ratification of the federal constitution was supposed to rectify.

From the very beginning of their new state's history, Vermonters themselves led in promoting a sense of imminent crisis. Ethan Allen and his friends demonstrated a remarkable flair for inspiring terror among their many opponents. The founding and survival of Vermont depended on intimidating its enemies through sheer bravado, wildly inaccurate rumors, and the occasional, well-timed, and highly selective use of force. The new state's leaders had to convince Vermonters, as well as Congress, neighboring states, and the British that Vermont had a right to exist. Manipulation of public opinion, at home and abroad, thus represented the new state's biggest challenge. In a June 3, 1779, proclamation Gov. Thomas Chittenden conceded that Vermonters themselves seemed to think "a public Acknowledgement of the Powers of the Earth is essential to the Existence of a distinct separate *State*."[12]

Of course, Vermonters enjoyed certain crucial advantages, most notably in their forbidding, easily defended, mountainous landscape. It was unlikely that New York, even with the support of Congress, ever would be able to reduce Vermont by force. This was a "Remedy" that Gouverneur Morris disavowed as early as June 6, 1778, in a letter to Gov. George Clinton, the first governor of New York.[13] After all, Morris wrote in early 1781, "America is now busied in teaching the great lesson, that men cannot be governed against their wills."[14] New Yorkers showed little ability or inclination to launch a campaign against the new state. Even Clinton proved toothless; the belligerence of his rhetoric was only surpassed by his uncanny ability to avoid a fight. (Perhaps the embarrassing showing of the state militia in 1781 skirmishes with Vermonters helped persuade him that he should rely on bluster alone.) For his part, George Washington had made it clear that Continental forces would not do New York's dirty work.

Under pressure of the Americans' apparently precarious situation (before news of the victory at Yorktown circulated), both Congress, in May 1781, and the New York Senate, in February, 1782, indicated their willingness to recognize Vermont's independence. Vermont's enemies were able to neutralize these efforts, but they were unable to take any real countersteps. The Vermonters, Clinton wrote disgustedly to Alexander Hamilton in late 1782, had received "secret assurances that Congress will not direct any coercive Measures against them."[15] Over the next several years, successive efforts to normalize relations failed. Vermont's independence was an acknowledged fact, but not one the other states appeared able to act on. The resulting impasse was both symptomatic of the legendary "imbecility" of the union and a source of growing danger to the confederated states.

The weakness of both New York and Congress stood in sharp contrast to the remarkable success of the new state in exercising its authority. Ethan Allen and his Green Mountain Boys set the tone for Vermont politics and diplomacy with brilliantly conceived and executed forays against New York officials and titleholders in the years before independence. Subsequently, and most conspicuously during the struggle for jurisdiction in Windham County, Allen orchestrated raids and show trials that quickly demoralized New York Loyalists and led many of them to support the Vermont cause.

On the broader stage of interstate diplomacy, the new state's imperialist adventures to the east and west — including the annexation of sixteen New Hampshire towns in June 1778, of another thirty-five towns east of the river in April 1781, and of twelve New York towns in June 1781 — sent similar shivers through neighboring governments. Governor Chittenden bluntly explained to Washington in a November 1781 letter that the eastern and western unions were designed to suppress "internal Divisions, occasioned by the Machinations" of New Hampshire and New York in Vermont. Now, he said, those states would "experience the Evils of intestine Broils."[16] Washington got the message: "So long as this Dispute of Territory subsists," he told President Meshech Weare of New Hampshire in a July 1782 letter, "the parties, Divisions and Troubles, both external and internal, will . . . encrease."[17]

Not coincidentally, in May 1781, the Vermont leadership opened up not-so-secret negotiations with Gen. Frederick Haldimand, British commander at Quebec. Seeking to secure recognition of their "independence" from the neighboring "claiming states" as well as of their rapidly expanding territorial claims, Vermont negotiators were apparently prepared to rejoin the British Empire — if the terms were right. But, of course, like the eastern and western unions, the Haldimand talks were also probably intended to shake Congress out of its chronic lethargy. In typically colorful language, Ira Allen described Vermont's basically ambivalent attitude: there was "a north pole" (the British in Canada) and "a south pole" (the American union); "should a thunder-gust come from the south, they would shut the door opposite that point and open the door facing the north."[18]

After all this excitement and intrigue, the next few years seem anticlimactic. The end of the American Revolution temporarily diffused the Vermont crisis, restoring the region to a brief and superficial calm. Abandoned by the British, Vermont's leaders prudently charted a less offensive policy, withdrawing to their old, although still unrecognized, boundaries and abandoning the eastern and western union towns to New Hampshire and New York. Having secured their old borders, those states tacitly accepted Vermont's original boundaries, and the new state was finally able to consolidate its control over dissident Yorkers.

Yet continued inaction would not make the Vermont problem go away. The ambiguous, potentially dangerous situation of the new state remained unchanged as long as it stayed outside the union. American statesmen were not likely to forget what had already happened — and what might have happened — in the Vermont region. During the war, Vermont demonstrated how an unrecognized, sovereign state jeopardized the common cause. Regardless of the Vermonters' patriotic attachment to the American cause, the pursuit of their state's vital interests necessarily led to violent boundary conflicts that could easily have led to interstate warfare and foreign intervention. The rapidly changing international situation as well as local political conditions might soon again be propitious for military and diplomatic adventures.

It was a maxim of international law that independent sovereignties confronted each other in a perpetual state of war, even when not actually belligerent. The connection between disunion and war was clear in the case of Vermont. The Vermonters let it be known in a sworn affidavit in 1782 that they had "strength enough to defend their State."[19] They "will establish their State by the sword," dispirited Yorkers reported to their governor.[20] New Hampshire supporter Jacob Bayley of Newbury warned in a February 1781 letter that the "mere suspicion" that Congress would seek to vindicate New York's claims would drive Vermont partisans into a British alliance.[21] In any case, John Sullivan of New Hampshire concluded in September 1780, "the continent must be involved in a war" to enforce its judgment.[22]

War appeared inevitable. It would take a war to reduce the new state to submission. As a small, weak, independent state, Vermont would attempt to secure itself by subverting the jurisdiction of powerful neighboring states in border areas or by extending its own jurisdiction at their expense. A policy of neutrality could not be sustained. Vermont needed allies; if the American states would not come to terms, it was only a matter of time before some sort of alliance with the British in Canada was concluded.

During the so-called "Critical Period" of the mid-1780s, proponents of constitutional reform portrayed the dangers of disunion and anarchy in precisely these terms. The chronic instability and violence of the greater Vermont region during the revolutionary years provided a chilling preview of the future course of American politics if the union collapsed. Interstate warfare would quickly lead to despotic rule as some strong man or self-proclaimed monarch reduced the warring states to order. In 1787, Daniel Shays was frequently mentioned as a likely candidate for this role. Earlier—in one of his more outrageous and playful moments—Ethan Allen nominated himself. Terrified Yorkers reported to Clinton in 1783 that Allen would "march into Albany with the Green Mountain Boys, and set up and be absolute monarch of all America."[23]

As nationalist sentiment began to coalesce in the mid-1780s, the continuing impasse over Vermont seemed increasingly unacceptable. "Vermont has long been viewed and considered as an independent State," a Philadelphia newspaperman noted in 1785. "No good reason can be assigned why new states and empires should not arise, and branch out from old ones," he continued, but Congress was still unwilling, or at least unable, to act on this increasingly conventional wisdom.[24] The political and constitutional obstacles to admitting states under the Articles seemed insurmountable. If Vermont could not qualify for admission, no new state could ever hope to join the union. And if this were so, the union would probably not survive.

The fragility of the union was reflected in Congress's inability to act, either to welcome new states and satisfy the political aspirations of frontier communities or to suppress them and secure old state jurisdictions. With many separatist movements breaking out from the Maine District to North Carolina, Vermont could no longer be dismissed as unusual. But the large states dug in their heels, warning that separatism would unleash centrifugal forces that would destroy the union. After all, as the committee report of a convention of towns of Cheshire County, New Hampshire, warned in 1780, "if every district so disposed, may for themselves determine that they are not within the claim of the thirteen states . . . we may soon have ten hundred states, all free and independent."[25] Yet it seemed equally likely that frustrated pleas for state division, the formation of illegal new states (following Vermont's notorious example), and foreign alliances would have the same effect. According to one commentator, "the unwieldiness of many of our present governments in extent of territory" meant that separations "must sooner or later take place."[26]

The large states were increasingly hard-pressed to maintain their authority in frontier regions. Again, the case of Vermont showed how frustrated frontiersmen might be tempted by foreign alliances. Because of their proximity to Canada, the Vermonters might "become a sore thorn in our sides," Washington wrote in early 1787, and "the Western Settlements without good and wise management . . . may be equally troublesome."[27] Growing intersectional tensions generated by John Jay's controversial offer to relinquish American claims to the navigation of the Mississippi made the threat of foreign tampering increasingly plausible. James Madison also made an explicit connection between Vermonters and westerners: alienated by Congress, the people of the West "by degrees . . . may be led to set up for themselves [and] . . . slide like Vermont insensibly into a communication and latent connection with their British neighbors."[28]

Like the rapidly opening West, Vermont also threatened the union by offering refuge to debtors, deserters, and other dangerous elements. Anti-expansionists argued vigorously against

161

permitting the depopulation and impoverishment of the old states. William Grayson of Virginia bemoaned the "fatal example" Vermont had set for the rest of the union: "[A] very considerable body of people residents of Vermont pay no taxes towards the support of the federal government, neither are they in fact a part of the Union; they also furnish a comfortable asylum to all those who are disposed to fly from taxation in the others."[29]

Vermonters shirked their tax burdens; by seizing lands to which they had no legal claim, they also set a disastrous precedent for settlers in other frontier areas from the Wyoming Valley in Pennsylvania, where Ethan Allen himself was reportedly spearheading a new-state movement, to the area northwest of the Ohio River where federal troops tried in vain to drive off illegal settlers.

Paradoxically, the logical conclusion of anti-expansionist logic was that Vermonters and other frontier separatists were probably better off *outside* the union: they would have access to better and cheaper lands while escaping heavy tax burdens. The old states' losses apparently translated into new-state advantages. This was the theme of a brief essay in a Baltimore newspaper, reporting erroneously in May 1787 that "Vermont has refused to accept a place in the confederation," supposedly to avoid making herself "liable to pay any of our unjustly accumulated debts."

> In a few years the new States will contain more inhabitants than the old. They will be free of debt, rich and happy; while we shall be divided into tenants and landlords and consequently miserable, with Governments truly aristocratic, and our States divided into confederated and unconfederated.[30]

As the Constitutional Convention prepared to meet in Philadelphia, many other commentators had also begun to calculate the advantages — and disadvantages — of the union. Disunion seemed increasingly likely because the immediate in-

"I can tell you this much. If we admit Vermont and Kentucky, we'll have to find a bigger place to go for lunch."

Drawing by Ed Fisher; © *1984. The New Yorker Magazine, Inc.*

terests of so many Americans seemed better served by alternative arrangements. If many frontier settlers believed they would be better off in their own new states, even if this necessitated alliances with foreign powers, many Easterners began to think seriously about breaking the existing union into three or four regional confederations in which it would be much easier to define and pursue common interests.

But disunion — in whatever form — entailed new and frightening risks. What was to prevent individual sovereign states or sectional alliances from waging war on each other? Divergent commercial policies as well as conflicts over boundaries or undeveloped territory would multiply occasions for hostilities, while encouraging hard-pressed combatants to seek support abroad. The Constitutional Convention had been called to prevent the collapse of the union and the Europeanization of American politics that would inevitably follow. Disunion would lead to an "anarchy" of hostile sovereign states confronting each other in a savage "state of nature" and would thus betray the continent's promise of unbounded prosperity and power.

Talk of disunion thus recreated the sense of crisis and danger characteristic of the Revolutionary War years. Reports of the Shaysite disorders in Massachusetts raised anxieties to a high pitch. Once again the British were seen to be plotting counterrevolution, and once again the diplomatic maneuvers of independent Vermont seemed to threaten the peace of the union. Sir Guy Carleton, the new British governor in Canada, had reportedly opened communications with Vermonters, Shaysites, and other frontier malcontents. And, just as the continued independence of Vermont came to seem intolerably dangerous to the common cause in 1781-82, pro-recognition forces renewed pressure for admitting the new state as fears of imminent disunion and counterrevolution gained strength in 1786-87.

Independent Vermont threatened the interests of all the confederated states, but Northerners had particular reasons to promote its admission into the union. Disgusted with Rhode Island's financial policies, a Massachusetts writer recommended dropping that state "out of the Union" and adding Vermont in its place: "the State of *Vermont* shines with far superior lustre, and would more than compensate the loss."[31] But other commentators saw an opportunity to add to northern voting power in Congress, not simply replace Rhode Island. New Englanders also agreed that as long as it remained independent, Vermont constituted a liability. "If they are not taken in, & remain exempt from taxes," New Hampshire's John Langdon stated at the Constitutional Convention, then it would be a "great injury" to his "and the other neighbouring states."[32] Such considerations led William Samuel Johnson to assert in the same debate that "Vermont ought to be compelled to come into the Union."[33]

Meanwhile, in New York, Alexander Hamilton and his allies challenged Governor Clinton's obstinate refusal to recognize Vermont. Seeking to promote regional interests as well as a more effective national union, New York Federalists made a strong case for coming to terms with the new state. What would happen, John Jay asked in 1787 in *An Address to the People of the State of New York*, if there were no union between New York and its neighbors? "What advantage Vermont in combination with others, might take of you, may easily be conjectured." With no union, Jay concluded, "every State would be a little nation, jealous of its neighbors, and anxious to strengthen itself by foreign alliances."[34] Vermont's flirtation with the British did not augur well, and New Yorkers were well aware that neighboring New Jersey and Connecticut chafed under New York's commercial domination. At the June 1788 New York State ratifying convention, Robert R. Livingston, another long-time advocate of the new state, was convinced that "Vermont [stood] ready to avail itself of our weakness" in the event of disunion.[35]

Hamilton developed and generalized these themes in the *Federalist* series. Jealous of New York State's "future power," the New England states, as well as small states like Maryland, had offered aid and comfort to the Vermonters, hoping thereby "to dismember this State." But any effort to assert New York's title by force would surely have shattered "the peace of the Confederacy." It was only by respecting and preserving the union, however illusory its foundation, that the dogs of war could be restrained. Those who would "lull asleep our apprehensions of discord and hostility between the States, in the event of disunion" were dangerously ignorant or artful. It is a "sort of axiom in politics," Hamilton concluded, "that vicinity, or nearness of situation, constitutes nations' natural enemies."[36] When Federalists predicted such dire consequences from disunion, they were not simply invoking familiar political axioms. In dealing — or failing to deal — with Vermont, Americans knew from experience what disunion meant.

At first, the return of peace apparently neutralized the Vermont threat. But the outbreak of new-state movements over the next few years revealed the dangers of complacency. If the old states crumbled and no provisions were made to recognize new ones, the union would necessarily fall apart. By the mid-1780s, many frightened commentators predicted that self-proclaimed new states would soon surround what remained of the old states. These states, in turn, would be ringed by hostile foreign powers and savage Indians. Rebuffed by the old states, they would be forced to form unholy alliances with America's traditional enemies. The "Goths and Vandals" would then descend in force on the embattled republic.[37]

This nightmare vision of disunion and counterrevolution lay at the heart of Federalist rhetoric. What was the solution? We began this discussion by looking at the new-state clause of the federal constitution. With a few well-chosen phrases, Article IV, Section III made it possible for the new government to provide for expansion of the union. Under the Articles of Confederation, Congress had been unable to admit new states and the calamitous results of this were increasingly apparent. But the language of Article IV shows that the new union was intended to include Vermont and Kentucky, as well as new states created by Congress in the national lands north of the Ohio. The answer to the counterrevolutionary threat was a stronger, more inclusive union.

In balancing the interests of old and prospective new states and by reconciling the need for jurisdictional stability with the imperatives of expansion, the framers fashioned the most momentous of all the related "compromises" that made the Constitution seem so miraculous. Focusing on shifting alliances among the state delegations at the Philadelphia convention, it is easy to overlook the problem of expansion. As a result, historians usually emphasize crucial bargains on representation, slavery, and commerce. Although Vermont and the other new states did not participate directly in these negotiations, the framers well knew that it would be perilous to ignore their demands. After all, if their goal was to form a more perfect union, the admission of Vermont represented a first, crucial step toward perfection. Accommodating future Vermonts, striking a durable bargain between the present and the future and between old states and new, was the critical challenge.

Why was the creation of such a union so important? Many answers can be given. In their Critical-Period rhetoric, Federalists often advanced negative arguments: disunion meant anarchy and war. But they also promoted a positive and widely appealing vision, one that many Vermonters had always shared. This was the idea that the union of Americans was a natural one, and that conflicts among the states over boundaries, taxation, and commerce were ultimately artificial.

Admission to the union had always been a primary goal of Vermont's leadership, even when engaged in diplomatic intrigues with the enemy. The new state's leaders had sought admission for practical reasons: they recognized their weakness and vulnerable strategic situation. They also considered themselves patriotic American citizens and identified their future prospects for prosperity and power with the development of closer economic as well as political ties with the old states. By 1787, many Easterners had come to similar conclusions about their own best interests. Let the frontier regions govern themselves, they argued, then guarantee old and new state boundaries against further changes, while encouraging economic development to create strong common interests and cement the union.

Boundary controversies epitomized the union created by the Articles of Confederation. The tendency of the old union was entropic, that is, it tended toward disunion. Policy was formulated, or not formulated, under the self-fulfilling conviction that the states had always sought to advance their interests at each other's expense. Endless squabbling over the New Hampshire Grants was only one particularly conspicuous case in point. In contrast, the new union seemed to transcend this problematic, increasingly fragile balance of state interests. River improvements and canals that brought Americans together, not the contested boundaries that kept them apart, were appropriate symbols of the new dispensation. This was the union that could save the American states from each other; it was the union that could, at last, admit the new state of Vermont.

168

NOTES

[1] Peter S. Onuf, *The Origins of the Federal Republic: Jurisdictional Controversies in the United States, 1775-1787* (Philadelphia: University of Penn. Press. 1983); Peter S. Onuf, *Statehood and Union* (Bloomington, Ind.: University of Indiana Press, 1987).

[2] Max Farrand, ed., *Records of the Federal Convention of 1787*, (New Haven, Conn.: Yale University Press, 1911-37), 2:455.

[3] Ibid.

[4] Ibid.

[5] Ibid., 2:456.

[6] Ibid.

[7] Ibid., 2:462.

[8] Ibid., 2:455.

[9] Ibid., 2:462.

[10] Ibid., 2:462-3.

[11] Ibid., 2:463.

[12] John A. Williams, ed., *The Public Papers of Governor Thomas Chittenden* (Montpelier, Vt.: Secretary of State, 1969), 458-9.

[13] Hugh Hastings, ed., *The Public Papers of George Clinton* (Albany, New York: State of New York, 1899-1914).

[14] "Letters to Livingston," Bancroft Collection, New York Public Library.

[15] Harold C. Syrett, ed., *The Papers of Alexander Hamilton* (New York: Columbia University Press, 1961-87), 3:230-31.

[16] Williams, 381.

[17] John C. Fitzpatrick, ed., *The Writings of George Washington* (Washington, D.C.: GPO, 1931-44), 24:449-50.

[18] Reported by Dr. George Smith, enclosed in a letter from General Schuyler to Washington, *Collections of the Vermont Historical Society* (Montpelier: Vermont Historical Society, 1870-71), 2:132.

[19] Eliakim P. Walton, ed., *Records of the Governor and Council of the State of Vermont* (Montpelier: J. & J. M. Poland, 1873-4), 3:240.

[20] Edmund B. O'Callaghan, ed., *The Documentary History of the State of New York* (Albany: Weed, Parsons & Co., 1850-51), 4:965-66.

[21] Washington Papers, Library of Congress.

[22] Otis G. Hammond, ed., *The Letters and Papers of Major General John Sullivan* (Concord, N.H.: New Hampshire Historical Society, 1930-39), 3:187-90.

[23] Benjamin H. Hall, *History of Eastern Vermont from its Earliest Settlement to the Close of the Eighteenth Century* (Albany, New York: J. Munsell, 1865), 2:496-8.

[24] *Pennsylvania Herald*, 11 June 1785.

[25] *State Papers of New Hampshire* (Concord: State of New Hampshire, 1877), 381-3.

[26] Philadelphia's *Freeman's Journal*, 15 June 1785.

[27] Robert A. Rutland, et al., eds., *The Papers of James Madison* (Chicago and Charlottesville: University of Chicago Press and University Press of Virginia, 1962-   ), 9:342-44.

[28] Ibid., March 1787 letter to Washington, 9:314-17.

[29] Edmund C. Burnett, ed., *Letters of Members of the Continental Congress* (Washington, D.C.: Carnegie Institution of Washington, 1921-36), 8:609-10.

[30] *Maryland Gazette*, 4 May 1787.

[31] *Cumberland Gazette*, 31 March 1787.

[32] Farrand, August 29, 2:456.

[33] Ibid.

[34] Paul L. Ford, ed., *Pamphlets on the Constitution of the United States* (Brooklyn, N.Y.: n.p., 1888), 84.

[35] Jonathan Elliott, ed., *The Debates in the Several State Conventions on the Adoption of the Federal Constitution* (Philadelphia: Lippincott, 1876), 2:212.

[36] Clinton Rossiter, ed., *The Federalist Papers*, 7 and 6 (New York: New American Library, 1961), 62, 59.

[37] *Maryland Gazette*, 10 March 1786.

PART IV

—— • ——

Past and Future

Memory, Commemoration, and the Storyteller's Creed:

Lessons about History and a Bicentennial Celebration

by Michael Sherman

One of the assumptions that lies behind events such as the Vermont statehood bicentennial celebration is that people have a craving for history. This may very well be true but as anyone who has lived through similar events will recall, it begs the question of what and who satisfies that appetite. For my part, I have reached the conclusion that history in commemorative celebrations is like MSG in a Chinese dinner: a little bit brings out the distinctive flavors; too much gives people a headache.

The 1991 bicentennial of Vermont's admission to the union as the fourteenth of the United States of America, the 1989 commemoration in Vermont of the two hundredth anniversary of the death of Ethan Allen, and intense and bitter debates over the merits or flaws in Vermont's community and regional planning legislation, "Act 200," have already provided instructive examples of how occasions shape debate about the character of Vermont, the correct interpretation of its history, and the role, if any, Vermont can or ought to play in leading the United States toward a new definition of federalism. Predictably, while these occasions have stimulated some political leaders and a few politically savvy scholars to present their research and/or meditations in public, much of this debate, whether carried on in the editorial and op-ed pages of newspapers or in public meetings and forums, has generated more heat than light about Vermont's past and future. Thus, alongside — or perhaps instead of — discussions of history, we hear a lot about "the Vermont myth."

Let's examine this phrase, "the Vermont myth." Invoked in a piecemeal fashion, Vermont's stories and history become exemplary tales that demonstrate characteristics like frontier individualism; white-Anglo-Saxon-Protestant ethnocentrism; Jeffersonian pastoralism; and naive probity. The tales we tell each other time and time again glorify Yankee pioneers coming into an empty, inhospitable wilderness and taming the forests where not even the native people of the Americas had chosen to settle before them; Ethan Allen capturing Ticonderoga in the name of Jehovah and the Continental Congress — neither of whom provided him with a verifiable commission; yeoman settlers filled with the spirit of democracy fighting off the domination of oligarchic Yorkers; a population fiercely antislavery and abolitionist nudging the nation toward Civil War and then making disproportionate sacrifices of men and money to pursue it. We invoke the virtues of political innocence and independence with stories of Vermont "going it alone" after the disastrous 1927 flood and quietly forget that in addition to bonds sold in the state, Governor John Weeks accepted federal funds to rebuild highways and bridges. Our history has made folk heroes of smugglers in the 1810s and 1920s; of U.S. senator Ralph Flanders slaying with puritan rectitude the dragon, Joseph McCarthy; of George Aiken slaying with homey wit old-boy politics in the Green Mountain State and deceitful foreign policy in Washington; [1] of Ben and Jerry slaying with "aw-shucks" naiveté the Pillsbury doughboy. [2] We talk with mixed pride and irony of more sheep than people in the 1830s, more cattle than people in the 1940s, and more flatlanders than real Vermonters in the 1990s.

Sometimes, our mythology even creates events that call upon us to refashion our history. Such was the case in 1990 when the

The Vermont Secession Debates, 1990. Drawing by Jeff Danziger. Courtesy Vermont Statehood Bicentennial Commission.

Vermont Statehood Bicentennial Commission sponsored a series of debates on whether Vermont should exercise its beloved but entirely fictitious right to secede from the union. According to popular wisdom, Vermont bargained for this option at the time it joined the United States but can only exercise it at the centennial anniversaries of statehood. The so-called secession clause, also called the "Brigadoon clause," enjoys wide credence and persistent popularity in Vermont. It reflect just those qualities of pugnacious independence that pop up elsewhere in our mythohistory. [3]

    The 1990 secession debates had the predictable result of overwhelming votes against continuing in the union. Behind the showmanship, mordant humor, and just plain orneriness of the event, however, lay some interesting observations and genuine concerns about the relationship between states and the federal government at the end of the twentieth century. These echo in a remarkable degree some of the issues about political identity, sovereignty, benefits and sacrifices of union that Daniel Buck and Nathaniel Chipman debated in 1791 and that Vermonters worked out through painful trial and error in the early years of statehood.

Used in this fragmentary way, Vermont's history demonstrates what Robert Fulghum means when, in the foreword to his best-selling book of popular philosophy and new-age innocence, *All I Really Need to Know I Learned in Kindergarten*, he proclaims himself an adherent to the storyteller's creed:

> I believe that imagination is stronger than knowledge
> That myth is more potent than history
> That dreams are more powerful than facts . . .[4]

There is a problem here: Fulghum innocently assumes that history is merely the recounting of objectively verifiable facts and that myth is merely the imaginative telling of fantasy. His rigid dichotomy assumes that history belongs to scholars and poetry belongs to the people. In fact, as we all know, historians do not always tell the truth — even when they know it — and poets are sometimes the best — or at least the most effective — tellers of history. Furthermore, and more to my immediate point, Fulghum fails to see that history and myth are two powerful ways of dealing with the question of how, as individuals and as a society, we harness the resources of human memory, recover and give shape to the past, impose orderly patterns on messy complexity, and establish narrative traditions and mimetic strategies in order to retain and celebrate community, however broadly or narrowly defined. The problem is not choosing between history and myth, but understanding the relationship between memory and commemoration as elements in recalling and using the past to build or strengthen the sense of community from generation to generation.

175

In the "Compulsory Preface" to their extraordinarily good and durable satire of English history, *1066 and All That*, authors W. J. Sellar and R. J. Yeatman tell us: "History is not what you thought. *It is what you can remember*. All other history defeats itself."[5] In the western tradition, ancient, medieval, and early modern European history is filled with accounts of the stunning feats of memory performed by statesmen, scholars, and orators. The *Jesuit Relations* — accounts of early European contacts with the native peoples of North America — also contain many stories of tribal chiefs, sachems, and elders who repeat verbatim long speeches that have just been recited by another member of the tribe or by the members of visiting delegations. In non-literate or proto-literate societies, where the spoken word is more powerful than the written word, information is highly coded and narration relies on commonplaces and formulaic turns of phrase that serve as guideposts for the memory, creating and recreating an account. We can see how this works in classic tales like the *Iliad* and *Odyssey*, saints' lives, and medieval chronicles. In her book, *Fiction in the Archives*, historian Natalie Zemon Davis explores the formulas of storytelling in sixteenth-century French pardon tales.[6] She explains that the stories told by individuals seeking the king's pardon had to conform to well-known criteria of evidence, circumstance, and formal presentation not only to qualify but even to receive a hearing. In the retelling of history, therefore, even the history of crimes for which there might be severe penalties, events and explanation were or became encoded to the categories of motive and deed acceptable and understandable in the context of society. Memory was thus aided by context and custom, even as action was shaped by convention. Seen this way the storyteller's task is to fit the narrative of events — fictional or historical — into comprehensible and contextually acceptable form. The storyteller must know the conventions of storytelling in his or her culture and be able to transform the raw data of the tale into those conventions. At

176

its best, this produces great stories: great myths, if you will, and great history.

Ethan Allen's account of his exploits from 1775 to 1778, for example, shows the power and possibilities of working within the conventions of storytelling. The literary archetype for Allen's *Narrative of His Captivity* is the enormously popular captivity narratives of the earlier eighteenth century. [7] These accounts of white male and female English settlers on the frontiers of colonial New England, who were carried into captivity by French and Indian raiders, generally followed a format that reflects the Puritan religious experience of separation, trial, confirmation, and return to the community of the faithful. An alternative interpretation, provided by anthropologists who look for wider models of common human experience, emphasizes the pattern of integration, separation, liminality (where all norms and forms of behavior are absent), and reintegration. [8]

Allen's autobiographical book is a variation on the traditional captivity narrative. He translated terms within the literary conventions, making the English the functional equivalent of Indians and his capture and transport to England as a prisoner of war the political equivalent of a spiritual journey of exile, trial, and reintegration into the community of the faithful — the revolutionary society from which he was forcibly separated in 1775. Allen's use of the old captivity narrative was an ingenious manipulation for propaganda purposes of a well-known literary genre. He effectively adapted rhetorical and cultural commonplaces with which his audience was thoroughly familiar to changed political circumstances. [9] This reading of his book allows us to see how history and myth are coded messages that guide memory. But if we forget the code, or if it changes, as it surely has in the two centuries since Allen composed his *Narrative*, we are in danger of misunderstanding the message and misinterpreting the story and its teller.

It is, of course, possible for the conventions to so far constrain the telling of the story and the storyteller that the audience learns nothing new or significant from a retelling of history *or* myth. Note, for example, this comment in a review of a book about the Battle of Cedar Creek: ". . . the work illustrates the basic problem in too many histories of the Civil War: they are aimed at a distinct popular audience that expects to hear the well-worn tale, like a group of Saxon warriors in the Mead Hall hearing again of Beowulf's deeds, and, therefore, *the story cannot be liberated from old forms.*"[10] When some of us complain that the history of Vermont has been and is being buried beneath the "myth of Vermont," I think we are saying that the conventions by which we have told the story of our history for many generations have become too constraining, that they no longer or imperfectly encode the behavior and beliefs of our society, and that they interfere with the creative and imaginative use of memory to tell usable stories.

Some scholars believe that myths are stories we tell to mediate cultural and social contradictions.[11] If they no longer do so, it is time to change the stories. But agreeing on new ones is difficult because it requires some consensus on what is important to remember and some agreement on who has the authority to express the consensus. A similar process occurs periodically in the writing of history, where not only new stories, but a new framework for the stories must be worked out and generally accepted.

Something like this has been happening in Vermont over the last decade. In 1981, T. D. S. Bassett catalogued the need for new studies and new directions in our history in the "Foreword" to his *Bibliography of Vermont*, produced for the Committee for a New England Bibliography.[12] He, too, noted the passage from long-accepted stories to new ones and pointed to some of the areas in social, economic, and institutional history that had either been neglected or needed re-examination in the light of new cultural beliefs and commonplaces. Some parts of

Mr. Bassett's program have been addressed; others await the revisionists who will write the new stories and the pioneers who will write the first story.

Work in those areas does not depend on and may, in fact, be retarded by commemorative events, for they generally have another, far more conservative agenda of enshrining old accepted beliefs. Surely, however, commemorative events can also provide a powerful stimulus for creating and inaugurating new versions of the old stories.

The *Oxford English Dictionary* tells us that the word commemorate derives from Latin roots: *com-memorare* — to bring to remembrance, make mention of — and gives these two, among other, definitions of the word: 1. To call to the remembrance of hearers or readers; to make mention of, relate, or rehearse; 2. To call to remembrance or preserve in memory, by some solemnity or celebration.

The first definition — retelling the story — reminds us of the ancient function of storytellers, of the poet Homer calling upon his Muse to help him recount details of battle and death of heroes on the field before Troy, [13] as much as the historian Herodotus soberly publishing his "researches" in the hope, he says, "of thereby preserving from decay the remembrance of what men have done and of preventing the great and wonderful actions of the Greeks and the Barbarians from losing their due meed of glory. . ." [14]

The second definition, which links memory to ceremony, brings us to our own bicentennial celebrations. Their purpose is to call to the remembrance of hearers or readers the events of two hundred years ago when Vermont joined a community of states. The commemoration is thus the *occasion* for remembrance. It is also the *vessel* into which we pour the contents of our collective memory, and as such it shapes that memory and is shaped by the interests, concerns, and norms of the celebrants.

When in 1921, Walter Hill Crockett described the celebration of Vermont's centennial of statehood in volume four of his history of Vermont, he placed it at the beginning of a chapter entitled "The Spanish-American War Period."[15] The content of the official celebrations a century ago was, indeed, military and militaristic, both in events such as the dedication of the Bennington Battle Monument on August 16, 1891, and the rhetoric, which time after time emphasized Vermont's contribution of soldiers to the Revolution and Civil War. Such details reveal with unmistakable clarity the tenor of the times and the issues that dominated public life. They reveal, too, the shape of late nineteenth-century nationalist mythology and historiography.

We have already embarked on the retelling of our myths and — to a noticeably lesser degree — the telling of our history in celebration of our bicentennial. When we have finished in 1992, we will leave behind a record that will reveal to future generations something about our historiography, a lot about our myths, and a great deal about our cultural, social, and political concerns. In many respects we have already shaped the vessel into which we shall pour our memory, and in some respects the commemoration has begun to shape the stories we are telling and retelling to each other. When we debate about secession, project Ethan Allen into the role of defender or opponent of Act 200, or invite our fellow citizens around the nation to think of Vermont as "home" and to come to a statewide "homecoming" we are reciting deeply held beliefs about our society and its history. Those invocations of ancient if perhaps fictitious or exaggerated privileges, heroes, and virtues reveal a core of truth and concern about self-governance and the role of the state, the interpretation of individual liberties, attitudes toward the land, definitions of work and leisure, social institutions and personal values that help us define family and community in our time.

The tellers of myths will surely play an important part in our commemorative celebrations. Our collective memory is tied to those myths, which come from the deep memory of society, where what we have been and what we are blend with what we wish to be. As we retell myths we reenact them — that is one of the functions of myth — and as we reenact them they guide us toward the ideal that they define.[16]

Historians, both inside and outside the academy, also have powerful and useful stories to tell, and we must be sure that we do not allow them to get drowned out by the din of neo-secessionist rhetoric or buried beneath the debris of commemorative belt buckles, T-shirts, and coffee mugs. Our stories are drawn from the diaries, account books, letters, words, deeds, and remains of physical structures built and used by our predecessors over the past two hundred and more years.

Historical stories are, like myths, synthetic constructions of a complicated reality that we cannot see whole and cannot experience directly. But unlike myths, historical stories are not prescriptive and we do not have to become again what we once were. Myths are always cyclical, bringing us back to the place where we were when the story started, sending us again around the loop of narrative.[17] Most of the history we write these days has freed itself from deterministic structures and intent. We are never free of our history, just as we are never free of our myths; but we are not wholly constrained by it.

I am not so naive to think that historians can nor always wish to remake the myths of society. However, the warning that history is "what you can remember" is cheering in its ambiguity. The forms of celebration and commemoration we use leave at least a few openings for telling new stories. Recited often enough, and with sufficient conviction, our stories may eventually bend the old myths in new directions and expand our collective memory to include people, ideas, and events that have formerly been overlooked or excluded. It would be interesting to know what stories are being told when Vermont celebrates its 250th anniversary.

NOTES

[1] I refer here to the famous "Aiken formula" supposedly proclaimed by U.S. Senator George D. Aiken on the floor of the Senate on October 19, 1966. Aiken is widely credited with having said that America's best course of action in Vietnam would be to "declare victory and get out." Recent scholarship, based on close study of the *Congressional Record* and the Aiken papers at the University of Vermont, has convincingly demonstrated that Aiken's advice to Lyndon Johnson was more complex and less radical than the epigram attributed to him.

[2] Calvin Trillin, "American Chronicles: Competitors," *New Yorker*, 8 July 1985, 31-45. Trillin reports on the "ice cream war" between Ben & Jerry's Homemade and Haagen-Dazs, owned by the Pillsbury Corporation. At the height of the campaign to get their product marketed nationwide, Ben & Jerry's sold a bumper sticker that read, "WHAT'S THE DOUGHBOY AFRAID OF?"

[3] The best indicator of the durability of both the secession clause myth and the rugged non-conformist attitude that keeps it alive is the enormous popularity of Frank Bryan and Bill Mares, *OUT! The Vermont Secession Book, or "We Won't Make That Mistake Again!"* (Shelburne, Vt.: New England Press, 1987). It was the success of this book that prompted the "secession debates" in 1990 and assured their coverage by the national press.

[4] Robert Fulghum, *All I Really Need to Know I Learned in Kindergarten. Uncommon Thoughts on Common Things* (New York: Ballantine Books, 1986), viii.

[5] W. J. Sellar and R. J. Yeatman, *1066 and All That. A Memorable History of England, Comprising All the Parts You Can Remember, Including One Hundred and Three* Good *Things, Five* Bad *Kings, and Two* Genuine *Dates* (New York: E. P. Dutton, 1931), vii.

[6] Natalie Zemon Davis, *Fiction in the Archives. Pardon Tales and Their Tellers in Sixteenth-Century France* (Stanford, California: Stanford University Press, 1987).

[7] Ethan Allen, *A Narrative of Ethan Allen's Captivity, Containing His Voyages & Travels, . . . etc.* [1779] (Vermont Heritage Press, for the Vermont Statehood Bicentennial Commission, 1988.) This is a reprint of the 1930 edition published by the Fort Ticonderoga Museum.

[8] For an excellent definition of myth from an anthropologist's point of view, and one that focuses on the concept of liminality, see Victor W. Turner, "Myth and Symbol," *International Encyclopedia of the Social Sciences* (1968), vol. X, 576-582.

[9] On the captivity narrative as a literary genre, its political implications, and Allen's use of it, see Capt. Greg Sieminski, "The Puritan Captivity Narrative and the Politics of the American Revolution," *American Quarterly* 42 (March 1990): 35-56; and P. Jeffrey Potash, "Fact or Fiction? An Irreverent Review of *A Narrative of Colonel Ethan Allen's Captivity,*" *Vermont Bicentennial*, Newsletter of the Vermont Statehood Bicentennial Commission, vol. 1, no. 4 (Spring 1989), 4.

[10] Michael C. C. Adams, review of Thomas A. Lewis, *The Guns of Cedar Creek* (New York: Harper & Row, 1988), *American Historical Review* 95 (February 1990): 262 (emphasis added).

[11] This is the theory of myth of French anthropologist and structuralist critic Claude Levi-Strauss. For a clear and concise exposition of this theory see G. S. Kirk, *Myth. Its Meaning and Function in Ancient and Other Cultures* (Cambridge: Cambridge University Press, 1970), 42-83.

[12] Thomas D. Seymour Bassett, "Foreword," *Vermont: A Bibliography of Its History* (Hanover, N.H.: University Press of New England, 1981, for the Committee for a New England Bibliography), xix-xxiv.

[13] *The Iliad of Homer*, I, 1-7, Richmond Lattimore, trans. (Chicago: University of Chicago Press, 1951), 59.

[14] Herodotus, *History of the Persian Wars*, Introduction to Book I, George Rowlinson, trans. (New York: Random House, 1942), 3.

[15] Walter Hill Crockett, *Vermont: The Green Mountain State* (New York: Century History Company, 1921), 4:197-300; see esp. 199-210 for an account of the centennial celebrations.

[16] The connection of myth to rituals is the fundamental insight of Mercea Eliade and has had a profound influence on other students of myth and literary criticism. See Eliade, *The Myth of the Eternal Return* (New York: Harper & Row, 1954); see also Kirk, *Myth*, 1-41, 252-285; Joseph Campbell with Bill Moyers, *The Power of Myth* (New York: Doubleday, 1988), 123-164; Northrop Frye, *Fables of Identity: Studies in Poetic Mythology* (New York: Harcourt, Brace and World, 1963), 14-18.

[17] Eliade, op. cit. Anna Russell, in her perceptive and entertaining description of Wagner's opera cycle, "The Ring of the Niebelungen," sums it up best when she notes in despair, "Sixteen hours, and you're right back where you started!"

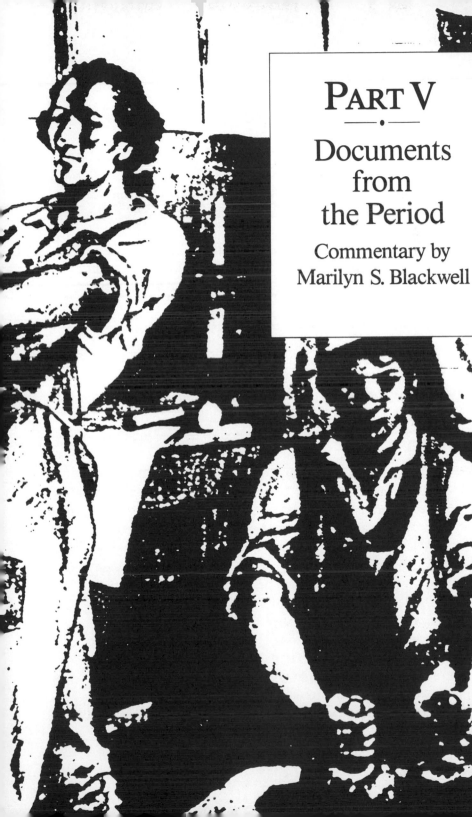

PART V
·
Documents
from
the Period

Commentary by
Marilyn S. Blackwell

"To the Inhabitants of Vermont"

April 11, 1777, Thomas Young

Using the name "New Connecticut," a group of residents of the New Hampshire Grants declared the territory a "separate, free and independent" state at Westminister on January 15, 1777. Identifying their cause with that of the American Revolution, these men approved the Declaration of Independence, agreed to support the war against Great Britain and sent a delegation to the Continental Congress requesting representation. The rebels asserted that the government of New York, while supporting "monopolizing land traders," had failed to protect their lives and property.

Dr. Thomas Young, the first to use the name Vermont in his open letter of April 11 and 12, 1777, was no stranger to the new state's problem with New York land-jobbers. While a resident of New York, Young had invested in a large land grant in Vermont territory. His failure to gain clear title from New York increased Young's contempt for the New York land system that placed property in the hands of wealthy officials and speculators and denied the rights of settlers on virgin land.

Young was also familiar with the leaders of the fledgling Green Mountain republic. While practicing medicine in New York and western Connecticut in the early 1760s, he had spent many hours discussing philosophy and political theory with the young Ethan Allen. Allen later published much of the doctor's philosophy in *Reason the Only Oracle of Man* (1784).

As an outspoken champion of republican principles, Young became an ardent patriot. He participated in mob actions in Albany and Boston, defending the rights of the common people to self-government. In an effort to escape the British, he moved to Philadelphia where he associated with radical Pennsylvanians in the Continental Congress. When delegates from the Grants arrived in Philadelphia to request recognition of their new state, Thomas Young eagerly supported their cause.

Young's broadside "To the Inhabitants of Vermont" was a bold publication. The new name he proposed symbolized the immediate encouragement he offered; it embodied his sympathies for the Green Mountain Boys and his familiarity with the history of "Les Montagnes Verds." He provided Vermonters with a copy of the congressional resolutions of May 10 and 15, 1776, which asserted American independence and encouraged the colonies to form new state governments. Recommending that Vermont adopt a constitution similar to Pennsylvania's, Young advocated a unicameral legislature and a weak executive council that would place governmental power with the people.

While Young exhorted Vermonters "to organize fairly, and make the experiment," members of Congress saw Vermont independence as a threat to the unity of the new confederation. They were also aware of the importance of New York's military strength to the Revolutionary cause. The delegates from Vermont returned home with Young's letter and a copy of the Pennsylvania constitution, but without an answer from Congress.

In June, after Young's advice had circulated and the Windsor Convention had chosen the name Vermont, Congress responded by dismissing Vermont's petition for representation. A congressional resolution affirmed the jurisdiction of the existing states, denied the right of the Grants' inhabitants to use the Declaration of Independence to justify their claims, and rebuked Thomas Young for his misrepresentation of congressional sentiments. Young was unable to appeal, for he died of fever June 24, 1777. Vermonters would have to press their case for independence without the support of a revolutionary committed to their cause.

M.S.B.

187

In Congress

May 15, 1776

Whereas his Britannic Majesty, in conjunction with the Lords and Commons of Great-Britain, has by a late Act of Parliament excluded the inhabitants of these United Colonies from the protection of his Crown: And Whereas no answer whatever to the humble Petitions of the Colonies for redress of grievances and reconciliation with Great-Britain, has been or is likely to be given; but the whole force of that kingdom, aided by foreign mercenaries, is to be exerted for the destruction of the good people of these Colonies: And Whereas it appears absolutely irreconcileable to reason and good conscience, for the people of these Colonies now to take the oaths and affirmations necessary for the support of any government under the Crown of Great-Britain, and it is necessary that the exercise of every kind of authority under the said Crown should be totally suppressed, and all the powers of government exerted under the people of the Colonies, for the preservation of internal peace, virtue and good order, as well as for the defence of their lives, liberties and properties against the hostile invasions and cruel depredations of their enemies: —

Resolved therefore, That it be recommended to the respective Assemblies and Conventions of the United Colonies, where no government sufficient to the exigencies of their affairs has been hitherto established, to adopt such government as shall in the opinion of the Representatives of the people best conduce to the happiness and safety of their constituents in particular and America in general.

Extract from the Minutes,
CHARLES THOMSON,
Secretary

To the Inhabitants of Vermont, a Free and Independent State, bounding on the River Connecticut and Lake Champlain

Philadelphia, April 11, 1777.

Gentlemen,

Numbers of you are knowing to the zeal with which I have exerted myself in your behalf from the beginning of your struggle with the New-York Monopolizers. As the Supreme Arbiter of right has smiled on the just cause of North-America at large, you in a peculiar manner have been highly favored. God has done by you the best thing commonly done for our species. He has put it fairly in your power to help yourselves.

I have taken the minds of several leading Members in the Honorable the Continental Congress, and can assure you that you have nothing to do but send attested copies of the Recommendation to take up government to every township in your district, and invite all your freeholders and inhabitants to meet in their respective townships and chuse members for a General Convention, to meet at an early day to chuse Delegates for the General Congress, a Committee of Safety, and to form a Constitution for your State.

Your friends here tell me that some are in doubt whether Delegates from your district would be admitted into Congress. I tell you to organize fairly, and make the experiment, and I will ensure your success at the risque of my reputation as a man of honor or common sense. Indeed they can by no means refuse you! You have as good a right to chuse how you will be governed, and by whom, as they had.

I have recommended to your Committee the Constitution of Pennsylvania for a model, which, with a very little alteration, will, in my opinion, come as near perfection as any thing yet concerted by mankind. This Constitution has been sifted with all the criticism that a band of despots were masters of, and has bid defiance to their united powers.

The alteration I would recommend is, that all the Bills intended to be passed into Laws should be laid before the Executive Board for their perusal and proposals of amendment. All the difference then between such a Constitution and those of Connecticut and Rhode-Island, in the grand outlines is, that in one case the Executive power can advise and in the other compel. For my own part, I esteem the people at large the true proprietors of governmental power. They are the supreme constituent power, and of course their immediate Representatives are the supreme delegate power; and as soon as the delegate power gets too far out of the hands of the constituent power, a tyranny is in some degree established.

Happy are you that in laying the foundation of a new government, you have a digest drawn from the purest fountains of antiquity, and improved by the readings and observations of the great Doctor Franklin, David Rittenhouse, Esq; and others. I am certain you may build on such a basis a system which will transmit liberty and happiness to posterity.

Let the scandalous practice of bribing men by places, commissions, &c. be held in abhorrence among you. By entrusting only men of capacity and integrity in public affairs, and by obliging even the best men to fall into the common mass of the people every year, and be sensible of their need of the popular good will to sustain their political importance, is your liberties well secured. These plans effectually promise this security.

May Almighty God smile upon your arduous and important undertaking, and inspire you with that wisdom, virtue, public spirit and unanimity, which ensures success in the most hazardous enterprizes!

I am, Gentlemen, Your sincere friend and humble servant,

THOMAS YOUNG

April 12, 1777.

Your Committee have obtained for you a copy of the Recommendation of Congress to all such bodies of men as looked upon themselves returned to a state of nature, to adopt such government as should in the opinion of the Representatives of the people best conduce to the happiness and safety of their constituents in particular and America in general.

You may perhaps think strange that nothing further is done for you at this time than to send you this extract. But if you consider that till you incorporate and actually announce to Congress your having become a body politic, they cannot treat with you as a free State. While New-York claims you as subjects of that government, my humble opinion is, your own good sense will suggest to you, that no time is to be lost in availing yourselves of the same opportunity your assuming mistress is improving to establish a dominion for herself and you too.

A Word To The Wise is Sufficient.

*Courtesy of Brooks Memorial Library,
Brattleboro, Vermont*

"To the Inhabitants of the State of Vermont"
July 13, 1779, Ira Allen

Major figures in the establishment of Vermont, Ethan and Ira Allen became its most active and vocal promoters as well. While Ethan preferred to remain outside official government channels, Ira served as both treasurer and surveyor-general. Ethan's effectiveness rested on his commanding personality, his brazen military ventures, and his patriotic rhetoric. Ira maneuvered in a less ostentatious manner, yet he was equally influential in defending the new Vermont community.

Both men, recognizing the importance of persuasion in a democratic republic, used the power of the printed word to rally their fellow Vermonters. Ira's circular of July 13, 1779, is just one example of the propaganda he published to convince the inhabitants of Vermont and those of neighboring states that the new government was legitimate.

One of the first threats to the struggling state and to the Allens' political power surfaced at the initial meeting of the Vermont Assembly in March 1778. Sixteen New Hampshire towns along the Connecticut River petitioned to join the new state, based on their affinity with neighboring Vermont towns across the river. Believing their interests were not properly represented in the New Hampshire legislature, these towns hoped to establish a more cohesive community centering on the Connecticut River. Vermonters on the west bank of the river were anxious to enhance their political power by the addition of the New Hampshire towns.

The Vermont Assembly accepted this Eastern Union, but the aggrandizement antagonized New Hampshire and weakened Vermont's status with members of the Continental Congress. More importantly for the Allens, the addition of New Hampshire towns shifted the balance of power in the Vermont assembly

192

to the eastern side of the Green Mountains. While the Allens maneuvered successfully in the assembly to dissolve the union, the Connecticut River towns, led by Jacob Bayley of Newbury, met at Cornish to pursue their aim of a government centered on the Connecticut. Their actions eventually spurred New Hampshire to reassert its claim to the Grants territory.

As an official agent of Vermont, Ira Allen traveled to Exeter several times to confer with the New Hampshire government on the boundary question. He took advantage of his excursions to stop at Dresden (Hanover), where Alden Spooner printed Ira's latest appeals to the people. In this handbill of July 13, 1779, Allen argued against New Hampshire's claim and reasserted Vermont's right to self-government, comparing Vermont's rebellion to that of the colonies against Great Britain. His concluding statements outlined the favorable circumstances that existed in Vermont, the state's liberal constitution and its lack of debt, arguments that he would continue to use to promote Vermont's status as a separate state and to encourage new settlers.

By July 1779, however, Vermont's leaders needed more than rhetoric to quell their enemies and achieve admission to the union. While Ira appeased New Hampshire officials, Ethan's show of military force, suppressing Yorker sympathizers in southeastern Vermont, enraged New York's powerful Governor George Clinton and further weakened outside sympathy for Vermont's claim to independence. As internal unrest and pressure from New York and New Hampshire heightened, Congress became increasingly hostile to Vermont's bid for statehood. Disheartened by their lack of success with Congress, Ethan and Ira Allen began pursuing negotiations with the British in mid-1780. Their discussions with General Frederick Haldimand, designed to protect Vermont from invasion and insure the state's independence, created another concern for Congress—fear of Vermont's defection to the enemy.

M. S. B.

To the Inhabitants of the State of Vermont

Friends and Fellow Citizens,

Pursuant to Appointment by the Legislature, and Instructions from the Governor and Council of the State, I waited on the General Court of *New-Hampshire*, at their Sessions in June last, and delivered the public Writings intrusted me by the Governor of this State, to the President, which were read in Council, and sent to the House for their Inspection: The House, after reading and considering the same, resolved into a Committee, to take into Consideration the whole Matter respecting *Vermont*, which was concurred in by the Hon. Board; and Thursday the 24th of June, the Committee met in the Assembly Chamber, and the Resolves of Congress of the 1st and 2d of June, respecting the Premises, and several other Papers were read; among which was the Appointment of Col. *Peter Olcott*, and *Beza Woodward*, Esq; impowering them as a Committee from the Committee of the *Cornish* Convention, to use their Influence with the General Court of *New-Hampshire*, to extend their Claim and Jurisdiction over the whole of the *New-Hampshire* Grants. A Question was put to said Committee, by a Member of the House, *How many Towns were represented in said* Cornish *Convention, on the West Side of* Connecticut-River? Answer, *About twenty-two in the Whole, and about Half of them West of said River*. Said Committee then proceeded to exhibit the Returns made on a Hand-Bill formed by the Committee of the *Cornish* Convention, on the 23rd of April last, and sent to the several Towns in this State, for the express Purpose of getting the Numbers of the Inhabitants that were willing *New-Hampshire* should extend their Claim and Jurisdiction over the whole of the Grants—their Returns were sixty-five Persons. They also alledged, that they had mislaid or lost the Returns from one Town, in which there were one hundred and twenty Families, and but four Persons acted in Opposition to connecting with *New-Hampshire*: That the Reason why more Persons had not acted on said Hand-Bill, was, that they had not circulated thro' the Grants, by Reason of their falling into the Hands of the New Statesmen, who secreted or burnt them: — That for eighty Miles up and down Connecticut-River, there were but two Members attended the Assembly of *Vermont*: — That so far as they had been able to collect the Sentiments of the People, they were very generally on the east Side of the Green Mountain, and a Number on the west Side said Mountain, for connecting with *New-Hampshire*: then refering to the Members of the House who lived contiguous to Connecticut-River, to inform what they knew respecting the Matter; Judge *Marsh* then arose, and with a Degree of Warmth asserted, That to his certain Knowlege, two-thirds of the Inhabitants of the Grants west of the River, would hold up both Hands to connect with *New-Hampshire*. A few more of the Members of the House, in Conversation with the other Members, had endeavored to insinuate Tenets nearly similar. I then proceeded to make my Defence; in which I observed, That it was strange those Gentlemen were at a Loss to determine how many Towns were represented in the *Cornish* Convention, as one was the Clerk, and both Members of the same: — That there were but eight Towns west of the River, represented in said Convention: — That the Town said Committee had Reference to, as having one hundred and twenty Families, was the Town of *Norwich*, in which Col. *Olcott* lived: — That I was informed by several respectable Gentlemen of that Vicinity, that all due Pains were taken to convene the legal Voters on Town-Meeting Day; some refused to attend, as they would not act against the State of *Vermont*; others were tired of Town Meetings, and neglected to attend; in all, thirty-one Persons met, twenty-seven for *New-Hampshire*, and four for *Vermont*: — That I had as good, if not a better Right, to count those who

195

did not attend the Meeting for *Vermont*, as they for *New-Hampshire*: — That said Hand-Bills had been sent into the County of *Bennington* in several Places; and that the People there did not take so much Notice of them, as to secrete or burn them: — That I was knowing to said Hand-Bills circulating thro' a very considerable Part of *Cumberland* County: — That in several Towns where they had Town-Meetings on other Business, said Hand-Bills were read, and the Towns unanimously voted to have nothing to do with them; in other Towns the Select-Men said, they knew nothing of "*F. Marsh*, Chairman;" and if they called a Town-Meeting at his Request, by the same Rule they might have a Town-Meeting every Day, if any Gentleman desired it; therefore they would have nothing to do with it: — That by this open and public Trial, they had proved that Gen. *Bailey*, at least, was mistaken when he asserted in his Petition (preferred to the General Assembly of *New-Hampshire*, at their Sessions in March last) That the Inhabitants of the Grants were, in general, desirous of an Union with *New-Hampshire* — That the eighty Miles mentioned by said Committee, where there were but two Members attended the Assembly of *Vermont*, was true; but Part of that Distance was Woods, consequently no Member could from thence attend; and some of the other Part was thinly settled, and several Towns joined to chuse one Member; but in that Distance, and for more than eighty Miles more down the River, thro' a settled Country, there were but four Towns on the River where they had got so much as one Man to act in favor of connecting with *New-Hampshire*; and not so much as one-fourth Part of the legal Voters in those four Towns — a very small Minority indeed in Favor of connecting with *New-Hampshire*.

I then proceeded to treat largely on the fundamental Arguments, viz. the Change of Jurisdiction in 1774 — the Proclamation issued by his Excellency *Benning Wentworth*, Esq; dated about Feb. 1765 — the Heads of the Grievances the Inhabitants of *Vermont* have suffered from *New-York*, since 1764, to the present Era—Expence in tending Agents to *Great-Britain*—*New-Hampshire* refusing to exert herself to recover her Jurisdiction, although often requested by the Inhabitants of the Grants, when they were put to the greatest Extremity by *New-York*—the Right the People had to assume Government since the present Revolution—Constitution and Code of Laws astablished—Officers of Government, together with the Freemen of the State, sworn to support the Constitution thereof, as established by Convention—Letters from the General Court of the State of *New-Hampshire*, in November last, giving their full Approbation to the State of *Vermont*'s being established by Congress as such, provided the People there, as a political Body, would dissolve all Connections with sixteen Towns east of Connecticut-River, which they alledged to be a Part of *New-Humpshire*: —That every Engagement on the Part of *Vermont* to *New-Hampshire*, was fulfilled: —That it was one Thing for said State to lay a jurisdictional Claim to the Territory of Vermont, and another to exercise Jurisdiction.—

The Committee of both Houses dissolved, and the House resumed the Subject, and voted to lay Claim to the Jurisdiction of the Whole of the *New-Hampshire* Grants, to the Westward of Connecticut-River; nevertheless, allowing and conceding, that if the Hon. Continental Congress should establish the State of *Vermont*, that in such Case the State of *New-Hampshire* will acquiesce therein; and that said State should not extend Jurisdiction farther West than the West Bank of Connecticut-River, till otherwise directed by Congress.—Councurr'd by the Hon. Board.—The General Court then chose a Committee to wait on the Committee of Congress, supposing they would come to the County of *Grafton*.

Although this Proceedure of the Court of *New-Hampshire* doth not appear to be to the Disadvantage of *Vermont*, but rather as a Bar against *New-York*; yet I must not omit to observe, that there are a Number of the Members of that Court, who would be exceeding glad to have the Territory of *Vermont* added to *New-Hampshire*. Their principal Motives to me appear to be these, viz. That the Addition of the Territory of *Vermont* to that State, would most certainly bring the Seat of Government into another Neighbourhood; but a greater Inducement is the unappropriated and Tory Lands within this State, which, if added to *New-Hampshire*, would help them in the heavy List of paying Taxes. — If said Lands are a sufficient Motive for some Part of the General Court of *New-Hampshire* to wish to enlarge their Government for a Share in them, surely it would not be for the Interest of the Inhabitants of this State, to take in so many Partners on that Footing, but to the Interest of each Individual to oppose such an ungenerous Extension of *New-Hampshire*; and warrantable for the following Reasons:

The State of *Vermont* is at this Time formidable against its old Adversary, *New-York*, and has little or nothing to fear from her Power in Arms or Influence at Congress. — In former Days, when under *British* Administration, for any Sett of Men to rise and oppose the Authority, was thought a most daring Thing: People in general were under a strong traditional Bias in favor of Government, and but few, how much soever they might be oppressed, had that Fortitude and Patriotism that they dare appear in Arms to defend their just Rights, in Opposition to the undue Exercise of Law, when attempted to be exercised by legal Officers of Justice; and when they did, seldom failed of losing some of their Lives, and being vanquished by their Adversaries — witness *Nobletown, Livingston's Manor, Bateman's-Patent,* &c. — In those Days the *Green-Mountain-Boys* were put to the sad Alternative of rising in Arms, and opposing the legislative and executive Authority of *New-York*, or of giving up their Lands and Possessions to the Land-jobbers of said Province. Then the *Green-Mountain-Boys* were few in Number, settled in a Wilderness Country, generally poor, but little more than the Heavens to protect them and their Families from the

Inclemency of the Weather, the Justice of their Cause not publicly known—a rich, powerful and intriguing Province to contend with, who did not fail to send their Emissaries amongst them, in order to make Divisions, by Commissions, and every other Way in their Power. In short, no Kind of Bribery or Corruption was too mean for them to be guilty of. Then were the Lives, Liberties and Properties of the People at Stake. In this Situation, a few small Companies of *Green-Mountain-Boys*, (stimulated by the same patriotic Spirit of Freedom which has since shined with a superior Lustre from one End of this Continent to the other) baffled all the diabolical Machinations of their inveterate Adversaries, for more than seven Years altogether. Can this be accounted for, without acknowledging the propitious Agency of the Deity? — In those Days, repeated Applications were made to *New-Hampshire*, to exert herself to obtain the Jurisdiction again; but her Language was then nearly similar to that of righteous *Job*; for *it was the King gave, and the King had taken away, and blessed be the Name of the King*: From that Day to this, said State hath not exerted herself to obtain Jurisdiction again.

It was by Virtue of a royal Edict, that *New-Hampshire* ever had a Right of Jurisdiction to the Westward of Connecticut-River, and by the same Authority, in 1764, the Jurisdiction was curtailed to the west Bank of said River; and the Assembly of said Province did then acquiesce therein. The Members thereof did publicly assert, that they had no Desire that their Province should extend any farther than said River; and that they would not do any Thing to obtain Jurisdiction over a Territory they did not want. — Had the People then submitted to the Jurisdiction of *New-York*, and since the present Revolution associated with them, and assisted in forming a Constitution, established Courts, &c. the Inhabitants would now have been effectually bound down to the Jurisdiction of said State, and it would have been now as much out of the Power of *New-Hampshire* to extend their Jurisdiction to their antient western Limits, as for the *Massachusetts-Bay* now to extend their Jurisdiction to their antient northern Limits, which I believe none are now so hardy as to think of.

By what has been already elucidated, it appears that the Inhabitants of the Grants, by their own Exertions, have saved themselves from the heavy Yoke of Bondage which *New-York* had prepared for them and their Posterity; and that the Right of *New-Hampshire* (so late in the Day) to the Territory of *Vermont*, must be very inconsiderable: And now, for a few of the Members of that General Court, with the Assistance of a few Individuals to the East and West of Connecticut-River (for sinister Views) to think of breaking up the State of *Vermont*, and connecting the Territory thereof again to *New-Hampshire*, is an idle Whim, a mere Chimera. — It is well known, that by Reason of Oppressions from *Great Britain*, *America* revolted from her, and published to the World a List of Grievances for the Vindication of her Conduct. — In like Manner the Inhabitants of the now State of *Vermont*, published a List of Grievances received from *New-York*, which to me appear as numerous and aggravating as those this Continent has against *Great-Britain*.

All governmental Power was given by GOD himself to the People; therefore the Inhabitants of the now State of *Vermont* did associate together, and assume to themselves that inestimable Blessing of Heaven, *civil Government*. This they did upon the same grand original Basis, or great Rule of eternal Right, that a Number of the present Powers of *Europe* revolted from the several Kingdoms to which they paid Allegiance, and on which the United States of *America* revolted from *Great-Britain*, and assumed to themselves civil Government. The Inhabitants of *Vermont*, for more than ten Years last past, have nobly exerted themselves for the Defence of their Liberties and Property, and in the present Revolution did most heartily join their Brethren for the joint Defence of the Liberties and Property of the

Americans in general, and have distinguished themselves to the World, as a truly brave and enterprising People; and it is conceded to by the United States, that they have done their full Proportion in this War, consequently they are intitled to equal Privileges with the Rest of their Brethren in *America*.

They have not delegated their natural Right of Legislation out of their own Hands: — Their Numbers and Territory are sufficient for a State; and they have now as good a Right to govern their own internal Police, as any one of the United States have theirs. By their noble Exertions in the Cause of Liberty, they have acquired the Esteem and Confidence of the United States — merited a Right to the Articles of Confederacy, and a Seat in the Grand Council of *America*. These precious Privileges, I conceive, will be the ultimate Reward of their many expensive Toils, Battles and Hazards, and for the Attainment of which they have suffered such an uncommon Share of concomitant Evils. — And as I have Reason to apprehend the Grand Council of *America* is composed of as great Patriots as any on Earth, doubt not but in due Time they will grant us our reasonable Request: — Indeed it is for the Interest of the United States to do it, as soon as the Circumstances of the Continent will admit; therefore we need not hurry them — It is an antient maxim, that *Representation and Taxation should go together*; and until this State is represented in Congress, no Continental Tax can justly be laid on it.

Is it not strange that any of the Inhabitants of this State, who have perused the Constitution and Laws, and duly considered the Advantages that would accrue to each Individual by being and remaining a distinct State, would be willing to give up those Privileges and connect with any other State? — Surely the Constitution is upon the most liberal Foundation — the Laws are well calculated to preserve inviolate the Liberties and Property of each Individual — the Act of Oblivion settles past Controversies, and puts those who made the Laws and those who opposed them on one Footing, each having a Right to the Protection of the same; and as one common Interest runs thro' the Whole, hope that past Animosities will be forgotten, and all join Hand in Hand to support their common Rights and Interests.

The Circumstances of this State, in some Respects, is different from every other State on the Continent; — it is not in Debt — I have as much Money in my Office, as is due from the State, except what I have taken in upon Loan; to balance which, I have in my Office about as much Money in Continental Loan Office Notes, so that on a Balance, the state is little or none in Debt, excepting what may be supposed to be this State's Proportion of the Continental Debt — (If any Individual in the State is not satisfied with this Stating of Accounts, I invite him to wait on me at my Office, and I will exhibit the public Books of Debt and Credit for the proof of the Assertion) — But there are several valuable Tracts of Land, the Property of this State; — how far those lands will go towards paying the Continental Debt, do not at this Time take upon me to determine.

Every one of the United States have emitted large Sums of Money, some Part of which has been called in, by giving States Loan Office Notes for the same, which are yet due. By this and other Proceedures of the several States, they are in Debt. The Inhabitants of the respective States, have received the Benefits of such Debts when they contracted them; but the Inhabitants of this State have received no Benefit from such Debts; and why they should, any of them, wish to connect with any such State, when they know they will be brought in to pay a Part of all such Arrearages, is a Thing almost unaccountable.

As there are four public Rights of Land in each Town in this State — one for the first settled Minister, one for Schools, one for the first settled Church Minister, and one for propagating the Gospel in foreign Parts — I propose for Consideration, whether it would not be advisable for the Assembly to direct each Town to lease out to the two latter, and the Avails to be by each Town appropriated for the Support of the Gospel in the same.

Lastly, I proceed to state two Matters that are Facts, which I believe will not be disputed by any; from which I shall ask two Questions.

Fact First. A certain Fraternity of Gentlemen, contiguous to Connecticut-River, after the Inhabitants of the Grants west of said River had declared themselves to be a free State, by the Name of *Vermont*, did assert that said State had a just Right to be a State; and that the Grants east of Connecticut-River were unconnected with any State, and had a just Right to join said State.

Question First. Did the Dissolution of the Union (so called) lessen the Right the State of *Vermont* had to be a State before the said Union took Place? — If it did, in what Manner?

Fact Second. It was also asserted by said Gentlemen, that *New-Hampshire* had no Right, Title or Colour of Jurisdiction to the West of the *Mason* Line — That the Grants West of the *Mason* Line, and East of Connecticut-River, had a good Right to form themselves into a State, and would do it, if the State of *Vermont* would not take them into Union. — The foregoing Assertions being granted;

Question Second. What Propriety is there now in requesting *New-Hampshire* to extend their Claim and Jurisdiction over the Territory of *Vermont*?

I am, Friends and Countrymen, your obedient and ever faithful Servant,

IRA ALLEN
Norwich, July 13, 1779.

Letter to "The Hon. Joseph Jones in Congress"
February 11, 1783, George Washington

By 1783 Vermont's ambiguous status as an independent state had hovered for six years as an irritating annoyance over members of the Continental Congress. Any movement toward recognition had been immediately forestalled by the powerful State of New York, whose militia was essential to the Revolutionary cause. As hostilities with Great Britain ceased and a peace treaty appeared likely, Congress, meeting in Philadelphia, began to grapple with internal problems, not the least of which was Vermont.

George Washington was as familiar with the Vermont question as anyone in Congress. He had already used his influence to encourage the state to dissolve the Eastern and Western Unions, assuring Governor Chittenden that Vermont need only relinquish this territory to insure its admission to the union. In January of 1783, however, relations between Vermont and Congress had reached a new crisis, and Washington felt obliged to intervene again.

After Vermont dissolved the two unions, Yorkers in the Brattleboro and Guilford area had attempted to reassert New York authority. With his usual military showmanship, Ethan Allen quelled the disturbance, banishing the Yorkers and confiscating their property. When the dispossessed appealed to Congress, they received a sympathetic response, for congressional representatives from several large states had aligned themselves with New York against Vermont's admission and New England interests. These states — Virginia, South Carolina, North Carolina, and Georgia — had claims to extensive unsettled western lands. Vermont's rebellion against New York indirectly threatened those claims by suggesting that settlers anywhere could create their own state governments.

204

On December 5, 1782, Congress censured Vermont for its actions, claimed congressional authority in the area, demanded the state make restitution to the dispossessed Yorkers, and threatened military intervention. Governor Chittenden responded with a printed remonstrance that reasserted Vermont's independence. He refused to recognize congressional authority over the state's internal police, blamed Congress for its indecision and, once again, expressed Vermont's desire to join the union.

When Washington wrote Joseph Jones, a personal friend and representative from Virginia, Congress had debated the advisibility of military action against Vermont. Hoping Jones would convey these sentiments to his congressional colleagues, Washington outlined the practical difficulties of using force on the Vermonters. He recognized the powerful influences in the state's favor, citing the many New Englanders and Continental Army officers who had become speculators in Vermont land. The state did house a fair number of Tories and deserters, for after 1780 Vermont officials had granted them asylum to encourage settlement. Washington was also wary of Vermont's flirtation with the British. Peace with the British was not yet assured, and the Allens had been secretly negotiating with the enemy for several years. Military intervention might simply confirm the tenuous Vermont-British connection.

Washington's arguments were effective in helping to sway congressional opinion against military action. The Vermont question, however, remained unresolved. Vermont's admission posed fundamental issues for the Confederacy: Could a territory carve itself out of an existing state? How would the union make provision for new states? How could regional interests be balanced and interstate hostilities avoided? As the thirteen states deliberated on these issues during the broader debate over federalism, the Vermont example tended to heighten fears of disunion and anarchy.

M. S. B.

The Hon. Joseph Jones in Congress

Newburgh Feby 11th 1783.

Dear Sir,

I am about to write you a letter on a subject equally important and delicate — which may be extensive in its consequences & serious in its nature. I shall confine myself to the recital of what I believe to be facts, & leave it with you to make deductions.

The printed remonstrance of Mr. Chittenden and his Council, addressed to the President of Congress & founded upon the Resolves of the 5th of December last, contains a favorable recital in their own behalf of what I suppose to be facts; but if my memory serves me, it is an uncandid performance, in as much as it keeps out of view an important transaction of theirs consequent of those Resolves. Be this as it may, matters seem to be approaching too fast to a disagreeable issue for the quiet of my mind. The Resolves on one hand & the remonstrance on the other, unless it should be annulled by their Legislature at their next meeting, which I do not expect, seems to leave little room for an amicable decision.

Matters being thus situated, permit me to ask how far, and by what means coercion is to be extended? The army I presume will be the answer to the latter. Circumstances alone, for no determinations when blood is once drawn, can prescribe bounds to the former — It has been said, but of this you can judge better than I, that the Delegates from the New England States in Congress — or the Majority of them — are willing to admit these people into the Union as an Independent & Sovereign State. Be this as it may, two things I am sure of — viz — that they have a powerful interest in those States, and have pursued very politic measures to strengthen & increase it, long before I had any knowledge of the matter & before the tendency of it was seen into or suspected; by granting upon very advantageous terms large tracts of land—in which I am sorry to find the army in some degree have participated.

Let me next ask, by whom is that district of country principally settled? and of whom is your present army (I will not confine the question to this part of it, but extend it to the whole) comprised? The answer is evident—New Englandmen.

It has been the opinion of some that the appearance of force would awe these people into submission. If the General Assembly should ratify & confirm what Mr. Chittenden & his Council have done, I shall be of a very different sentiment. —and moreover that it is not a trifling force that will subdue them, even supposing they do derive no aid from the Enemy in Canada—and that it will be a very arduous task indeed, if they should—to say nothing of a diversion which may & doubtless will be created in their favor from New York, if the war with G Britain should continue.

The Country is very Mountainous, full of Defiles, and very strong. The Inhabitants for the most part are a hardy Race, composed of that kind of People who are best calculated for Soldiers; in truth who *are* soldiers—for many, many hundreds of them are Deserters from this army who having acquired property there, would be desperate in the defence of it, well knowing that they were fighting with halters about their necks.

It may be asked if I am acquainted with the Sentiments of the army on the subject of this dispute? I readily answer no: — not intimately—it is a matter of too delicate a nature to agitate for the purpose of information—but I have *heard* many officers of Rank & discernment, and have learned by indirect enquiries, that others, express the utmost horror at the very idea of shedding blood in an affair of this sort— comparing it in its consequences, tho' not in its principles, to the quarrel with Great Britain, who thought it was only to hold up the rod and all would be hushed. I cannot at *this time* undertake to say there would be any difficulty with the army if it should be ordered upon this service, but I should be exceedingly unhappy to see the experiment made — for besides the reasons before suggested, I believe there would be a great unwillingness in it to embrue their hands in the blood of their brethren.

I have to add, that almost at the same instant, a number of the printed copies of the remonstrance were disseminated thro' every part of the army. I do not know what effect it may have, but the design is obvious.

I promised in the beginning of this letter that I would content myself with a simple relation of facts. I shall therefore only lament that Congress did not in the first commencement of this dispute act decidedly. This matter, as you much know, was much agitated last winter, & a Committee of Congress with whom I had the honor to be in conference, and of which I believe you were one, saw Mr. Chittenden's letter to me — & approved of my writing him an answer to the effect it was given. — With great esteem & regard and in much haste as Col. Pickering is waiting

I am Dr. Sir
Yr. most obed. & affect. Ser.

G. WASHINGTON

PS. Altho there can be no doubt of Congress having received the letter I have alluded to in this letter, I send, nevertheless, one of the printed copies.   GW

Courtesy Friends of the Vermont State House

Act of the Convention of the State of Vermont for Adopting the Constitution of the United States
January 10, 1791

Congress of the United States
February 18, 1791

In fall 1790, 109 Vermont towns elected delegates to attend a constitutional convention at Bennington. Vermonters saw ratification of the Constitution as the decisive step in convincing Congress that they wanted to be part of the union. The agreement with New York over the land claims issue and the common boundary would be invalid unless Vermont became a state. In fact, New York was now anxious that Vermont be admitted in order to maintain the northeastern states' majority in Congress.

During the convention, which met from January 6 until January 10, 1791, Nathaniel Chipman and Stephen R. Bradley were the leading spokesmen for ratification. Chipman, a Supreme Court justice, had been active in public affairs since 1780, when the state began relying on his legal advice. Opening the convention debate, he outlined Vermont's weak position as an independent state, the benefits of participating in a strong national government, and Vermonters' affinity with American ideals.

Stephen Bradley had championed Vermont's recognition since the earliest days of independence. In 1780, under the direction of the Governor's Council, he had written *Vermont's Appeal To The Candid And Impartial World*, detailing the state's right to independence based on revolutionary principles. On several occasions he had gone to the Continental Congress to plead Vermont's case. In his convention statements, Bradley emphasized Vermont's weak military position, the state's inability

209

to defend its sovereignty or protect its citizens, and its lack of negotiating strength against the strong federal union.

Delegates from towns in Windsor County, a locus of unrest fostered by debt-ridden farmers, opposed adoption. Hoping to delay the proceedings, these delegates stressed the need for further study of the Constitution. Vermont would have to sacrifice its vital interests to that of the federal union, they argued, and to assume a share of the national debt. Moreover, there was no indication from Congress that a majority of states would accept Vermont as a new state. These objections reflected the delegates' apprehensions about the security of their property as well as opposition to the political leadership of Chipman and Bradley.

Despite these arguments, the convention passed the act of ratification after four days of debate on a vote of 105 to 4. The delegates who had spoken against the measure now concurred, but representatives from the Windsor County towns of Andover, Chester, Bridgewater, and Rochester remained firmly opposed.

The agreement with New York and ratification of the Constitution cleared the way for Vermont statehood. In February Congress passed an act stipulating that on March 4, 1791, the "'State of Vermont,' shall be received and admitted into this Union, as a new and entire member of the United States of America."

M. S. B.

Act of the Convention of the State of Vermont for Adopting the Constitution of the United States, Jany 10, 1791

STATE OF VERMONT

In Convention of the Delegates of the People of the State of Vermont.

Whereas, by an Act of the Commissioners of the State of New York, done at New York, the Seventh day of October, in the fifteenth year of the Independence of the United States of America, one thousand seven hundred and ninety, every impediment, as well on the part of the State of New York, as on the part of the State of Vermont, to the admission of the State of Vermont into the Union of the United States of America, is removed; — In full faith and assurance that the same will stand approved and ratified by Congress; —

This Convention, having impartially deliberated upon the Constitution of the United States of America, as now established, submitted to us by an Act of the General Assembly of the State of Vermont passed October the twenty seventh one thousand seven hundred and ninety, DO, in virtue of the power and authority to us given, for that purpose, fully and entirely approve of, assent to, and ratify the said Constitution; and declare that immediately from, and after, this state shall be admitted by the Congress into the Union, and to a full participation of the benefits of the government now enjoyed by the states in the Union, the same shall be binding on us and the people of the State of Vermont forever.

Done at Bennington, in the County of Bennington, the tenth

day of January, in the 15. year of the Independence of the United States of America, one thousand seven hundred and ninety one. — In testimony whereof we have hereunto subscribed our Names —

THOS. CHITTENDEN,
President,
MOSES ROBINSON,
Vice President

Tim^o Brownson	Isaac Lyman	Wm. Perry
John Fassett	Daniel Jewet	Joseph Warner
John Strong	John Forgason	Asahel Smith
Jonathan Hunt	Reuben Thomas	Simeon Smith
Gideon Olin	Thomas Jewett	John Shumway
Stephen R. Bradley	Asaph Fletcher	Silas Hathaway
Janna Churchill	Elijah Lovell	Thos. Porter
Ebenr. Wilson	John Rich	John Smith
John White	John Barron	Elisha Barber
Daniel Shearman	Amos Brownson	Wm. Ward
Abel Waters	David Hopkinson	Joseph Beeman
James Shefter	Danl. Kingsbury	Heman Durkee
Edward Aiken	Saml. Harrison	E. Case
Simon Stevens	Michl Flynn	Peter Pennock
Abel Thompson	Cornelius Lynde	Martin Chittenden
Joshua Wood	John N. Bennet	Josiah Pond
Nathl. Chipman	Jonathan Brewster	Wm Slade
Thos. Hammond	Jona. M'Connell	John Spafford
Benja. Holcomb	Benj. Henry	Peter Sleeman
Peter Briggs	Samuel Lathrop	Jonas Whitney
John M'Neile	Oliver Pier	Nath^{el} Niles
Oliver Gallup	Nathl. Stoughton	Alex^r Harvey
Lem. Chipman	Martin Powel	Wm Chamberlain
Samuel Miller	Nathan Daniels	Daniel Buck
Israel Smith	Jason Duncan	Daniel Farrand
Benj. Greene	Elias Curtis	Abraham Morrill
Andrew Selden	Samuel Beach	Beriah Loomis
John Marsh	Benj^a Emmons	Asahel Jackson
Gardiner Chandler	Alex Brush	Jon^a Arnold
Timo^y Todd	Daniel Gilbert	Saml Gatt [Gates]
Calvin Knoulton	Ira Allen	Eben^r Allen
Timothy Bliss	Timothy Castle	Enos Wood
W. C. Harrington	Eleazer Claghorn	Saml Hitchcock
Josiah Edson	Silas Tupper	
N. Lee	David Palmer	

State of Vermont fr. Bennington Jany 10th 1791

The foregoing ratification was agreed to, and signed by one hundred and five, and dissented to, by four, which is a majority of one hundred and one.

THOS. CHITTENDEN,
President

Attest, *Rosl. Hopkins*, Sccy of Convention

State of Vermont

In Convention Bennington Jany 10th 1791

Resolved (the Governor of this State being President) that the Vice President be and hereby is directed to transmit to his Excellency the Governor Duplicates of the act of this Convention ratifying the Constitution of the United States of America to be by him transmitted to the President of the United States and the Legislature of this State.
Attest, *Rosl. Hopkins*, Sec^y

Congress of the United States

At the Third Session,
Begun and held at the City of Philadelphia, on Monday the fifth
of December, one thousand seven hundred and ninety.
An ACT for the Admission of the State of Vermont into
this Union.
THE State of Vermont having petitioned the Congress to be admitted a member of the United States, Be it enacted by the SENATE
and HOUSE OF REPRESENTATIVES of the United States of America
in Congress assembled, and it is hereby enacted and declared,
That on the fourth day of March, one thousand seven hundred
and ninety-one, the said State, by the name and title of "the State
of Vermont," shall be received and admitted into the Union,
as a new and entire member of the United States of America.

Frederick Augustus Muhlenberg,
Speaker of the House of Representatives.

John Adams, *Vice-President
of the United States*, and *President of the Senate*

Approved, February the eighteenth, 1791

George Washington, *President of the United States*

Courtesy of Vermont Historical Society

Vermont Gazette
March 21, 1791

Vermonters on the west side of the Green Mountains read about the proceedings surrounding statehood in the *Vermont Gazette*, Anthony Haswell's weekly Bennington newspaper. On March 21, 1791, Haswell printed this account of a celebration held at Rutland several days after admission. A group of "federal citizens of Vermont" raised the "federal standard" and drank "federal toasts," accompanied by the firing of cannon.

Anthony Haswell (1756-1816) came to Vermont to fulfill the need for a state printer. Born in England, Haswell became a printer's apprentice in Boston during the Revolution, when he firmly attached himself to the patriot cause. After moving to Bennington in 1783 at the request of Vermont leaders, Haswell began issuing his *Vermont Gazette*, the state's second newspaper. His press also produced official state records, books, magazines, and pamphlets. Despite his share of state printing, he struggled to keep his paper going. Under his hand, the *Gazette* appeared regularly until 1797 and with interruptions until 1806. Relatives continued to use the masthead until 1850.

A fair measure of Haswell's local fame came from the ballads and folksongs he wrote for festive occasions in Bennington. Imbued with Revolutionary spirit, his verse inspired fellow citizens with patriotism. A believer in republican principles, Haswell defended Matthew Lyon in 1800 and was jailed under the Alien and Sedition Acts for his outspoken defense of freedom of the press.

Haswell's support of Vermont statehood was evident as early as December 1789. Shortly after New York and Vermont appointed commissioners to negotiate a settlement, he began using both Vermont and United States seals on the masthead of the *Vermont Gazette*. He placed the Vermont seal on the paper's right side, the place of honor, and the United States seal on the left. Soon after Vermont was admitted to the union, he reversed the position of the two seals.

With his account of the Rutland celebration, Haswell informed his readers of popular sentiments on statehood. Celebrants, expressing their patriotism for both Vermont and the union, were willing to forget past differences and look to a bright future. A salute to the State of New York appeared among the fifteen toasts. After twenty years of animosity toward Yorkers, Vermonters recognized New York's crucial role in furthering Vermont statehood.

M. S. B.

Vermont Gazette, March 21, 1791

Copy of a letter from Rutland, dated March 9

Yesterday a numerous collection of the federal citizens of Vermont, met at the town square in this town to cellebrate the accession of this State to the federal union.

The federal standard was hoisted at six o'clock in the morning, ornamented with fifteen stripes, and the field emblazoned with two stars, representing the state of Vermont and the new state of Kentucky. About five in the afternoon, a large body of citizens assembled at Williams's inn, consisting of the judges of the supreme federal court, the attorney general and other officers of the court, the rev. clergy of the vicinity, with a large number of respectable citizens from this and the neighboring states.

After an economical collation the following federal toasts were drank, under the discharge of cannon, fired by the volunteer corps of artillery, under the direction of capt. Samuel Prentiss.

1. The president. A discharge of fifteen cannon.
2. The vice president and congress.
3. The allies of the united states.
4. The state of Newyork.
5. His excellency governor Chittenden.
6. The union of Vermont with the united states, — may it flourish like our pines and continue unshaken as our mountains.
7. May the new states soon rival the old in federal virtues.
8. May the federal officers of the district of Vermont act with integrity and merit the confidence of the people.
9. May the patriotism of America secure it from venality.
10. The union of states, interests and hearts.
11. Arts, science, manufactures and agriculture.
12. The clergy, may they unite to dispel the clouds of ignorance and superstition.

13. The memorable 16th of August, on which was fought the glorious battle of Bennington.

14. The conjugal union and rising generation.

15. May we never experience a less happy moment than the present under the federal government.

The following song composed for the occasion was sung by a select choir of singers, accompanied by the whole. [*Tune Washington's birthday*.]

COME every federal son.
Let each Vermonter come,
And take his glass,
Long live great Washington,
Glory's immortal son;
Bright as the rolling sun,
O'er us doth pass.

Hail hail this happy day,
When we allegiance pay,
T' our federal head,
Bright in these western skies,
Shall our new star arise,
Striking our enemies
With fear and dread.

Come each Greenmountainboy,
Swell every breast with joy,
Hail our good land,
As our pines climb the air,
Firm as our mountains are,
Federal beyond compare,
Proudly we stand.

Fill fill your bumpers high,
Let the notes rend the sky,
Free we'll remain,
By that immortal crown
Of glory and renown,
Which our brave heroes won
On bloodstain'd plain.

Then come join hand in hand
Like a firm federal band,
Bound by our law,
From our firm union springs
Blessings unknown to kings,
Then each shout as he sings
Federal huzza.

Volunteer toast. May the Vermonters become as eminent in the arts of peace as they have been glorious in those of war.

The festival was concluded with continued demonstrations of joy. In the evening the ladies of the vicinity honored the youthful part of the company with their presence at a ball.

Courtesy Vermont Department of Libraries

About
the
Contributors

Gary J. Aichele, an associate professor of political science at Juniata College, received his J.D. (1976) and Ph.D. (1983) from the University of Virginia. A former U.S. Supreme Court Judicial Fellow (1980), he is the author of *Oliver Wendell Holmes, Jr.: Soldier, Scholar, Judge* (Twayne, 1989) and *Legal Realism and Twentieth-Century American Jurisprudence: The Changing Consensus* (Garland, 1990).

Michael A. Bellesiles received his Ph.D. from the University of California at Irvine. Dr. Bellesiles is a member of the history faculty at Emory University and in 1990-91 a guest professor at the University of Augsburg in Germany. His article, "The Establishment of Legal Structures on the Frontier: The Case of Revolutionary Vermont" (*Journal of American History*, March 1987) received the Pelzer Award. A forthcoming book, *Revolutionary Outlaws*, is a study of Ethan Allen and the formation of Vermont.

Marilyn S. Blackwell holds a masters degree in American history from the University of Vermont. As a volunteer, staff member, and independent scholar, she has been associated with the Vermont Historical Society for nearly twenty years. She has contributed articles to both *Vermont History* and *Vermont History News* and coauthored *Across the Onion: A History of East Montpelier, Vermont 1781-1981* (1983).

Paul S. Gillies has served as Deputy Secretary of State for Vermont since 1981. He claims that he has utterly failed to resist the temptations of history, given the proximity of the State Archives vault some twenty feet below his desk. He has written a monthly column on the progress of Vermont statehood and edited the *Vermont Bicentennial Calendar*. He received his law degree from the University of Maine in 1978.

Samuel B. Hand is a professor of history at the University of Vermont. He is coeditor of *In a State of Nature: Readings in Vermont History* (1982, 2nd ed., 1985) and has written extensively on both the New Deal and oral history. A book on the Vermont Republican party is in progress. In 1989 Dr. Hand was named a University of Vermont University Scholar.

Peter S. Onuf received his Ph.D. from Johns Hopkins University and has taught at Worcester Polytechnic Institute, Southern Methodist University, and University College, Dublin. He is now professor of history at the University of Virginia. His publications include "State-Making in Revolutionary America: Independent Vermont as a Case Study" (*Journal of American History*, March 1981); *A Union of Interests: Political and Economic Thought in Revolutionary America* (with Cathy D. Matson), University Press of Kansas, 1990; *The Midwest and the Nation: Rethinking the History of an American Region* (with Andrew R. L. Cayton), Indiana University Press, 1990; and numerous other works.

P. Jeffrey Potash, associate professor of history at Trinity College of Vermont, received his Ph.D. degree in American history and religion at the University of Chicago. His dissertation, "Toward a New Rural History: Patterns of Community Organization in Three Addison County Towns, 1761-1850," will be published in 1991 as part of the Chicago Series on American Religion (Carlson Press).

D. Gregory Sanford is the Vermont State Archivist and a member of the Vermont Statehood Bicentennial Commission. His most recent publication (with Eleazer Durfee) is *A Guide to the Henry Stevens, Sr. Collection at the Vermont State Archives* (1989). With Paul Gillies, he plans to publish the journals of Vermont's Council of Censors.

Michael Sherman is Director of the Vermont Historical Society. He received his Ph.D. in history from the University of Chicago. His publications include articles on pageantry, propaganda, and historical writing in early sixteenth-century France, and essays on the role of history and the humanities in public life. He edited *The Views from Montaigne's Tower: Essays on the Public Uses of the Humanities* (with Shelly Simek, 1980); *What Portion in the World. New Essays on Public Uses of the Humanities* (with Cynthia Buckingham and Steven Weiland, 1982); and *Productivity: A Concept in Political Economy Reconsidered* (1984).